EVERYDAY REASONING

Evelyn M. Barker

UNIVERSITY OF MARYLAND,
BALTIMORE COUNTY

PRENTICE-HALL, INC. Englewood Cliffs, N.J. 07632

Library of Congress Cataloging in Publication Data

BARKER, EVELYN M
    Everyday reasoning.

    Includes index.
    1. Reasoning.   2. Fallacies (Logic)   3. Thought
and thinking.   I. Title.
BC177.B28   160   80-21177
ISBN 0-13-293407-8

Editorial/production supervision and interior design by Peter Roberts
Cover by Saiki Design
Manufacturing buyer: Harry P. Baisley

© 1981 by Prentice-Hall, Inc., Englewood Cliffs, N.J. 07632

Printed in the United States of America

10 9 8 7 6 5 4 3 2 1

PRENTICE-HALL INTERNATIONAL, INC., *London*

PRENTICE-HALL OF AUSTRALIA PTY. LIMITED, *Sydney*

PRENTICE-HALL INTERNATIONAL, INC., *London*

PRENTICE-HALL OF CANADA, LTD., *Toronto*

PRENTICE-HALL OF INDIA PRIVATE LIMITED, *New Delhi*

PRENTICE-HALL OF JAPAN, INC., *Tokyo*

PRENTICE-HALL OF SOUTHEAST ASIA PTE. LTD., *Singapore*

WHITEHALL BOOKS LIMITED, *Wellington, New Zealand*

To the Memory of

ANIELLO and MARY VERNA MASI

Contents

chapter 4

Immediate Inference   58

chapter 5

The Logic of Categorical Statements   74

chapter 7

Deductive Reasoning: Truth-Functions   **139**

chapter 10
Other Kinds of Everyday Reasoning   226

chapter 11
Further Principles for Everyday Reasoning   251

ACKNOWLEDGMENTS

This book owes much to UMBC students, whose questions and answers have shaped my treatment of its subject matter. I am also indebted to other writers on logic and philosophy, whose notions and techniques I borrow or adapt; in particular, to Stephen F. Barker, who read the original draft and made many valuable criticisms and suggestions. I am grateful to Brenda Bland for cheerful efficient secretarial help. Charles and George Barker have given aid and encouragement from the book's inception to its publication.

I wish to thank the *Baltimore Sunpapers* for their kind and generous permission to reprint 41 items from their publications, *The Sun, The Evening Sun* and *The Sunday Sun.*

chapter 1

Logic and Everyday Reasoning

1A   REASONING IN DAILY LIFE

What one person needs or wants to know in the conduct of his life may differ greatly from what his neighbor, co-worker, or fellow student wants or needs to know. But the *ways* in which we learn what we know are not so different: We observe for ourselves, take the testimony of those we meet, read what has been recorded by others, and recall things from our own past and human history. We extend such knowledge by *reasoning:* going on from things we believe to be true to infer other things whose truth seems to us to follow. Our own time is often said to have produced a "knowledge explosion"; modern techniques of observation, experimentation, and information-gathering have yielded such a number, variety, and complex of facts and theories that neither expert nor ordinary citizen can hope to comprehend the whole. Nevertheless, in such a mass of "knowledge claims," it would be naive to accept at face value as true all that is claimed to be so. We know the individual human mind to be fallible; science exhibits its fallibility in its continuing correction of its own knowledge claims. Therefore, each one of us must in some way cope with the truth claims that bombard us as members of an advanced technological civilization, in which knowledge itself is one of the most important artifacts.

The subject of this book is the kinds of reasoning we employ in daily life and encounter in the special sciences. Its purpose is to explain in clear language the principles of such reasoning and how to put them to use. In succeeding chapters we shall develop strategies to distinguish reasoning whose conclusions are worthy of belief from those that deserve questioning and rejection. To know that a conclusion is dubious, and to know how dubious it may be, is often as useful and important as knowing that a statement is flatly true or false. The study of principles of reasoning has historically been called *logic*. Traditionally, logic is primarily concerned with the kinds of reasoning used in mathematics and the special sciences, that is, deductive reasoning and inductive reasoning, respectively. We shall study such reasoning in Chapters 4 through 9 inclusively. However, we shall consider these reasoning processes only insofar as they are relevant to the arguments we find in everyday thinking, rather than as a basis for specialized work in mathematics or the special sciences.

We begin in Chapter 2 with a detailed study of the logic of statements, taking up various matters which often cause difficulty in dealing with statements in full-blown arguments. Chapter 3 distinguishes three types of definitions commonly used in reasoning and formulates rules for judging the adequacy of definitions offered in the course of reasoning. The remaining chapters, 10 and 11, consider distinctive types of reasoning that figure in everyday life but are ignored or inadequately treated in many logic texts. In particular, reasoning by analogy, although prominent in ordinary thinking and even in the sciences, is often undervalued in logic texts; normative reasoning, that is, arguments advanced to prove a thing desirable or undesirable, frequently occurs in everyday thinking, but its special character is seldom analyzed. We shall propose specific criteria for assessing the soundness of such arguments, which are neither expendable nor replaceable by deductive or inductive reasoning.

1B   WHAT LOGIC CAN AND CANNOT DO

At the outset we must recognize what logic can do and what it cannot do. Reasoning proceeds *from* things already known or believed to be true; that is, from indisputable facts, reliable generalizations, justified or generally accepted assumptions. These starting points of argument logic cannot in general provide, especially when the reasoning is of the kind we employ in everyday affairs. For them students must consult their own experience, reflect upon their own observations as well as those of others, and study the special sciences, literature, history, philosophy, religion, and art. A mind well stocked with accurate information and sound conceptions is essential to good reasoning, but logic does not supply it with them.

Logic can give us a few basic truths, but not those we need to carry on the kind of reasoning necessary for making our way in the world. For example, early in the history of logic, the so-called *laws of thought* were formulated. These laws are principles, presupposed in all reasoning, to which all valid reasoning must conform. One way of stating them is as follows:

1. *A thing cannot both have the property* A *and lack the property* A, *whatever* A *may be.* For example, a thing cannot be both wet and not wet, moving and not moving, electromagnetic and not electromagnetic. This principle is called the *law of contradiction* (or sometimes, more accurately, the *law of noncontradiction*). A little reflection should convince the student of its truth, once an obvious objection is met. A particular dress may be wet at the top and dry at the bottom. But it cannot be wet at one place on the top and not wet at that very same place on the top. When we understand the principle with the qualification that a thing cannot be both A and not-A *in exactly the same respect,* we can see that it holds true of anything in the world that it cannot be both A and not-A. However, this truth does not tell us whether any given thing is A at all, whatever A may be, whether hot, white, moving, or electromagnetic. For such information we pass beyond logic.

2. A second principle is that of the *law of identity.* It states that A *is A, whatever* A *may be:* A galaxy is a galaxy; Julius Caesar is Julius Caesar. Although seemingly trivial, such truths may provide an essential step in a chain of argument. For example, if we know that Julius Caesar was assassinated and we learn that Julius Caesar was the husband of Calpurnia, we may infer, by means of the *law of identity,* that the husband of Calpurnia was assassinated.

3. The third law of thought is called the *principle of excluded middle: A thing must be either* A *or not-*A, *whatever* A *may be.* This principle says that a thing must be a dog or not a dog, a galaxy or not a galaxy, a true statement or not a true statement, an argument or not an argument. It assures us that a galaxy beyond the scope of our observation either is a spiral galaxy or not a spiral galaxy, but it will go no way toward proving which shape that galaxy actually has.

These three laws illustrate the kinds of truths that logic by itself puts forward; clearly they do not take us very far. The laws of thought are very general principles which are true of anything whatsoever, and they can be known by reflection alone. In ordinary reasoning, we commonly make use of general principles of more limited extent, which apply only to specified classes or varieties of things. For example, the law of gravitation is called a universal principle, but it still applies only to things that have mass. The "golden rule," although a very general moral rule, relates primarily to our conduct toward fellow humans. The general principle that rapid inflation diminishes a nation's real income is generally true in the economic sphere

of human life. Such generalizations are not known to us simply by reflection; to arrive at them we must take in the significance of many
particular facts or put a variety of facts together in a coherent way. Our
knowledge of these facts is gained from our perceptions of the world in
which we live and act. The substance of our ordinary reasoning is in the
main outside logic.

Given particular facts and general principles, however we come by
them, we can and do build upon them, progressing to new particular facts
and general principles. It is here that logic comes into its own: It monitors
our steps from already established truths to projected new truths. Logic
can say how confident we should be when we go from observing that there
is a ring around the moon tonight to predicting that there will be a storm
tomorrow (from one particular fact to another particular fact). Logic
enters in when we form the causal generalization that smoking causes lung
cancer from statistics showing the large number of lung cancer victims
who are heavy smokers (moving from particular facts to generalization). In
applying the generalization that brown-eyed people have brown-eyed
children to the case of brown-eyed parents (to yield the inference that
their children are also going to be brown-eyed) we employ logic as we
move from a generalization to a particular instance. In passing from the
generalization that alcoholic mothers are more apt to have babies with
birth defects than non-alcoholic mothers to the generalization that pregnant women should refrain from excessive drinking, logic is relevant.
Taking steps of these kinds—from one particular fact to another; from
particular facts to generalizations; from generalizations to particular fact;
from one generalization to another—can be justified or condemned by
principles of reasoning.

I C   REASONING AND THE SPECIAL SCIENCES

In speaking of everyday reasoning as the primary concern of this text we
are not suggesting that there is any essential difference between it and the
reasoning to be found in the sciences. On the contrary, it is continuous
with scientific reasoning, which has evolved from the kind of thinking we
humans exhibit when faced with practical problems, puzzled by the course
of events, or simply curious about the world around us.

There are points of difference, nonetheless: Much scientific reasoning looks precise and highly systematized because it is able to employ
a formal language which largely eliminates the ambiguity of natural
language, the medium of our everyday reasoning. Furthermore, the scientist in a special field has the luxury of artificially limiting the scope of his
reasoning, excluding matters with which he cannot deal successfully at a
given stage of investigation. He operates on the basis of a body of

knowledge, the results of previous reasoning, generally accepted by experts in his field. Finally, the scientific reasoner can refrain from drawing any conclusion at all or hedge his inferences when the evidence is insufficient or points in contrary directions. For such reasons, scientific arguments, for those versed in the subject, are easier to follow and to criticize from the logical point of view.

Ordinary reasoning operates under quite different conditions, which complicate the task of the logician. The everyday thinker must decide on evidence presently available whether he or she ought to have a flu shot, and the government official must reach a conclusion as to the desirability of undertaking a program of mass inoculation, even though there are conflicting considerations. We cannot arbitrarily limit our reasoning to the economic aspects of unemployment, overlooking the political or moral dimensions of the problem; nor can our conclusions on abortion be dictated solely by medical or biological evidence. In such reasonings the assumptions from which we argue are often themselves controversial: Instead of being presented with a generally accepted body of knowledge which can be used to initiate an argument, the everyday thinker often confronts the problem of having to formulate a set of beliefs whose truth his or her hearers will not dispute. The everyday reasoner must learn to express himself (or herself) so as not to be misunderstood, without resorting to a symbolism that will fix the meaning unequivocally.

Above all, the everyday reasoner of our time and place must be able to assess scientific reasonings themselves. It has become our practice to seek out the opinions of experts in various fields on the whole range of social issues. Not infrequently serious matters of social policy are settled on grounds provided by the research of scientists. Court decisions on school busing, for example, were much influenced by the results of one study made by a sociologist. Many years later, he maintained that its results had been misused and that the subject of the investigation itself was skewed by the uniform political viewpoint of the members of the agency that commissioned the study. It is no longer surprising to us to find that equally expert psychiatrists hold contradictory views on the mental condition of a defendant in a law case, and that the view of each psychiatrist supports the case of his cilent. Such observations make us suspect that the objectivity of science may on occasion be influenced, perhaps quite unintentionally, by the human partiality of the scientist. Thus a responsible citizen should be able to review the evidence as well as the conclusions of a scientific investigation in order to form an opinion concerning its validity and to decide what weight to give to its results.

We must not conclude from the foregoing that everyday reasoning is something we just muddle through. We can apply principles of reasoning, but we cannot do so *mechanically*. Some relevant principles are those of the inductive and deductive reasoning which characterize the sciences;

some point out fallacies inherent in the workings of natural language; still others turn on the human and moral dimensions of the subject matter. Aristotle, the Greek logician who first formulated the principles of everyday reasoning in the fourth century B.C., noted that arguments can be found to support a false conclusion as well as a true conclusion. But he also reminds us:

> Nevertheless, the underlying facts do not lend themselves equally well to the contrary views. No; things that are true and things that are better are, by their nature, practically always easier to prove and easier to believe in.
>
> *(Rhetoric,* 1355a)

1D   HOW TO RECOGNIZE AN ARGUMENT

The aim of logic is to go beyond the obvious facts to test whether the "underlying facts" support the argument. Not every piece of writing that is informative is an argument. Our first task is to learn to identify an argument. Consider the following bit of wisdom, which is, nevertheless, *not* an argument:

> You can fool all of the people some of the time, and you can fool some of the people all of the time, but you cannot fool all of the people all of the time.

Three different statements are made in this example, each of which is asserted to be true. They have a common subject, the capacity of a person to fool others. But the truth of each statement is asserted independently of the other two. The third and last statement, "You cannot fool all of the people all of the time," does not follow from the truth of the first two statements. On the contrary, the truth of the third statement is unexpected, given the truth of the first two. It contradicts a statement that we might be tempted to infer from them, namely, "You can fool all of the people all of the time." What we have is a series of three statements, all of which deal with the same subject, but no one of them depends for its truth on any one of the others. Such a series of statements is not an argument; it is called *exposition,* putting forward a series of facts which are true independently of one another.

The Elements of Argument

In an argument there must be a statement, the *conclusion,* whose truth depends on the truth of some other statement or statements, which are the *premises,* or *evidence* for it. Suppose we add one more statement to the preceding series, as follows:

You can fool all of the people some of the time, and you can fool some of the people all of the time, but you cannot fool all of the people all of the time. Therefore, honesty is the best policy.

Now there *is* an argument, for the truth of the statement, "Honesty is the best policy," purportedly follows from the statement which precedes it, "You cannot fool all of the people all of the time." In an argument the statements are not related merely by having a common subject: They are related *logically;* that is, the truth or falsity of one statement (the conclusion) hinges on the truth or falsity of the others (the premises, or evidence). An argument must consist of at least two different statements: One of them, the *premise,* the argument assumes to be true or reports as true; the truth of the other, the *conclusion,* is proved in the argument itself. The point of the argument is to prove the truth of the statement that is called the conclusion, because it is the end or goal of the argument. The premises, or evidence, are the starting points of the argument. The term *inference* is sometimes used to refer simply to the statement that is the conclusion; at other times it refers to the process of moving from a given set of premises to a conclusion. In an argument one is often said *to make an inference;* that is, to draw a *conclusion* from given *premises* or *evidence.*

How can one tell whether a series of sentences constitutes an argument? One must observe whether the statements are tightly connected to each other in the way just described: whether the points being made are all heading in one definite direction, to a statement which is an end point. If so, that end statement is the conclusion. Statements that are premises have two different features: (1) The statements say something that leads one to believe that the conclusion is true; the *premises* offer reasons or grounds to support the conclusion, as the earth supports a building. (2) The premises must be known to be true *independently* of the conclusion.

Thus, in order to function as a premise a statement must be either (1) a matter of common knowledge or a generally accepted assumption, which doesn't itself require proof; (2) newly discovered evidence being reported by the argument; or (3) a statement just proven by a subargument to the main argument. For example, we might take the conclusion to the argument just discussed, "Honesty is the best policy," and use it as a premise in a main argument designed to prove that it is wrong for college students to cheat in examinations. One of the most common errors in reasoning is to confuse the premises with the conclusion. Some think that the statement that is unquestionably true is the conclusion, but such a statement is much more likely to be a premise. If a statement were unquestionably true, we would not need an argument to prove its truth.

Ordinary language provides verbal clues to the presence of arguments. Words like *hence, therefore, thus,* and *so* are almost always signs of an argument, and the words following them express the statement that is the conclusion of the argument. Phrases such as these usually indicate that the statement *following* them is the conclusion of an argument:

> it follows that . . . ; it may be inferred that . . . ; one may conclude . . . ; in consequence . . .

The words *since* and *because* often point to arguments, with the statement *preceding* them being the conclusion and the statement *following* a premise. The same holds true for phrases such as these:

> . . . for the reason that . . . ; . . . on grounds that . . . ; . . . on the assumption that . . . ; . . . due to the fact that . . . ; . . . given the circumstance that . . .

A number of locutions are used more loosely and may indicate that the statement following is either a premise or conclusion:

> it is undeniable that . . . ; it is evident that . . . ; it must be true that . . . ; it must be the case that . . . ; it is reasonable to believe that . . . ; I maintain that . . . ; I hold that . . . ; I assume that . . . ; it may be supposed that . . . ; it is likely that . . . ; it is unlikely that . . .

In analyzing a passage, the student should note words and phrases such as those above, for they are cues to the presence both of arguments and of statements that function as premises or conclusion. However, one must avoid use of these hints too mechanically: It is essential that one reflect on what is asserted in order to determine whether the statements are logically related to one another as premise and conclusion. Careful reading is indispensable in detecting arguments and in spotting the premises and the conclusion correctly. It often happens that an argument is put forward that uses none of the words and phrases listed, nor any equivalents.

Subarguments and Chain Arguments

It seldom happens that any substantial piece of writing contains just one argument or argument alone. More commonly, arguments are interspersed with exposition. This serves to illustrate or explain premises or the conclusion, or to give additional information on the subject. As previously mentioned, an argument will often contain a subargument. A *subargument* is simply an argument that is part of a larger argument. Its function is to prove a premise of the larger argument to be true. A subargument will have as its conclusion the premise of the larger argument. Also, the subargument must have for its premises some other statement or statements to support the subargument's conclusion.

Frequently, a further conclusion will be drawn from the conclusion reached in an argument, as in the following instance:

Honesty is the best policy. So, students are better off not cheating in examinations. Therefore, they ought to do their work diligently if they want good grades, rather than look for opportunities to cheat.

In the argument above, the word *so* indicates that the statement "Students are better off not cheating in examinations" is a conclusion derived from the preceding statement (and perhaps others not mentioned). The word *therefore* shows that the statement following is another conclusion, derived from "Students are better off not cheating in examinations." The latter statement has two different roles in this little argument: It is the conclusion of one argument, whose premise is the preceding statement; and it is the premise of a second argument, whose conclusion is the statement following the word *therefore*. (Alternatively, if one considered that statement to be the *main* conclusion, the first argument would be a subargument proving its premise, "Students are better off not cheating in examinations.") A whole series of statements that dovetail into one another—so that a statement that is a conclusion becomes a premise for the statement following it—is called a *chain argument.* A chain argument can extend to some length, and various types will be considered in our chapters on deductive reasoning.

More commonly, however, arguments have a looser structure, especially those we make use of in daily life.

Different Lines of Argument

In many arguments a number of different considerations are all presented as reasons for a particular conclusion, so that the premises are independent of one another (as opposed to a chain argument). In the argument on cheating, for example, the conclusion that students ought not to cheat on examinations might be buttressed by reasons such as the following:

If a student is caught cheating, he or she will have the grade lowered, perhaps fail the course, or even be expelled. Even if not caught, the student's not having learned the material may make him or her miss out on some knowledge necessary or useful in the future. Cheating is disapproved of socially, and the cheater will lose the respect of others, and perhaps suffer the disadvantages of a poor reputation. Cheating violates an important moral principle. One who cheats may develop a bad character and not be able to respect himself, and also lose the trust of others. The cheater will suffer from a bad conscience and be uncomfortable in the presence of others, who may have observed him.

The statements listed above are different reasons for believing cheating to be bad; one could accept any one of them, while rejecting the others. They represent several *different lines of argument* all leading by different routes to the conclusion that students ought not to cheat on examinations. Usually specific words or phrases point out statements that stand for independent lines of argument:

not only ... but also ... ; in addition ... ; furthermore ... ; moreover ... ; secondly ... thirdly ... ; finally ...

Many arguments, especially the most serious of them, not only provide evidence for a conclusion but also take account of facts that go against it. When these facts are very obvious, a reasoner may need to provide them in order to gain credibility; a strong argument seeks to disarm the opposing facts as one means of proving its own conclusion. Such statements, which count against the conclusion as opposed to leading to it, are *counterconsiderations.* In our first example of an argument, on page 7, the first two statements are really counterconsiderations; instead of leading to the conclusion, they lead away from the conclusion, suggesting circumstances in which one can get away with fooling the public. A number of terms in ordinary language signal the counterconsiderations:

but ... ; although ... ; despite ... ; however ... ; yet ... ; to the contrary ... ; even though ... ; it may seem strange ...

When an argument makes reference to counterconsiderations, its conclusion may be introduced by terms which suggest that the conclusion follows soundly from its premises, making allowance for the counterconsiderations:

nevertheless ... ; however ... ; nonetheless ... ; despite ... ; even so ... ; still ...

Sometimes an argument will even include a whole *counterargument,* that is, an argument that reaches an opposite conclusion from the main argument itself or one of its main premises. For example, a counterargument against the conclusion that it is wrong for students to cheat might run as follows:

Cheating is not really bad. It's done by most students at some time or other, and they don't think any the worse of anyone for cheating. Even if the instructor catches you, usually you can bluff it out or intimidate the instructor—it's often just the instructor's word against yours. If you're accused before a review board, the students on it seldom vote to convict a student. So it's quite safe and not a big deal at all.

In dealing with an argument that contains a counterargument, the student should be careful to distinguish the two from one another; otherwise, it is possible to misinterpret the whole drift of the reasoning. The citation of a counterargument is common; to do so is an effective strategy for disproving the counterargument and, thus, for supporting one's own argument indirectly. Showing that the case for the opposition does not hold strengthens one's own case.

To disprove a counterargument, one proceeds, just as in attacking any argument, to do one or both of the following: (1) prove that one or more of the main premises are false; (2) prove that the premises do not support the conclusion. In order to criticize an argument effectively, it is thus necessary to pick out correctly the statements that are the premises and to distinguish them from the statements that express the conclusion. A most common and most avoidable error in reasoning is the failure to analyze the elements of the argument properly. A study of graduate students who were given papers in their own fields to analyze came up with surprising results: A number of them took the conclusion to be a premise or one of the premises to be the conclusion—which suggested they understood neither the evidence nor the line of reasoning. Others took the conclusion or a premise to be negative when it was affirmative, or affirmative when it was negative, a mistake that shows they failed to get the drift of the argument.

It is also important to understand the *structure* of the argument: One needs to note subarguments and their exact connection with the premises of the main argument; it is essential to distinguish different lines of argument from counterconsiderations and counterarguments. Otherwise one may find oneself disputing the wrong premises entirely. The structure of an argument is a clue to its logic and can indicate its points of weakness or strength. A chain argument is by nature vulnerable: Since it is a series of separate arguments in which the conclusion of one argument becomes the premise of the succeeding argument, proving one argument to be unsound also weakens all the following arguments and, ultimately, the main conclusion. For example, consider the chain argument below, one advanced by a number of distinguished scientists:

If life once emerges on a planet, one can expect the subsequent evolution of intelligent beings within some period of time. If there are intelligent beings on other planets, some of them may have been in existence for a longer span of time than ourselves. If that is the case, they have probably developed a technology superior to our own, one capable of communicating over vast distances in space and time. In that case, intelligent beings may have been beaming messages around the universe in search of other intelligent beings for quite some time. Therefore, it is not unreasonable to expect some form of communication from intelligent beings at a great remove from us in space and time.

This ingenious argument depends on the truth of a large number of premises, and also on the plausibility of the succession of conclusions derived from them, and thus is vulnerable at many points. For example, even if one granted that life is likely to emerge on many planets, that this life would evolve toward intelligent forms, and that these intelligent species might in some cases have existed longer than ourselves, one could reasonably doubt whether these intelligent species would develop a technology at all, much less one more advanced than our own. Rejecting one link in a chain of argument tends to destroy the power of the argument to establish the main conclusion. Thus, it is usually the case that a chain argument is undermined by the weakness of any one link in the chain.

Reasoning that contains several different lines of argument converging toward one conclusion is not so vulnerable. The soundness of the argument as a whole may not be seriously affected by the falsity of just one premise or the weakness of some one or other of its lines of argument. In some types of argument no one line of argument may be conclusive, but the cumulative effect of several lines of argument may be overwhelming. Nevertheless it should not be supposed that the soundness of an argument is guaranteed by the number or variety of its premises or lines of argument. Just as one good excuse is better justification than many feeble ones, so one strong premise may outweigh a number of inconsequential ones.

EXERCISE 1D

1. Underline the conclusion and bracket the premises of the arguments below. List any word or phrase signaling an argument, premise, conclusion, different line of argument, counterconsideration, or counterargument. Which premises are dubious? Which premises tend to support the conclusion?

    a. Since the pointer of the gas gauge is on Empty, the car will soon run out of gas.

    b. In this snapshot there is snow on the ground and the people are dressed in heavy clothing. So it must have been taken in the winter.

    c. The Emperor Augustus Caesar could not have been Julius Caesar's heir, for Caesar and his wife were childless.

    d. Mice given large quantities of saccharin develop bladder tumors. It follows that humans who eat saccharin may also develop cancer, because substances that cause cancer in mice usually cause cancer in humans.

    e. Marijuana users do not smoke as much as nicotine smokers but the burn is much hotter. Therefore marijuana smoking may have harmful physical effects, though not as bad as nicotine smoking.

    f. Drinking alcohol often makes people violent and offensive whereas smoking marijuana usually makes a person calm and agreeable. Doesn't that prove that smoking pot is good and drinking is bad for you?

2. List some counterconsiderations or construct a counterargument to any of the preceding arguments.

1E DETECTING GENUINE ARGUMENTS

Circular Argument

Ordinarily it does not make sense to use as a premise in an argument a statement that is just as doubtful as the conclusion drawn from it and thus needing proof itself. When the truth of a premise even presupposes the truth of the conclusion, logicians speak of *circular reasoning*. A familiar instance of circular reasoning goes as follows:

> The "Son of Sam" killer must be insane, for only a madman would commit murders such as these.

The conclusion that the killer is insane here depends on the premise that the acts he committed could only be performed by one who is insane—instead of, for example, by one who is vengeful, amoral, or acting under the influence of drugs or some passion. But this premise needs to be proved just as much as the conclusion that the killer is insane. Indeed, the latter statement would be part of the evidence for holding that only a madman would commit crimes such as these.

Circular reasoning is fallacious when the circular relationship of premise and conclusion is not recognized. The recognition of circularity in reasoning is useful: By revealing what we must know to be the case if we are to arrive at a given conclusion, we are able to identify vulnerable points in the reasoning. Circular reasoning is not necessarily fallacious. Some philosophic and scientific treatises employ circular reasoning: The interconnection of facts or concepts is sometimes such that it is not possible to separate the evidence for one from what would be evidence for another of the statements in the argument. As the American philosopher C. I. Lewis remarked, circular reasoning is not bad when the circle is big enough—if the reasoning follows a course through its subject matter that enables us to understand its windings and turnings and charts the territory for us.

Begging the Question

Circular arguments in the strictly logical sense are not overly common. More frequent are arguments in which the dubious premise and the conclusion are not so directly related as to make the argument circular. An argument obviously fails to prove its point when its main premise is as questionable as the conclusion it supports. Here is a common one:

All acts of murder are wrong. Since abortion is murder, abortion is clearly wrong.

But people who deny that abortion is wrong will usually also deny that abortion is murder, so the argument is hardly convincing, its premise being as controversial as its conclusion. Whenever an offered premise is dubious or controversial but not recognized to be so by the reasoner, the argument may be said to *beg the question.* An argument of this kind fails to meet one of the basic requirements of a sound argument, that it provide premises that are true and also support the conclusion. Of course, fallacious circular arguments also beg the question, that is, assume the truth of a premise requiring proof independently of the conclusion.

It is not always easy to determine whether a given text contains an argument. In a piece of writing, various points may seem to converge, yet there may be no definite place in the text where they are brought to a focus and a conclusion is drawn from them. In such cases, the best way to interpret the passage may be to supply a conclusion that does follow *from what is said.* If this cannot be done plausibly, it may be that there simply is not an argument, even though the writer may think he or she is presenting one. This does happen, even when a specific question is raised, and what we have is a *pseudoargument,* something that is only thought to be an argument. Students' answers in examinations sometimes fall into this category: The reasoner is unaware that he or she has not carried the thinking through to any conclusion; the student does not see that he or she is only listing facts or loosely associating ideas on the subject rather than working out logical connections from premises to conclusion. The first step in logic is to become aware of one's own deficiencies in reasoning as well as those one encounters elsewhere. For, as Socrates suggests in the *Symposium,* ignorance of these deficiencies is the greatest barrier to achieving knowledge:

> The truth of the matter is this: No god is a philosopher or seeker after wisdom, for he is wise already; nor does any man who is wise seek after wisdom. Neither do the ignorant seek after wisdom. For herein is the evil of ignorance, that he who is neither good nor wise is nevertheless satisfied with himself: he has no desire for that of which he feels no want.

Diagramming an Argument

Sometimes it is difficult to recognize the presence of an argument because it is expressed so as to be rhetorically effective, and the logical structure of the reasoning may not be apparent. Did the reader notice the pattern of reasoning in the preceding quotation? It contains several arguments and makes a number of points in a condensed way (as often happens in everyday reasoning) to establish its conclusion about the evil of ignorance. To show the logical structure of an argument, number each statement that expresses a premise or conclusion in serial order as it actually occurs:

(1) No god is a philosopher or seeker after wisdom, for (2) he is wise already; (3) nor does any man who is wise seek after wisdom. (4) Neither do the ignorant seek after wisdom. (5) For herein is the evil of ignorance, (6) that he who is neither good nor wise is nevertheless satisfied with himself: (7) he has no desire for that of which he feels no want.

Diagram the argument as follows: Draw a line, writing the number of the conclusion below the line and the numbers of its premises above the line. The above argument contains several interrelated arguments. The first argument is a short one expressed in the first sentence, whose conclusion, (1), is introduced by the phrase, "The truth of the matter is this," and whose premise is indicated by "for":

2   Every god is wise already
1   No god is a philosopher

Statement (3) is also a conclusion, drawn from an unstated premise which is like premise (2) but applied to wise men according to the *law of identity.* For such implied premises, we can use a new number, putting it in brackets as follows:

[8]   No one who is wise already seeks after wisdom.
2   No wise man seeks after wisdom.

Statement (4) is a parallel conclusion to (1) and (2) and follows from statement (6); statement (6) is itself an inference from statement (7). Finally, statement (5) follows from statement (4). When the conclusion of one argument is used as a premise of a succeeding argument (a subargument or chain argument), simply draw another line under it, to show its double function, as happens with statements (6) and (4):

<u>7</u>   An ignorant man has no desire for that of which he feels no want.
<u>6</u>   An ignorant man . . . is nevertheless satisfied with himself.
<u>4</u>   An ignorant man does not seek after wisdom.
5   The ignorant man's not seeking after wisdom is the evil of ignorance.

Paradoxical Reasoning

We are now ready to consider whether the premises of these arguments are true and whether they support the conclusion. The first argument is plausible, for omniscience is an attribute of divinity, making it unnecessary for gods to seek wisdom. But in the second, the supplied premise (8) is not obviously true, even though it does support conclusion (2) that wise men do not pursue wisdom, a conclusion most would find paradoxical. The conclusion of the third argument is also paradoxical, for we assume that the ignorant who lack knowledge will seek it. A *paradox* occurs when an apparently false statement is claimed or proved nevertheless to be true.

Rhetorical techniques such as paradox and irony are often used to jar us out of fallacious assumptions or to sharpen our reasoning. These two paradoxical arguments tempt us to infer that no one at all pursues wisdom, since neither the gods do nor do wise men nor ignorant men. But in drawing the conclusion that no men at all pursue wisdom, we are assuming that all men are either wise or ignorant. We readily suppose this to be true, taking "Each man is either wise or ignorant" to be an instance of the *law of excluded middle* (A thing must either be *A* or non-*A*, whatever *A* may be). But such an inference is mistaken, for the logical opposite of "wise" is "non-wise," not "ignorant." It is not the case that a man is either wise or ignorant: There is an intermediate state in between wisdom and ignorance, the state of the man who knows that there are things he does not yet know that are worth knowing. The paradoxical reasoning shows us that wisdom and ignorance are not true opposites, so that we cannot suppose that every man fits into one category or the other (a pattern of thinking—often fallacious—that logicians call *black-and-white thinking.* A fuller discussion of this pattern of reasoning is found in Chapter 11.) The whole argument shakes our common assumption that those who seek after knowledge are wise men who value it or ignorant men who need it: That the wise do not seek wisdom is a sign that they already possess this good, but in the ignorant the failure to pursue knowledge is a sign of their defectiveness. The evil of ignorance is that it tranquilizes the ignorant person in his imperfect state.

Elliptical Arguments

Even though we supplied one implicit premise in analyzing the logical structure of the *Symposium* extract, we still have left out some premises which are assumed by the argument but not expressed in so many words. We often need to fill in things that are not said in the text, but that are matters of common knowledge, in order to complete the connections required for the argument. For example we need to connect *not knowing* that one is lacking wisdom with not·being *bothered* by that lack with a generalization, such as "Those who are not aware of their defects are not bothered by them." Like many arguments, this argument is somewhat *elliptical;* that is, it leaves out premises or intermediate conclusions that the reader must supply.

It is not unusual, especially in everyday reasoning, for arguments to leave out essential steps; nor is an argument defective for doing so. It makes sense to leave out very obvious statements to render the reasoning more eloquent and less tedious and mechanical. When the premises or conclusions left unstated are obviously true or credible, no harm is done. If any one of them is questionable or implausible, however, then an inattentive reader can be taken in. Therefore, it is important to reconstruct an argument in enough detail to be sure that no dubious statement essential to the argument has been left out, thus making the argument look stronger than it is.

Rhetorical Questions and
Rhetorical Conditionals

Two other rhetorical features are commonplace in everyday reasoning: the rhetorical question and the rhetorical conditional statement. A *rhetorical question* is one in which the context or the way in which the question is posed makes clear what the answer to it is; it can thus be an alternative way of expressing the premise or conclusion of an argument. Both the premise and conclusion of an argument appear as rhetorical questions in the following:

Why shouldn't teachers have the right to strike? Don't they deserve annual cost-of-living increases just as much as auto workers?

Few of us would doubt that anyone who raised such questions was arguing that teachers do have the right to strike, and that his or her grounds for saying this are that he or she believes it is true that teachers deserve an annual cost-of-living increase just as much as auto workers.

In a *rhetorical conditional*, a whole inference from premise to conclusion is made by a conditional statement. A conditional statement is one of the form: *If* such-and-such is the case, *then* so-and-so is the case. One of the statements following the *if* or *then* is the conclusion of the argument; the other, the premise. Usually the statement following the *if* is the premise, and that following the *then* is the conclusion, as in the well-known saying,

If you can't take the heat, then you ought to get out of the kitchen.

However, one must read carefully to interpret correctly. Note which statement is implied to be a fact and what conclusion follows from that fact. The following conditional makes an inference:

If our society indeed cared about children, we would not spend more money on liquor than we do on schools. . . .

The burden of this hypothetical statement is clear: The writer is asserting that our society *does* spend more money on liquor than on schools and that this fact proves that we don't really care about children. The tone of disapproval implies that we ought to care about children, and the conclusion of the argument is that we ought to spend more money on things essential to their welfare.

Distinguishing a Genuine Argument

Genuine Argument and Ordinary Hypotheticals   An ordinary hypothetical statement does not express a whole argument all by itself, as the rhetorical conditional does. Usually it describes a state of affairs in which the occurrence of one thing is a condition for the occurrence of another sort of thing:

If it stays cold, the water in the pond will freeze.

All by itself, the above statement is not an argument. Of course, it could be one premise in an argument, as in the following:

If it stays cold, the water in the pond will freeze. Since the weather prediction is for an extended cold snap, we'll surely be able to skate on the pond in the next few days.

Genuine Argument and Motive-Giving Statements   It is sometimes difficult to distinguish a genuine argument, which seeks to prove that something is the case (the conclusion), from a statement explaining the motive or reason for something that has happened. The following is an example of the latter:

The actress shot her lover because she was angry at his leaving her.

Recalling a previous lesson, one might be tempted to interpret this as an argument, reasoning as follows: The sentence asserts two statements, "The actress shot her lover" and "She was angry at his leaving her." The latter statement is preceded by the logical particle "because," which often indicates the reason for the conclusion of an argument.

But we are now misinterpreting the whole sentence, for by this interpretation the point of the argument would be to prove that the actress shot her lover. Whereas in fact the point of the sentence is a different one: That the actress' shooting her lover was caused by her anger at his leaving. The whole sentence would be proved false if it turned out that the actress was relieved at her lover's leaving or shot him in self-defense; but then the truth of the statement that she shot her lover would not be affected. However, such is not the case with a genuine argument. Thus the sentence does not express a genuine argument. One must also be careful with particles such as *due to . . . , the reason being . . . , on account of . . . ,* which similarly often indicate a reason or motive being given for an event rather than a genuine argument to prove that an event has occurred. Particles such as *in order to . . . , so as to . . . , for the sake of . . .* seldom indicate arguments; they quite regularly point out the purpose of an action, as in "He confessed to the crime, in order that his wife might go free."

Statements attributing motive or purpose, like conditional statements, may function as the premises or the conclusion of an argument. For example:

The actress shot her lover because she was angry at him. Therefore, the shooting was not an accident.

Here the motive-giving statement is the premise of the argument. Occasionally, motives are offered as premises to prove that something is the case. The following, for example, is an argument that cites the existence of a motive as a reason for the conclusion:

The actress could not have killed her lover, because she loved him so passionately.

The following rule is helpful in determining whether a sentence containing terms such as *because, due to,* and so on should be interpreted as being an argument: *Such a sentence contains an argument if and only if it can be broken into two separate sentences, one of which functions as premise and the other as conclusion, without changing the original meaning of the statement.*

Genuine and Sound Arguments   To say that something is a genuine argument is very different from saying that it is a *sound* argument; a genuine argument is simply the kind of discourse to which we can apply logical principles in judging whether it is sound or unsound. Only a small part of what is said or written does in fact contain arguments; and it is only that fraction on which logic can pronounce.

Arguments are an important kind of thinking, and it is for this reason that logic is useful. But much thinking of great significance in private and public life, and in the continuing life of the mind, takes forms other than argument. Such thinking may be in the background of arguments we analyze; the strength or weakness of an argument may lie in the shallowness or depth of these background notions rather than in the explicit premises or conclusions of the argument. Reasoning is one kind of thinking that informs these conceptions; but other forms of conscious experience also contribute: aesthetic and moral perceptions; the insights of philosophy, history, religion, and literature; and our shared human and personal lives. The domain of logic is not the whole of human thinking, but at the same time we cannot separate its domain from that whole.

EXERCISE 1E

Which of the following are *genuine* arguments? Which of the genuine arguments appear to be sound:

1. The union will not go on strike in order to obtain more fringe benefits, but it will strike if its wage demands are not met.
2. Taking pills is the best method of birth control. Using contraceptive devices requires planning ahead, is troublesome, and interferes with pleasure. But all you need to do is take a pill a day and then do as you please.
3. I know that smoking heavily may lead to heart or lung disease and that sex with many partners can cause venereal disease, but I still believe that we should be merry while we can.

4. When Percival Lowell trained his telescope on Mars, he saw numerous lines crisscrossing the planet in a regular pattern. Since the lines were regular, he inferred they could not be natural phenomena, but must be artifacts. From this he speculated that Mars was or had been inhabited by intelligent beings. Because Mars also showed signs of desertism, he thought it probable the lines were canals built to transport water from one part of the planet to another.
5. If the lines observed on Mars are canals, they must be many miles wide in order to be seen from the earth.

Review Exercise for Chapter 1

1.* Can a genuine argument be constructed from the following statements of a CIA spokesman? Can the facts about the research at the hospital be made into premises leading to a conclusion about the CIA's purpose in sponsoring the research?

A San Diego hospital has been conducting experiments for the Central Intelligence Agency for two years on how the human brain reacts to what the eye sees, a CIA spokesman said yesterday. But the CIA spokesman denied published reports that the $100,000 contract with the Children's Hospital was to develop a sophisticated lie-detector system that electronically probes at the brain. . . . "It's so that we can better understand how the human brain absorbs and processes information . . . how the brain interprets visual materials. I want to stress that no children and no drugs are involved. . . . They are following very strict, existing federal guidelines on medical research involving humans."

The hospital's research director is supervising the experiments at the facility's Speech, Hearing, and Neurosensory Center, using volunteers from among the staff and friends. The responses in the cortex of the brain to what the eyes see are electronically recorded from brain waves and analyzed by computers, the *San Diego Union* reported yesterday. The volunteers respond to pictures of faces flashed on screens, with each picture evoking a different brain wave pattern. The computer can then determine which pictures are familiar and which are not even if the subject says nothing, the newspaper said. The director also has paired names and faces and has presented logical problems for which true or false answers produce certain brain waves, the newspaper said. "Using a good computer," he was quoted as saying, "the brain

*Reprinted by permission of the *Baltimore Sunpapers*.

wave confirmation of material presented to the volunteers can be available in a minute. The experiments have an accuracy rate of 80 percent so far."*

2. Analyze the following argument, showing premises, intermediate conclusions, and final conclusion. Does it "beg the question"?

Everyone must agree that capital punishment is "cruel and unusual punishment," and, consequently, that it ought to be abolished in a truly civilized community. For nothing can be more cruel than to put a person to death. Furthermore, there are nowadays very few cases in which the death sentence is imposed, and even fewer ones in which the sentence is actually carried out. Thus there is added to the cruelty of the sentence itself the agony of the condemned wondering whether the execution will take place at all.

*Reprinted by permission of the *Baltimore Sunpapers.*

chapter 2

The Logic of Statements

2A STATEMENTS AND SENTENCES

To obtain a sure grasp of the principles of reasoning we need to understand the logic of statements, which are the linguistic units of arguments. We have been speaking about statements and sentences in a casual way hitherto; now we will make the distinction between sentences and statements more carefully in line with logical practice. A *sentence* is a string of marks or sounds arranged in accordance with the grammatical rules of some natural language (that is, a language used by some linguistic community). In English we commonly categorize sentences into four different types:

1. Declarative: "The sun is shining."
2. Interrogative: "Is the sun shining?"
3. Imperative: "Shine on, sun!"
4. Exclamatory: "How brightly the sun shines!"

The distinction between these four types of sentence is a *grammatical* one: The characteristic arrangement of the grammatical parts of the sentences differs (the placing of verb, subject, adverb, and so on) as does the punctuation of them (the use of the period, comma, exclamation point, or question mark). There is also a difference of *logical* significance in the intent of a speaker in using one or the other of the sentence types. In an exclamatory sentence, the speaker expresses surprise, admiration, sorrow, or the like; imperatives are characteristically used to give commands; interrogatives, to ask for information; and declarative sentences, to put forward items of information.

A *statement,* in the logical sense, is a sentence used to say something true or false. The distinction between a statement and a sentence is not a grammatical one but a *logical* one, hinging on whether the sentence says something that correctly can be called *true* or *false.* We may not know whether the statement is true or false, but that does not matter. What matters is whether the sentence is used to say something capable of being true or false. In logical terminology we say a statement is a sentence having *truth-value;* that is, it is a sentence to which one can assign truth or falsity.

One may judge a speaker's expression of emotion to be strong or weak, sincere or hypocritical; a command may be more or less harsh, justified, or arbitrary. But it would be inappropriate to call exclamations or commands "true" or "false"; imperative sentences and exclamatory sentences do not characteristically make statements to which we can assign truth-value. Declarative sentences are the usual vehicles of statements: The speaker using a declarative sentence generally makes a claim about some fact. The existence of a fact corresponding to what the sentence says makes that statement true; the nonexistence of such a fact renders it false.

Interrogative sentences generally ask for information and thus they are usually not statements. But rhetorical questions, as noted in the previous chapter, are couched in such a way as to assert a fact, and so count as statements. Even when the question is not a rhetorical one, a speaker may sometimes give information in the course of asking a question. In asking the question, "Is this book, whose purpose is to explain the principles of everyday reasoning, hard to follow?" the assertion, "This book's purpose is to explain the principles of everyday reasoning" is included.

In the foregoing example, part of a sentence contains a statement, even though the sentence as a whole is not a statement. Any kind of sentence may contain a statement as a part, even imperative and exclamatory sentences. Consider the exclamatory sentence

Shine on, sun, as you have shone four billion years!

It contains the statement, "The sun has been shining for four billion years." Similarly the exclamatory sentence

How brightly shines the sun, the symbol of Apollo!

contains the statement, "The sun is the symbol of Apollo"—a sentence which is true or false.

When a sentence is compound, it may contain more than one statement. A compound sentence consists of two or more independent sentences linked together by a conjunction. For example, the conjunction *but* links two statements in the compound sentence

The sun is shining today, but it rained all day yesterday.

However, the compound sentence

The sun is shining today, but will it be shining in four billion years?

only asserts one statement, "The sun is shining today"; the other sentence is interrogatory.

A grammatically *complex* sentence usually makes just one statement; a complex sentence contains a subordinate clause which does not function independently of the main part of the sentence. An example of a complex sentence is

The sun shines in order that plants may grow.

This sentence makes only one assertion; "plants may grow" is not an independent statement. Statements attributing motive or purpose, which we distinguished from arguments in the previous chapter, are usually complex sentences. A complex sentence which contains only *one* statement cannot be an argument. An argument requires *two* independent statements: one to serve as premise, the other as conclusion.

On the other hand, compound sentences often do express arguments, for example, "Since there is snow on the ground, it must be wintertime." Here, "There is snow on the ground" is a statement acting as premise, and "it must be winter" is the conclusion inferred from it. However, the statement, "It's a long time since I saw you last." is clearly no candidate for being an argument, as it is a complex sentence containing one statement only. The word *since* is an adverb denoting time, not a logical conjunction, in this sentence.

In analyzing a piece of reasoning, it is essential to separate correctly the various statements made in the sentences of the text. Such statements—that is, sentences capable of being judged true or false—function as premises or conclusion. Whether a given statement is a premise or conclusion depends entirely on the specific sentences of the argument. Consider the sentence

It is winter, so there will be snow on the ground some of the time.

In this argument, "It is winter" is the premise, and "There will be snow on the ground some of the time" is the conclusion. Thus this argument is entirely different in its premise and conclusion from the argument of the preceding paragraph. Since the soundness or unsoundness of an argument turns on which statements are asserted as premises and which as conclusion, correct identification of statements is required before we can apply any principles of reasoning to the argument.

To summarize: Statements that may function as premise or conclusion of an argument are to be found in declarative sentences, subordinate clauses of any kind of sentence, independent parts of compound sentences, rhetorical questions, and rhetorical conditionals.

EXERCISE 2A

What statements are contained in the following sentences? Which sentences contain arguments?

1. If the sun turns cold, can life on earth survive?
2. Life on earth is possible because the earth is close enough to the sun to be warmed by its rays, but not so near that it is scorched by the sun's heat.
3. No star the size of the sun will ever become a black hole.
4. The sun not only lights up the day but also the night, for moonshine is reflected sunlight.
5. I pray that the sun may shine for four billion years more!
6. Sirius, the brightest star in the night sky, is at such a great distance from the earth that it must be many times larger than our sun.
7. God said, "Let there be light," and there was light.
8. Apollo is the god of the sun and Artemis the goddess of the moon in Greek mythology.
9. Why should we worry about the sun turning cold in four billion years when we won't any of us be around then?

2B   MEANING AND TRUTH-VALUE

In the previous section we in effect defined a statement as a sentence or part of a sentence having truth-value, that is, as capable of being judged true or false (regardless of whether we know which judgment is the correct one). We shall now distinguish between a sentence having meaning and a sentence having truth-value. Students sometimes become confused in applying criteria of reasoning because they fail to make this distinction. Every kind of sentence has *meaning*: Declarative, imperative, interrogative, and exclamatory sentences differ in the kind of meaning they convey, but they are all meaningful. The only requisite for a sentence to be meaningful is that it must be a *well-formed sentence*; that is, its words must be genuine words of a language and arranged in accordance with the linguistic conventions and grammatical rules of its language. But not every kind of sentence has *truth-value*: Declarative sentences generally do, interrogative sentences occasionally do, but imperative and exclamatory sentences generally do not.

Every sentence has a meaning, but not every sentence has truth-value. The meaning of a sentence is a function of the meaning of its words and their grammatical arrangement. The two sentences

1. The cat is on the mat.
2. The mat is on the cat.

contain exactly the same words but differ in meaning because these words are arranged differently. The two sentences

3. Is the cat on the mat?
4. Is the book on the table?

have the same grammatical arrangement but differ in meaning because they contain different words in that arrangement. Sentences 1 and 2 both have truth-value but are different in meaning. They might have the *same* truth-value; that is, they might both be true or both be false; or they might have *different* truth-values: 1 true and 2 false, or 1 false and 2 true. Sentences 3 and 4 have different meanings; being interrogative sentences, neither of them has truth-value. We can ask about the *meaning* of any kind of sentence; but we can raise the question of truth or falsity only about those sentences that qualify as statements. To ask whether a statement is true is not the same as to question its meaning.

The term *truth* has a rich connotation, which in some contexts overlaps that of *meaning*. We speak of "moments of truth," for example, as supremely meaningful occasions. We apply the notion of truth to experiences, to religious figures such as Christ or Buddha, to doctrines such as Christianity or Marxism. However, for the purposes of logic, we restrict our use of the terms *meaning* and *truth* without thereby implying that the logical use of these terms is the sole correct one. The work of logic is better done if we distinguish meaning from truth and restrict our use of the terms *true* and *false* so that they apply *primarily* to statements. Using the technical term *truth-value* will help to remind us that we are using the terms in a restricted sense. Still, we must keep in mind that there are only two truth-values, true and false, and that a false statement has truth-value just as much as a true statement.

One may well ask, what do we mean when we say that a statement is true? This philosophical question has been answered in various ways and is a subject of dispute. The theory best applicable to logic and common-sense thinking is the *correspondence theory of truth: To say that a statement is true is to say that there is some fact to which it corresponds; to say that a statement is false is to say that there is no such fact.* To say "The cat is on the mat" is true is to affirm the existence of a fact of a kind readily intelligible. The existence of facts corresponding to more complicated sorts of statements is harder to grasp, yet the notion may serve to define truth sufficiently for our purpose of distinguishing the truth value of a statement from its meaning.

We can know what a statement means without knowing whether the statement is true or false. We know the meaning of the statement, "There are intelligent beings on planets other than the earth," although we do not know its truth-value, that is, whether the statement is true or false. In order to tell whether a sentence is true or false, however, we need to know its meaning with some degree of clarity; otherwise we cannot tell whether some fact corresponds to it or not. One task of reasoning is that of clarifying the meaning of statements so as to be able to determine truth-value; we shall give attention to issues relating to the meaning of statements in this chapter and succeeding ones. To reason effectively, one must have not only a knowledge of the relevant facts but also the ability to express this knowledge in statements whose meaning is clear and unambiguous.

The meaning of a statement is conveyed by the grammatical arrangement of the specific words of the sentence; the truth or falsity of a statement is determined by the relationship between the arrangement of words and the world of facts. Thus the meaning of a statement and its truth-value are not two unrelated things; but the meaning of a statement typically depends on the grammatical ordering of the words in the sentence, whereas the truth of the statement typically depends on the ordering of facts in the world.

In the rest of this chapter we shall categorize statements into two different logical types, the first type involving meaning and the second type relating to truth.

In the first chapter we distinguished various types of reasoning in the following way: reasoning from one particular instance to another particular instance, reasoning from particular instances to generalities, reasoning from a generality to a particular instance, and reasoning from one generality to another generality. We shall now describe these steps of reasoning as *inferences* from one kind of statement to another statement of the same kind or a different kind. We can classify statements as singular statements or general statements, a classification which depends on the meaning of the statement.

A *singular statement* is a statement that has for its grammatical subject a word or phrase that is supposed to refer to an individual item—an object, event, or entity of the past, present, or future. These are singular statements:

The Hope diamond is in the Smithsonian Museum.

President Kennedy was a Roman Catholic.

The star Vega is in the constellation Lyra.

This cup of coffee is bitter.

The winter of 1978 was one of the coldest on record.

In contrast, a *general statement* (or generalization, or generality) has for its grammatical subject term a word or phrase that, merely in terms of grammar, could apply to an indefinite number of things, all of which come under the same heading. The following are *generalizations*, or general statements:

Diamonds are the hardest substance known.

No American president can be under 35 years of age.

All stars shine by their own light.

Drinking coffee is habit-forming.

Any winter in Baltimore is milder than a Boston winter.

In the set of singular statements the subject term refers to some particular thing which we can mark off from other things of the same or different kind: the Hope diamond, President Kennedy, Vega, this cup of coffee, the winter of 1978. In a generalization, however, the subject is a whole class of things, to which no limit is set other than a thing's having a certain property: diamonds, American Presidents, stars, drinking coffee, a Baltimore winter.

The distinction between a singular and a general statement is important because either one may function as the conclusion of an inference; but different kinds of reasoning and criteria of judgment apply, depending on whether the conclusion is singular or general. The kind and amount of evidence we need to draw a conclusion about the Hope diamond obviously differs from the evidence required to support a conclusion about diamonds in general. Singular statements often have a proper name ("Hope diamond," "President Kennedy") for a subject term; or a demonstrative term (*the, this, that*) precedes the subject term ("the winter of 1978," "this cup of coffee"). Generalizations have a plural noun for the subject term (diamonds, stars) or start with words like *all, no, every, none, any, most, few.*

We must be careful to distinguish a statement like the following from a genuine generalization:

All the people in this room have brown eyes.

In its normal use, such a statement refers to a limited group of people, not to an unlimited or indefinite number. To know whether such a statement is true, we need only summarize a limited number of singular statements, each of which applies to one person present: "Jones has brown eyes," "Smith has brown eyes," and so on. Such statements are sometimes called *accidental generalizations* (to differentiate them from the *essential* generalization); these may logically be regarded as shorthand summaries of a definite number of singular statements. But a true generalization is not just a summary of true particular statements. Take the statement:

All women have a set of XX chromosomes.

This statement applies to every woman of every era, past, present and future. It does not hold merely for all those women whose chromosomes have actually been observed but for any woman whatsoever. This is the mark of an essential generalization, which thereby makes a much broader claim than an accidental generalization.

EXERCISE 2B

Say whether each of the following is a singular statement or a general statement. Is any statement an accidental generalization?

1. All the stars visible in the night sky belong to the Milky Way.
2. An American president is the highest ranking elected official in the United States.
3. No American president has been Jewish.
4. Two stars in the Big Dipper are moving in a different direction from the other five.
5. The Big Dipper constellation is also called Ursa Major.
6. All the stars in the Big Dipper can be seen with the unaided eye.

7. Every voter in a primary election is either a Republican or Democrat.

8. The Three Musketeers were French noblemen.

9. Women presently comprise about 53 percent of the U.S. population.

10. The Man in the Iron Mask was the twin brother of Louis XIV.

2C NECESSARY AND EMPIRICAL STATEMENTS

We will now consider a very different way of categorizing statements, based not on meaning but on *how we know the statement to be true or false.* Again examine the statement, "All women have a set of XX chromosomes." In order to assert the truth of this statement, a large number of studies were run, theories elaborated, and data assembled from observations of actual women. To assert a simpler generalization, such as "Women have softer skin than men," doesn't require such formidable evidence, only more easily made sense perceptions. Even less observation is needed to verify a singular statement, such as "Marilyn Monroe was fair-skinned." A statement requiring that we actually observe things in the world (whether that observation is easily made or complicated) is called an *empirical* statement. (The term *empirical* comes from a Greek word which means "finding out by using the senses.") An empirical statement may be false or true, just as a generalization may be false or true. The point of calling a statement empirical is to indicate that we need to investigate something by some technique of sense perception to find out whether it is true or false. Empirical statements are sometimes called *contingently true* or *contingently false,* since their truth or falsity is contingent, or depends on, what the empirical facts happen to be.

A contrasting group of statements are *necessary statements,* statements that are necessarily true or necessarily false whose truth or falsity does not depend on what the empirical facts are. An example is "All women are female." To know that statement is true, one does not need to make a check of the women of one's acquaintance; one only needs to know what the word *woman* means. The word is tightly linked in our language with the idea of a female, so that if one understands what *woman* means one sees that being a woman has a necessary connection with being female. A necessary statement is one that asserts some kind of necessary connection of meanings. Many necessary statements turn on the meaning of the subject term in the sentence, as in "All women are female." In such a statement, the meaning of the predicate term in the sentence is contained in the meaning of the subject term, as being female is a necessary part of being a woman. This type of necessary statement is sometimes called an *analytic* statement, since it analyzes or breaks down the meaning of the subject term into one or more of its components. (In contrast, an empirical statement is one in which the predicate term *adds to* the meaning of the subject term, and is thus called *synthetic,* as in "All women have an XX set of chromosomes.")

Some necessary statements are more complicated. Instead of analyzing the meaning of the subject term, the statement asserts that a logical connection exists as a result of the whole logical structure of the sentence or the interrelationships among the terms of the sentence. In the necessary sentence, "Things equal to the same thing are equal to each other," we have to consider not only the meaning of *equality* but how things that are equal to the same thing stand in relation to each other. To know whether such a statement is true we need to think through the relationships which exist among our basic notions.

A related distinction which has been important in the history of philosophy is between *a priori* and *a posteriori* statements. Empirical statements, such as "All women have a set of XX chromosomes," are only known to be true *after* we have made observations that confirm them, or *a posteriori*—the Latin term means "following or subsequent to experience or observation." But an a priori statement, such as "Things equal to the same thing are equal to each other," we know to be true independently or before observation, just by thinking the matter through in our minds. The Latin term *a priori* means "knowable independently or before observation." The so-called *laws of thought* described in Chapter 1 are a priori truths. The statements that express laws of logic and mathematics are put in the category of a priori knowledge, whereas statements expressing laws of the natural and social sciences are typically empirical.

Just as empirical a posteriori statements may be true or false, so may necessary a priori statements. The statement "Three apples and two pears are four things in all" is necessarily false; the statement "Three apples and two pears are five things in all" is necessarily true. A statement that is necessarily true is called a *tautology*; one that is necessarily false is a *contradiction*.

The distinction between necessary and empirical statements is useful in reasoning because it helps us to know how to go about questioning the truth of premises in a given argument. If a premise is an empirical statement, we need evidence from observation of facts to dispute it; at some point we will need to use inductive reasoning. If a premise is a necessary statement, a different kind of evidence is called for, requiring us to think through the meaning of terms or the relationships existing among basic notions. Thus, determining whether a statement is empirical or necessary may be an important preliminary step in assessing an argument.

Consider the following statement, which appeared as a filler in the column of a daily newspaper:

All the matter in the solar system consists of chemical elements.

If this statement is meant to be an empirical one, then evidence from observation is relevant to its truth or falsity: Is there anything in the solar system that is not a chemical element? Such things as free electrons, cosmic rays, and photons occur in the solar system, yet we would not classify them as bits of hydrogen, helium, chlorine, and so on. Thus if this statement is meant to be an empirical statement, as we would expect a newspaper filler to be, it is false, not true.

It sometimes happens, as may be the case with the above example, that a necessary statement is mistakenly taken as an empirical statement. The statement may mean to say that all material particles of the solar system are composed of one or more elements in the periodic table, thus excluding free electrons and photons and cosmic rays from the category of material things. Taken this way, the statement would seem to be defining what it is to be a material particle and making a necessary statement analyzing the meaning of "matter in the solar system." In this case, whether the statement is true or false will depend on whether we accept the implied definition of "matter in the solar system." In the next chapter we will formulate principles for correct definition. These principles would be relevant for deciding the matter, because definitions are a kind of necessary statement often encountered in reasoning.

As the above example shows, it is not always clear whether a given statement is necessary or empirical; there are genuinely controversial cases as well as borderline cases. However, the distinction marks an important difference in our ways of knowing the truth or falsity of a large class of statements and serves a useful function in ordinary reasoning.

We will take note of one objection which may have already occurred to the reader. We have spoken of a statement as being necessary when its truth or falsity follows from our knowing the meaning of the statement, and as being empirical when knowing the meaning does not suffice—we need to observe the things in the world to which the statement refers. Yet in order to know the meaning of many words, we must observe some of the things to which a word refers. For example, one cannot know the meaning of *red* or *color* unless one has at some time perceived red things or discriminated colors. Thus we need to clarify the notion of a necessary statement to take account of this circumstance; we must not assume that *no* experience or observation at all is required; merely that *no other* experience is needed beyond what is required to understand the meaning of the word or the statement in question. With this qualification we can say that even one who is color-blind is able to say that the statement "Red is a color, not a sound" is a necessarily true statement. Of course there is a sense in which such a person would not understand the meaning of *red* as fully as a non-color-blind person would, but his or her understanding would be better than that of a person without sight. However, insofar as each of the three understands how the words *color* and *red* function in language, they would all take the statement to be necessarily true, not empirically true or false.

It happens not infrequently that the meaning of a term undergoes change in the course of time, often because of increases in our knowledge. The statement, "The sun is a star," ranks as a necessarily true statement given our present state of astronomical knowledge, but it might well have been a statement of surprisingly empirical fact to a cultured citizen of fifth-century Athens or even to a child in our own time. We cannot insist that every statement is unambiguously or uncontroversially necessary or empirical: Our criteria for distinguishing between necessary and empirical statements must include reference to the common knowledge current in a community of language users.

EXERCISE 2C

Say whether each of the following statements is necessary or empirical.

1. Whenever equals are added to equals, the sums are equal.
2. A straight line is the shortest distance between two points.
3. Acids turn blue litmus red.
4. Bases turn blue litmus red.
5. Warlocks are male humans with magical powers.
6. All living things have the capacity to reproduce.
7. Mary Shelley was the sister of the poet Percy Shelley.
8. Mary Shelley wrote the horror story *Frankenstein.*
9. A body in motion will continue in motion unless stopped by an external force.
10. Bachelors are neurotic.

chapter 3

Three Types of Definition

Definitions are found in all kinds of reasoning, everyday as well as scientific. Reasoning is used in formulating a definition, and reasoning is called for in judging its soundness. In what follows we examine three common types of definition and list rules for judging them: (1) standard definition, (2) stipulative definition, (3) real definition.

To apply these rules to definitions effectively, we have to give some attention to the existence of different kinds of words or terms that occur in language. Logicians classify the words that appear in sentences into three different groups: *proper names, general terms,* and a miscellaneous group called *syncategorematic terms.* General terms are the usual subjects of definition. Proper names hardly need explanation: Each reader has a proper name which he and others use in sentences about him. The point of a proper name is to single out the exact thing referred to by the words that make up the name. Statements whose subject term is a proper name are *singular statements.* Ideally a proper name ought to belong to only one thing; for this reason people with common names like Smith or Jones use initials or other means to make the name apply uniquely to them. It is not, however, the function of a proper name to describe the characteristics of its bearer but simply to identify him or her. (Many proper names do have an archaic connotation of a trait, occupation, or place of residence, such as Smith, White, or Hamburger.)

In the case of the general terms—the most common subject of a generalization—the situation is quite different. The function of a general term is not to make a unique reference, as a proper name does, but to refer correctly but indefinitely to an unlimited number of things. The proper name, "Rosalynn Carter," refers to just one person; but the general term, "American First Lady" refers to an indefinite number of women, some living, some dead, and others not yet born (Jacqueline Onassis, Dolly Madison, and others). Of course, the things to which a general term correctly applies or refers (its *referents*) are decided by the connotation of the general term. The *connotation* is the set of properties that a thing must have in order for the term to be true of it. In the case of the term, "American First Lady," the usual connotation is "wife of the President." Since on occasion (in the case of a President without a wife), the term is used of a daughter, sister, or niece of the President, the connotation stated more broadly would be "a close female relative of the President, entrusted with carrying out the official duties of the President's wife."

It is important to separate the connotation of a general term from its referents because the rules for definition make use of this distinction. The connotation of a term can always be expressed *in words* and indicates a property or set of characteristics associated with something, as the connotation of "American First Lady" is expressible as "the wife of the President, or a close female relative who carries out the duties of the President's wife." The referents of a general term are the *very things* in the world that do possess the properties indicated in the connotation: Rosalynn Carter, Jacqueline Onassis, Betty Ford, Mamie Eisenhower, and so on. In common speech the term *meaning* covers both connotation and reference, but in our study of definitions it is important to specify the dimension of meaning at issue. (Logicians also use the terms *intension, designation,* or *signification* for the dimension of meaning here called *connotation*; the words *denotation, extension,* or *comprehension* for what we are calling *reference.*)

The difference between connotation and reference emerges quite sharply when we compare proper names and general terms with the third type of words, *syncategorematic* terms. Syncategorematic terms are words such as *of, for, how.* These words are grammatical particles such as adverbs, conjunctions, pronouns, demonstratives, and prepositions, and have no sense apart from their use in sentences or sentence parts. Syncategorematic terms do have connotation—the word *above* is opposite in connotation to *below,* or example—but there are no entities, events, or properties to which they refer. To signify or refer, they have to be embedded in a phrase or sentence with other words which do have reference. For example, there is no entity that is the referent for the word *sake,* although the word has a connotation we employ successfully in the exclamation "For goodness' sake!" and in phrases like "for John's sake" and "for the sake of honor." In summary, syncategorematic terms have connotation but no reference, proper names have reference but no connotation, and general terms have both connotation and reference.

3A STANDARD DEFINITIONS

General terms are the usual candidates for definition. What we most commonly recognize as a definition is a *standard* definition: a statement that analyzes the connotation of a general term in the standard usage of a linguistic community. Although dictionaries supply much of the connotation of a term, a dictionary citation is often only a starting point when dealing with a piece of reasoning which calls for a definition. A dictionary entry usually points out the connotation of single words, indicating other words that may replace the given term in various contexts; often a dictionary will report very specialized uses of a term which are not part of its ordinary connotation. The full meaning of a term is not to be found in the words occurring beside it in the dictionary. Words interact with other words and therefore context is always a crucial index of a word's meaning. Also, words have a history in the written works and common speech of a culture which provides a framework for their understanding.

When a definition occurs in a piece of reasoning, some particular subject matter is under consideration; what is called for is a definition that incorporates the connotation of the term as it is used in significant true statements dealing with the subject matter. Thus a definition should not limit itself to listing words that might replace the term in a variety of sentences, but should seek to analyze its connotation in the context of the appropriate subject. Often a definition should be fleshed out with examples in order to make its referents clear. Also, counterinstances of its reference range can be given, or sometimes one can relate its connotation to that of other closely connected terms used in the subject.

Just as it is essential in following an argument to distinguish the statements that are premises from those that represent the conclusion, so we have to be able to recognize a statement as a standard definition. A definition should not be confused with an empirical statement of fact about the things talked of; unless we distinguish a definition from an empirical statement we are not in a position to judge it properly. Standard definitions are necessary statements; thus the proper way to find out whether a standard definition is true or false is to reflect on the meaning of the subject term of the statement. It is not always the case that a standard definition is announced by words like *definition, connotation,* or *meaning.* Sometimes the presence of a definition is implied by the context of the reasoning rather than made explicit. The presence of a standard definition is frequently indicated by phrases such as the following:

To say that *X* is to say that *Y.*

By a thing's being *X* one knows that it is *Y.*

Whatever is *X* is also *Y.*

To be *X* is the same as being *Y.*

To call a thing *X* is to imply that it is *Y.*

Anything that is *X* must be *Y.*

If a thing is *X* it necessarily follows that it is *Y.*

All *X* are *Y.*

All and only *X* are *Y.*

The words indicated by the *X* position represent the term being defined; the words in the *Y* position, the connotation being supplied to it in the definition. For example, look at this definition:

To say that something is a statement is to say that it is a sentence which may be called true or false.

The term being defined is *statement*; the connotation supplied in the definition is "sentence which may be called true or false." The term being defined is often called by the Latin term, the *definiendum* (meaning, *the term to be defined*), and the phrase that does the defining by the Latin term *definiens.*

We will understand better the rules for judging a standard definition once we review its main purposes. One purpose is to explain the meaning of a term previously unknown or not well known to a particular person or group. When the term is just one word, like *pugnacious*, a dictionary can often supply the wanted meaning. However, when the meaning of a combination of words is at issue, like *bilaterally symmetric*, the dictionary may not be enough; it may tell us what *bilateral* means and what *symmetric* means, but that knowledge may not enable us to understand what the two words mean together. This problem often occurs when some specialized knowledge is being related to nonspecialists: In an article describing studies of hypertension in children, the writer may expect his readers to be aware that hypertension has to do with having abnormally high blood pressure. But he could not expect them to understand the difference between *primary hypertension* and *secondary hypertension*, even though they also know the meaning of *primary* and *secondary.*

Often it is desirable to define ordinary words of a language which reflect notions crucial to the course of reasoning, in order to make a point more effectively. For example, a definition of *desire* would make the line of reasoning in the *Symposium* passage discussed in the first chapter more intelligible. The German philosopher Heidegger criticized contemporary ways of thinking for not being mindful of significant philosophic distinctions and nuances of meaning present in the terms we use to describe our experiences. This carelessness in speaking, he maintained, is inseparable from a debasement in our thinking. The work of philosophers such as Quine, Wittgenstein, Austin, and Ryle, though undertaken from a very different philosophical viewpoint, also demonstrates that an understanding of the workings of ordinary language is essential in dealing with issues relating to the basic concepts with which we operate both in science and in everyday life. An important function of standard definitions is to preserve the distinctive meanings of terms that are put to significant use in various forms of reasoning.

Since a standard definition analyzes the connotation possessed by a term in the actual practice of a linguistic community, it is a statement which is either necessarily true or necessarily false, in accordance with the distinction made in the preceding chapter. Whether the definition is true or false depends on whether it embodies faithfully the connotation the term has in its primary significant uses. We check for truth or falsity by determining whether the connotation offered in the definition (the *definiens*) matches that of the term being defined (the *definiendum*). By applying the following five rules we can reach a conclusion about the correctness of a definition.

Rules for Standard Definition

1. The defining term (*definiens*) should point out the crucial properties a thing must have so that the original term applies correctly.
2. The defining term should be better understood than the original term.
3. The *referents* of the defining term should coincide with the *referents* of the original term.
4. The *connotation* of the defining term should be consistent with the *connotation* of the original term.
5. The defining term should not be viciously circular.

We shall explain and illustrate the rules above by considering some definitions of the term *mother*. The meaning of this term is so obvious that the reasons for the success or failure of the definitions offered will be evident and will enable the student to grasp the point of the rules above.

1. *The defining term should point out the crucial properties possessed by those things to which the original term applies.* This rule relates to the *connotation* of the terms in the definition. The connotation of a term is regularly associated with a set of ideas and is expressed in words. Many or few ideas, of a simple or complex kind, may be associated with a term. Some may be very closely associated; others may be marginal. Some may be known by all users, whereas others may be quite idiosyncratic. The connotation of a term not only may vary from one user to another but may also even shift from one generation of users to another. Although the connotation may not be absolutely constant, this variability is not a defect in and of itself; it reflects the fact that language is an instrument responsive to changes in the knowledge, outlook, interest, and practice of its human users. Some deviations in connotation arise because language can be misused as well as used; a standard definition can reveal these kinds of deviation.

To function as a word in language a term must have some fixed core of meaning which is relatively permanent, in relation to which we can measure fluctuations in usage. The connotation of a term is not so much a solid block as it is a "planet"—a solid core of meaning to which other ideas are attached more or less firmly, with more peripheral notions, subject to change in the course of time, serving as the planet's "atmosphere." A definition ought to expose the solid core, which is the basis for notions closely connected with the term, but it cannot be expected to include all of those peripheral notions which are more subject to individual variations and cultural outlook. To apply some previously discussed terms, a definition ideally will account for the necessary connections of the general term but need not cover all or even most of its contingent associations.

Take the word *mother,* one of the oldest words in our language. It is a word that almost universally suggests a person to be respected, one who shows unselfish devotion to a child. Recent trends are eroding many of these sentimental associations, even expectations, about the behavior of mothers. Nevertheless there remains a fixed constant meaning to the term, which enables us to debate the issue of what a mother ought to be or whether motherhood is a worthy ideal at all.

The "planetary core" of the term *mother* is quite obvious: a female who has given birth to offspring. We necessarily include the notions of being female and of having at least one child in the connotation of *mother.* Is this combination of ideas the whole of the word's connotation? We have a number of terms which are spinoffs from the word *mother,* like *foster mother, stepmother, godmother, motherly, motherless;* their connection with it is not intelligible if these two biological attributes constitute the whole of its connotation. Closely connected with the biological attributes is the notion of a social role: A mother is one who rears or takes care of a child. Many ideas closely or loosely connected with the term revolve around this part of the connotation, which itself has strong causal and cultural bonds with the biological features of the connotation.

A definition of a term is not defective for omitting features more loosely associated with the term, as long as it includes those features that enable us to understand the term's significant uses in typical sentences of the language. In the case of *mother* we need to include the social role. If we say of someone, "She is an excellent mother" or "She is a terrible mother," we are quite unlikely to be praising that person, or blaming her, for her aptitude for delivering children; we are understood to be speaking of how she carries out the duties of child care.

2. *The defining term should be better understood than the original term.* This criterion holds for all definitions, whose function is to make the meaning of a term clearer than it was initially. The person who is formulating a definition must choose words that not only give an accurate analysis of the features of the connotation but which are also easy to understand. The appropriateness of a definition depends on those to whom it is addressed: An audience of specialists may find intelligible a definition phrased in technical language, but children or laymen need simpler ordinary terms illustrated with concrete examples. In the case of *mother* a definition like "female progenitor" is hardly likely to be helpful to one who did not understand the original term.

3. *The referents of the defining term should coincide with the referents of the original term.* In applying this rule we compare the *referents* of the original term with those of the defining words or phrase. The things to which the defining term applies should be *all* and *only* those things to which the original term applies. Anyone correctly called *mother* should be female and have at least one child of her own to care for. Conversely anyone correctly described as "a female with a child of her own to care for" should be a mother. Both conditions have to be met, or the defining phrase will not capture the connotation successfully. The defining term may be *too broad*—it may be true of some things to which the original term does not apply. The definition of *mother* as "animal with offspring" is too broad: It covers all mothers but it also applies to all fathers. A defining term is *too narrow* when it fails to cover all the things to which the original term applies. If we defined *mother* as "woman with offspring" this phrase would be too narrow, as it leaves out all nonhuman animal mothers. A definition often fails by being both too broad and too narrow at the same time, leaving out some things that belong and bringing in others that do not belong under the original term. The definition of *mother* as "a woman whose prime occupation is the care of children" would leave out animal mothers (who ought to be included) and cover female pediatricians, day-care attendants, and nurses (who ought to be excluded).

In testing the correctness of a definition, it is essential to compare the referents of the original term with those of the defining phrase. However, with abstract terms of complex meaning such as *justice,* it is often difficult to find a defining phrase which covers all and only the things to which the original term applies—there may be cases genuinely hard to decide. In defining such terms we must content ourselves with insisting that a defining term cover the significant and noncontroversial cases on the one hand, and also exclude what the original term would exclude, on the other. A definition of *justice* that requires us to include putting to death an innocent person as an instance of it would hardly do; nor would a definition that excluded the paying of one's debts.

4.   *The connotation of the defining term should be consistent with the connotation of the original term.* A defining term is inconsistent when it includes in its connotation an attribute that cannot logically coexist with some part of the connotation of the original term. In the case of a term of straightforward meaning, like *mother*, the inconsistency is apt to be glaring, but inconsistency may creep into definitions of less familiar phrases. Suppose we define *mother* as "one who sires offspring," for example. Here the notion of *siring*, which is part of the connotation of the defining term, is inconsistent with being *female*, an essential part of the connotation of *mother*. The inconsistency may also appear within the connotation of the defining term itself, as would be the case were we to define *mother* as "a female who sires offspring." Here the two elements of the connotation, "female" and "one who sires offspring," contradict one another. Such a definition would break the law of non-contradiction, mentioned in Chapter 1 as a basic logical law, and would be unsound.

5.   *The defining term should not be viciously circular.* A definition is viciously circular when the defining term provides a connotation that includes part of the original term but does not dispel the obscurity in the original term that makes it puzzling. A definition of *mother* as "one who mothers a child" is an example of vicious circularity: A key attribute of the defining term, "one who mothers," sends us back to the original term, so that there is no real advance in understanding. A definition may be circular, but not *viciously* circular. This occurs when part of the connotation of the defining term repeats the original term but the remainder of the connotation of the defining term succeeds in clearing up what was puzzling in the original term. In defining "Gold Star Mother," we might say, "a mother whose son has lost his life in battle under heroic circumstances and who has been posthumously awarded a medal for bravery by the United States Congress." Here the word *mother*, which appears in the original term, is repeated in the connotation of the defining term; but as it might reasonably be taken as not needing explanation, the definition as a whole is not viciously circular.

The preceding five rules point out what to look for in judging the correctness of a definition offered in reasoning, and also in criticizing any definition a reasoner himself constructs. The following procedures are useful in framing a definition:

1. First, determine what kind of thing is referred to in the original term to be defined—is it a material thing, a process, a property, an activity, a place, a mental state, and so on. Choose as a basic term for the connotation of the definition a word whose referents are the same type of thing. For example, suppose one is asked to define *pewter*. Pewter is a material thing that is a kind of metal. Thus the term *metal* can serve as a basic part of the definition.

2. Review the characteristics that differentiate the kind just determined from other things of the same kind; that is, what distinguishes pewter as a metal from other metals? Pewter differs from other metals in being *semiprecious*, so that we can add that term to our definition. Continue this procedure, adding to the definition until the connotation built up includes in its referents all and only those things that come under the referents of the original term. That is, consider how pewter is to be distinguished from other semiprecious metals and express these features in a complete definition which might begin: "Pewter is a semiprecious metal. . . ."

When the original term to be defined is of a grammatical kind such that the above procedure cannot be carried out, try a contextual definition; that is, put the term to be defined in a sentence that gives the verbal context in which the original term is generally found. This procedure is useful in handling the definition of a term like *bilaterally symmetric*. We construct a sentence showing its typical context, such as "A figure which is bilaterally symmetric is one. . . ," then we complete the sentence by specifying the features of the term in accordance with the procedures just indicated. If the definition is correct, the sentence is a necessarily true sentence.

In distinguishing the meaning of one term from another (a task often demanded of a student on examinations), the rules and procedures for definition just described are applicable. The procedures may be adapted as follows: (1) Indicate the main point(s) of similarity between the two terms. (2) Specify the crucial differences between the two, within the point(s) of similarity. For example, in distinguishing the meaning of *primary hypertension* from *secondary hypertension,* one could say: "Both are physical disorders involving abnormally high blood pressure [point of similarity]; in primary hypertension the abnormal blood pressure is caused by some improper state or malfunctioning of the arteries, whereas in secondary hypertension it is a symptom of disease in some other bodily organ, such as the heart or kidneys [point of difference]."

EXERCISE 3A

1. Apply the rules for definition to determine whether the following standard definitions are correct.

    a. Pewter is an easily worked semiprecious metal.

    b. To call someone a philosopher is to say that he or she knows the unknowable.

    c. Whatever is bilaterally symmetric always has two equal and opposite sides.

    d. The disease named *blackspot* is a serious and persistent fungus disease which causes black spots on the leaves and stems of roses.

    e. By *mode of production* is meant the way in which people produce and exchange the means of life—food, clothing, shelter.

2. Construct a standard definition for the following, using the procedures outlined in the text. Check for correctness by applying the rules for definition.

    a. Stainless steel

    b. Foul ball

    c. Standard of living

    d. Thriftiness

    e. Point of no return

3. Distinguish between the following terms, using the procedures outlined in the text.

    a. *Line drive* and *pop fly*

    b. *Property rights* and *civil rights*

    c. *Wisdom* and *cunning*

    d. *Collision insurance* and *liability insurance*

    e. *Boiling point* and *freezing point*

3B FURTHER USES OF STANDARD DEFINITION

Standard definitions are useful in eliminating errors of reasoning caused by vagueness and ambiguity of language. A term (or phrase or whole sentence) is *vague* if it does not convey any one precise meaning. *Ambiguity*, on the other hand, occurs when a term, phrase, or sentence offers more than one meaning. Vagueness and ambiguity cannot be entirely eliminated in the language we use and are not in themselves faults of language. On the contrary, ambiguity makes it possible to express very many things with a relatively small vocabulary and with uncomplicated grammar, which can be an advantage in the use of a language. Most readers and listeners are skilled enough in dealing with the vagueness and ambiguity in language that they can pick out the intentions of the speaker with remarkable accuracy. Computers, which operate with the actual strings of words in sequence, have difficulty in distinguishing which of the logically possible meanings is correct. Formal definition is not always called for in eliminating vagueness or ambiguity; often more careful rewording will suffice. Consider this statement, made in a discussion of morality and contemporary culture:

> To prevent the expression of everything: that is the irreducible function of culture.

This statement is both vague and ambiguous, but we can make its meaning more precise and resolve the ambiguity without recourse to definition. The problematic phrase is "To prevent the expression of everything." Remembering its context in a discussion of morality and culture, we can spell out the probable meaning as follows: "The irreducible function of culture is to prevent people from expressing all their urges or desires in action; culture forces people to repress some urges and permits or encourages the expression of others." Eliminating the vagueness by more specific rewording also helps to resolve ambiguity. "To prevent the expression of everything" could be a way of saying "To prevent the expression of some things," or it could mean "To prevent the expression of anything whatsoever." The latter meaning would not ordinarily recommend itself to a reader, since it hardly makes sense to say that the function of culture is to reduce men to paralysis. The ambiguity does not greatly impede understanding, because the latter meaning seems too ludicrous to be the correct one.

Much vagueness and ambiguity is of this kind: It doesn't interfere with understanding so much as it detracts from the effectiveness of the reasoning. The common human background shared between reader and writer often enables the reader to discard possible constructions of the words and to interpret them appropriately despite the vagueness and ambiguity of what is said. This common human background cannot ensure communication, however, when the subject is unfamiliar, or when the writer's thought is unconventional. It may happen that the vagueness and ambiguity of language lead the writer himself to overlook the wooliness of his own reasoning. In such cases standard definitions of key terms or phrases may reinforce the argument and expose weaknesses in the reasoning even to the writer himself.

Equivocation and Question-Begging

Standard definitions help one to detect mistakes in reasoning caused by (1) *equivocation* and (2) *question-begging definitions*. Both are to be found in this argument:

Is there life after death? This age-old philosophical problem of the immortality of the soul may now be solved by evidence that demonstrates conclusively that human consciousness does survive the death of the body. To say that the soul is immortal is to say that the soul retains the capacity to think, perceive, and feel even though the body's vital functioning has ceased and death has taken place. Reports of persons who have been returned to life by medical teams after all their vital signs had ceased for substantial lengths of time prove that the soul continues to operate after the death of the body. These patients say that during the period of death they perceived the actions of the medical teams upon their bodies as from a vantage point above the scene; many heard and saw dead relatives speak and beckon to them; some experienced feelings of peace and tranquility, and others felt fear and anxiety. These experiences prove that the soul does continue to have conscious experience after death, and that it is, therefore, immortal. There is indeed life after death!

In this argument the word *death* is *equivocal*; that is, it has two distinct meanings. In the first and the concluding sentences the connotation of the term is the usual one: an irreversible state in which the body falls into decay. But in the rest of the passage the word denotes a very different state: the stopping of the body's vital functioning for a limited period of time, after which it is restored by medical intervention. To indicate the difference, this state is sometimes called *clinical death.* The presence of human consciousness in the latter state of clinical death cannot be identified with its presence in ordinary death. But in this argument the proof of the soul's power to survive death depends on the correctness of identifying the two states by calling them both *death.* When a term shifts its meaning in the course of an argument, the term is said to be equivocal; in cases such as the preceding one, in which the soundness of the argument depends upon this shift in meaning, the argument is said to commit the *fallacy of equivocation.*

The *fallacy of question-begging definition* is also illustrated in the foregoing argument. This fallacy involves circular reasoning, as its name suggests, in which the dubious premise is a definition. A correct standard definition is a necessarily true statement, and so qualifies to be the premise of an agument. The soundness of an argument containing a standard definition as a premise turns on (1) the correctness of the standard definition and (2) whether the subject of the conclusion of the argument is properly included in the connotation or reference of the original term.

In the third sentence of the argument *immortality of the soul* is defined in such a way that the experiences of clinically dead humans are given as instances of the immortality of the soul, and thus said to constitute the so-called "proof" that the soul outlives the body and is immortal. But we would not attribute immortality of soul to persons whose vital functions had stopped and been subsequently restored; such persons still face the prospect of eventual death and are far from immortal. A different definition of immortality of the soul, in which the experiences of persons who have been "clinically dead" are excluded, is obviously in order and would destroy this argument.

When a conclusion follows from a definition of a term and the definition turns out to be false or controversial, then we have an argument that commits the fallacy of question-begging definition. In general we cannot settle a substantive question, such as whether or not human beings continue to enjoy conscious existence after the physical death of the body, by constructing a definition that leads verbally to the conclusion. Only genuinely verbal disputes can be settled by standard definitions. A verbal dispute is one that appears to concern disagreement over the facts but actually rests on differing uses of a term.

Suppose, for example, that one party maintains that all conscientious objectors should be excused from military service, whereas a second insists that some objectors on grounds of conscience should not be exempted, and they argue somewhat in this fashion:

> *Jones:* I think all those who object to war on grounds of conscience should be excused from military service. The government should not force a man to violate his deepest moral convictions.

> *Smith:* I disagree. If you begin excusing men from war service because they say they are pacifists or believe that a war is unjustified, pretty soon there will not be enough men to protect the country at all in time of war.

> *Jones:* That's not what I mean by a *conscientious objector:* I mean one who has a long-standing belief in a religious doctrine according to which taking a human life is a sin, even in wartime. People who object to war on political grounds or who believe some particular war is unjustified don't qualify as conscientious objectors at all.

In a case such as the foregoing the difference between the two speakers appears to be *verbal,* turning on the different connotations of the term *conscientious objector:* Jones is taking the term to have a more specific connotation than is Smith. Their disagreement may well disappear once each realizes how the other understands the term, or once they settle the correct meaning of the term by a standard definition.

It would be comforting to believe that many of our disputes may be settled by a standard definition which will reveal that our disagreements relate to the meanings we attach to terms. Unfortunately, it is more often the case that disagreements which appear to be verbal, and to concern different meanings attributed to terms, turn out to be *substantive,* at least in part. We use different terms, or the same term differently, because we have different beliefs about the things in question or conflicting estimates or assessments of the facts. If, for example, Jones in the previous dialogue insisted on using the term *conscientious objector* to include those who object to war on ideological grounds or those who object that a particular war is unjustified, the dispute would no longer be a verbal one. Substantive disagreements cannot be settled by a standard definition, but require different and more complex strategies, which we shall treat subsequently. But even in disputes that are substantive at least in part, standard definitions may narrow the subject of dispute or focus the point of controversy to make resolution of the matter more possible.

EXERCISE 3B

1. Is there any equivocation or question-begging definition in the following?*

   a. People who want to murder others really want to kill themselves, as psychological studies of actual murderers show them to be suicidal and lacking in self-esteem. So, in giving murderers the death penalty one does not really punish them at all; on the contrary one is satisfying their desires. Therefore, capital punishment is not justified as an appropriate penalty for murder.

   b. "You state that the television dramatization of Alex Haley's novel *Roots* was 'political.' ... That is quite true. But the clear implication of so characterizing *Roots* seems to be that what we normally experience in the mass media and in our educational system is somehow not, or less, 'political.' Is it not, for example, extremely political to portray working-class people as quaintly mindless boobs, as so much of TV does? ... My understanding is that all of these are political, although the content and visibility of the politics may differ from case to case. It is not only the handful of TV shows, movies, and books that move people to a *new* consciousness of the forces that shape our lives that are political."

   c. In understanding assertiveness training, it is important to distinguish assertive behavior from aggressive behavior. Whereas both involve the direct and open expression of feelings and preferences, aggressive behavior disregards the rights and feelings of others and seeks only to meet the needs of the aggressive

*Letters b and c reprinted by permission of the *Baltimore Sunpapers*.

individual. Assertive behavior is concerned with the rights of both sides and aims toward the establishment of mutually satisfying solutions.

2. Construct a standard definition of any term in the above arguments that will either (a) strengthen the argument or (b) reveal a defect of the argument.

3C   STIPULATIVE AND REAL DEFINITIONS

Another type of definition often met with in reasoning is a *stipulative definition*. In this definition a meaning is proposed for the term which may vary to a considerable extent from its usual connotation; the speaker does not pretend to be employing a current or standard usage but is consciously imparting a specialized meaning to the term. Thus stipulative definitions, as opposed to standard definitions, are not necessary statements which we can judge true or false; they do not claim that a meaningful bond exists between the terms in the definition in the world of common linguistic usage. Rather they propose that whenever the term given stipulative definition comes up in some named context, we should understand it to have the connotation that the speaker assigned to it in the stipulative definition.

Stipulative definitions are often called for because a term may be so consistently vague or ambiguous in ordinary language that a standard definition may be hard or even impossible to construct. If we must be sure of what it does or does not correctly apply to (its *referents*), the best recourse is often to specify its referents by means of the connotation presented in a stipulative definition. Laws, institutional rules and regulations, income tax forms, and the like frequently and appropriately make use of stipulative definitions. Occasionally stipulative definitions are given for symbols or coined words that did not have any previous meaning or for new combinations of words to which a special meaning is being assigned, such as *minimax, cruise missile,* or *sociobiology.*

Often terms given a stipulative definition are put in quotation marks to indicate that the speaker is using the term in a somewhat different sense from its ordinary one; occasionally the particular context is specified, as "in law," "in medicine," "for income tax purposes," "according to the club constitution." Other cue words and phrases are the following:

By X is here meant Y.

I therefore understand X to be Y in the following.

Whenever X is meant I use the term Y in this document.

From the viewpoint of Z, the term X is equivalent to Y.

Although we cannot judge a stipulative definition to be true or false (as we can a standard definition), we can judge it to be *acceptable* or *unacceptable* by applying criteria appropriate to it. Some of these criteria are rules which apply to standard definition and which do not need any further explanation:

1. The connotation provided by the stipulative definition is easier to understand than the original term. In particular it should fix the reference of the term unambiguously.
2. The stipulative definition avoids vicious circularity.
3. The stipulative definition is free of inconsistency.

Further rules for stipulative definition arise from its relationship to ordinary language and its special function as a language tool:

4. The connotation in the stipulative definition does not differ so radically from the standard connotation of the original term as to cause confusion or error.
5. The definer has the authority (if required) to stipulate the meaning of the term.
6. The stipulative definition holds in a limited context clearly marked off from general or ordinary use of the term.
7. The connotation stipulated is serviceable in its limited context.

These further criteria for a stipulative definition are needed because, as we remarked at the outset, the meaning of a term is not completely arbitrary. A speaker may not simply choose to supply whatever connotation he wishes to any term in the language, even if he announces his intention openly. The meaning of a term cannot be isolated from its relationship to other terms in the language. It may have an opposite, as *cowardice* is the opposite of *courage*; it may have synonyms, as *daring* is synonymous with *bold;* it may have cognates, as *foolish* is cognate with *folly* and *foolhardy*; it may be one term in a range of terms with close ties to each other, as *justice* goes with *fairness* and *rightness*; it may mark a moral difference or shading, as *bold* differs from *rash*. Furthermore it may occur in expressions or sayings that constitute informal conventions of usage. A stipulative definition best respects the ties of a term in ordinary language by not defining a term so as to snarl them or to lead to misunderstanding or equivocation.

For example, a business form that defined *self-employed* so as to include being employed by a spouse or parent as part of the definition would be unacceptable. Such a definition would clash not only with our notion of self-identity but would also raise the question of *nepotism,* an important term in professional ethics.

A speaker's prerogative to give his or her own special meaning to a term in general use is clearly justified only when this special use can be separated from the ordinary meaning of the term, as occurs in the writing related to an occupation or profession. However, in discussing abortion, for example, a speaker may not define *fetus* any way he or she pleases. If *fetus* is defined in such a way that it follows from the definition that a fetus is nonhuman or not a person, the definer would be foreclosing one of the issues at stake. Such a procedure is neither rationally nor morally acceptable, and is an instance of the fallacy of question-begging definition discussed in the previous section. In such matters of general human concern, standard definitions (or real definitions, next to be discussed) are required.

The stipulative definitions that occur in legal forms or state eligibility requirements ought to be put forward or approved by those who execute the laws or supervise the matters to which the definitions relate. In a profession or intellectual discipline, the definer ought to select a connotation acceptable to others engaged in the same pursuit and consistent with its canons. It would be unwise, for example, for this text to use the term *truth* in a way that deviates sharply from its use in other works of logic.

Finally, the stipulative definition ought to do the job it sets out to do: Set forth a meaning that functions effectively within its particular context. We have a right to expect that the definition of *self-employed* in Internal Revenue Service forms will enable the Service to easily distinguish those who come under that category from those who do not, and also enable the taxpayer to decide without trouble in what tax category he or she belongs. The definer needs to use a connotation related to the particular use to which the term will be put: Whether a wife or child is a *guest* in accordance with a club's rules is an issue for the club to decide by its own lights, not an ideological or moral issue. The definition of man as a *tool-using animal* is appropriate within anthropology, less acceptable in comparative zoology (where reference to physical attributes is preferable), and probably unsuitable in a treatise on theology.

Real Definition

The third type of definition we must consider is *real definition.* This term has been widely used by philosophers for this type of definition, although both the term and the practice have been unpopular with many modern logicians. Yet the practice is to be found in much scientific and ordinary reasoning, and we shall keep the name because of its aptness as well as its history. In the case of both standard and stipulative definitions we may fairly be said to be dealing with *words* in their ordinary and specialized uses. But sometimes in reasoning we come across definitions whose purpose is not to explain the meaning of a word or phrase but to characterize a type of thing or phenomenon which some word and its synonyms designate. The term *real* suggests that we are interested in defining the reality to which the term applies (its referent) and analyzing its nature.

Real definitions are often proposed as the culmination of serious and extensive reasoning, and they may reflect advances in knowledge or controversial changes in our conceptions of what they define. They require different standards of assessment from both standard and stipulative definition, although they share some of the characteristics of each. Like a stipulative definition, a real definition offers a connotation intended to replace the ordinary one; it may significantly broaden or narrow the reference of the original term. Like a standard definition, a real definition makes a claim to truth; its general application may have far-reaching consequences for knowledge or action. But the truth claim it makes is not about the standard use of a *word*; rather the real definition claims to distinguish the essential features of the *reference* of a word more accurately than past or standard use have done. The change in connotation is here not a convenience for a special purpose, as in stipulative definition, but is an alleged refinement or improvement in our ways of thinking about the things defined.

Real definitions are often found when a thinker develops theories that depart markedly from prevailing views on the subject. It is well known that the physicist Albert Einstein found it necessary to rethink the conception of *time* in formulating relativity theory; the proper definition of *mass* was a theme of Newtonian physics; the definition of what constitutes *life* has been a question in biology and in speculations about the existence of life in other parts of the universe. Many philosophical works center around real definitions of concepts such as *justice, truth,* or *value.* The results of new knowledge may bring about the revision of some notion, a revision expressed in the form of a new definition.

Since real definitions play an important role in reasoning, and differ both from standard and stipulative definitions, our logic would be lacking if we did not approach the issue of the truth or falsity of such definitions. Yet the process for testing real definitions differs markedly from that involved in standard definitions in that it often demands considerable knowledge of a subject matter and reflection on interrelated notions or theories of an advanced nature. The bases for a real definition include not only the primary uses of the terms both past and present, as in standard definition, but also evidence obtained from the types of reasoning to be studied in subsequent chapters. Nevertheless, we can outline the various considerations which may be brought to bear in judging a real definition.

Two criteria of standard and stipulative definition also hold for real definition: *It must be (1) free of inconsistency and (2) free of vicious circularity.*

A third criterion shared by standard and stipulative definition must be revised for real definition: We cannot insist that the new definition be easier to understand than the original term; it may very well introduce features or notions unfamiliar to us and difficult to grasp at first, as in Einstein's revisions of the terms *time* and *contemporaneity.* Instead we look to the new connotation for a better understanding of the thing; its specifying characteristics may expose causal or conceptual connections that help provide insight into the nature of whatever is being defined. To use an old-fashioned term, the real definition reveals to us the *essential properties* of the thing. Ideally, the real definition fixes its object more firmly within some system of knowledge, perhaps revealing unrecognized relationships to other things, filling in previous gaps in knowledge, or explaining hitherto puzzling phenomena.

Thus, our third rule for a real definition is that *it (3) reveals the essential nature of a thing more effectively than prevailing thinking on the subject.*

Our final rule relates to changes in the reference of words in ordinary use which may result from the application of the real definition. A real definition, as we have already noted, may alter the reference of the terms in which the subject of a real definition is expressed: It may connect the things to which these terms ordinarily apply to different ranges of phenomena and disturb their old relationships. The real definition of lightning as a form of electricity relates it to friction phenomena (like shocks when touching metal after walking on a deep-piled rug) and weakens its associations as a weapon of supernatural punishment. Ideally a real definition should be one whose main terms—those that embody its connotation—preserve enough of its standard meaning that the truth-value of widely accepted statements on the subject is not reversed or altered. The main terms in standard use should continue to refer to those things that by general agreement are prime examples of them (so-called *paradigm cases*). For example, a real definition of *justice* that has the effect of permitting Jack the Ripper's killings to be called *just acts* is objectionable. Even though a real definition deals with things, not words primarily, we need to attend to the effect of the proposed real definition on the ordinary usage of terms. Although we cannot prohibit changes in language, we may set limits to the radical interference with common usage which real definitions may produce.

Thus, our final rule is the following: *(4) Any significant deviation in the standard use of terms which a real definition produces is rationally defensible.*

By *rationally defensible* we suggest that powerful supporting reasons for the change are available and are strong enough to disarm objections.

Thus we may reasonably expect some new theory about the subject in question or empirical findings put forward in connection with the definition. Some amount of reasoning in support of a real definition is in order and is one of its distinctive marks.

A real definition is usually signaled by such words as "really," "actually," and "in truth." In some cases these words are qualified by phrases such as "from my point of view," "in accordance with my theory," "in this way of thinking". Such qualifications may lead the reader to suppose the definition to be stipulative; but the deciding factor is the role the definition plays in the reasoning, not the words or even the intention of the proposer of the definition.

Although they are so different, stipulative definitions are often confused with real definitions. Speakers sometimes introduce what is actually a real definition in phrases which make it appear that they are giving a stipulative definition; their words make it clear that they recognize that their use is non-standard and suggest that we accept the definition as their own stipulated meaning for a term. But if a speaker's talk suggests that his or her meaning improves on or corrects the usual meaning, or if the speaker draws consequences of a substantial kind from his or her definition, we should assume that a real definition is being offered, and it should be judged accordingly.

We conclude by reviewing the differences between these three types of definition, since each type of definition prescribes which set of rules or criteria are applicable to it. A standard definition tries to say what meaning a *word* already *has*; a stipulative definition arbitrarily assigns a *new* meaning to a *word*; a real definition tries to characterize the essential nature of a kind of thing referred to by a word.

Rules for Stipulative Definition

1. The connotation offered is easier to apply than the original term.
2. It avoids vicious circularity.
3. It is free of inconsistency.
4. The connotation offered does not differ so radically from the standard connotation as to cause confusion.
5. The definition is proposed for a clearly limited context.

Rules for Real Definition

1. It reveals the nature of the thing defined better than prevailing thinking on the subject.
2. It avoids vicious circularity.
3. It is free of inconsistency.

4. Any significant deviation in the standard uses of the term produced by the real definition is rationally defensible.

EXERCISE 3C

1. Identify the term given a stipulative definition and apply the rules for assessing its acceptability.

   a. In law an *act of God* is any occurrence not caused by human negligence or intervention.
   b. *Mainstreaming* is a seemingly innocuous, and, to most observers, laudable goal of returning handicapped children to the regular classroom as quickly as possible through special assistance and instruction.
   c. You are liable for self-employment tax if you have income of $400 or more from operating a business or profession as sole proprietor, in partnership with others, or as an independent contractor.

2. Assess and compare the following real definitions of alcoholism.

   a. Alcoholism is a condition of metabolism: a physical, functional, and progressive illness.
   b. When I speak of an alcoholic, I mean anyone who craves and is dependent on alcohol, drinking regularly and excessively, so that it interferes with his or her work, home life, and normal relationships with other people.

Review Exercise For Chapter 3

What kind of definition occurs in the following?* Assess each by applying the appropriate rules. Is there ambiguity removable by rewording or definition?

1. The Maryland Court of Appeals yesterday held that a tear-gas pistol which cannot be converted into a firearm is not a handgun under state law. The court held that to be a firearm a device "must propel a missile," and that the substance projected by the tear-gas device "is not a missile within the natural and ordinary signification of the term."
2. Angelo Asciolla of Laconia, N.H., had had his new car less than a week

*Numbers 1, 2, 4, 5, and 6 reprinted by permission of the *Baltimore Sunpapers*.

when it began to make "a big screaming whine." He was told the car needed transmission repairs, had water in parts of its body, and had rust on the brake drums, drive shaft, and exhaust pipe. He contended he was entitled to a new car, and last week the New Hampshire Supreme Court agreed. Justice Douglas said he agreed with Mr. Asciolla's "assertion that a new automobile is more than the sum of its various components. It is the integrity of the vehicle as a whole which is the essence of the consumer's bargain."

3. According to tax regulations, custody is defined as the right to custody under the court decree or separation agreement, rather than physical custody.

4. The Hemingway hero is on the way out. Today, the ideal man combines self-confidence, success, and the willingness to fight for his family and beliefs with warmth, gentleness, and the willingness to lose. These findings, and others, emerged from a survey designed for *Psychology Today.* Half of the women thought intelligence was essential for both sexes, but for some reason only a third of the men did. There was no single trait that readers overwhelmingly applied to men but not to women, or vice versa. Men were more likely than women to think the ideal man is competitive (38 percent to 27 percent) and takes risks (34 percent to 25 percent). But neither sex thought men should be especially aggressive; only some 30 percent thought this trait was essential or very important.

5. A divorced man has been ordered by the state's highest court to keep paying $160 a month in alimony to his former wife who is living "openly and notoriously" with another man. Alimony payments in New York normally end only with the death or remarriage of a former wife, but this case turned on an obscure section of a 1938 law which allowed the cutoff of payments in instances where an ex-wife is living with a man and "holding herself out as his wife." The court majority held that the woman must actually try to pass herself off as legally married to the man before she can lose her alimony payments. Such actions would include applying for utility or bank accounts using his name and making statements to other people.

6. Susan Brownmiller, in her definitive book on rape, *Against Our Will: Men, Women and Rape,* calls rape an exercise in power. I agree, and further would define it as an act of political terrorism designed to keep women "in their place," consciously and unconsciously. In manner and message it is similar to lynchings and pogroms. I would further claim that rape exists any time sexual intercourse occurs when it has not been genuinely initiated by the woman out of her own affection and desire.

7. An investment broker says it's important to call attention to the moral

difference between a tax shelter and a tax loophole. A tax shelter is an intentional benefit to the taxpayer specifically written into the law to stimulate investment in enterprises which contribute to a desirable social goal; but a tax loophole is an unintended benefit that accrues to a taxpayer because of overlapping tax laws.

chapter 4

Immediate Inference

4A CONSISTENCY AND INCONSISTENCY
OF STATEMENTS

In all forms of reasoning, it is essential to know whether statements are consistent or inconsistent with one another. Consistency of its statements with each other is the *minimum* logical requirement for a sound argument. Lack of consistency condemns an argument as unsound. Inconsistency of the premises indicates that at least one of the premises is false and must be rejected; inconsistency of the conclusion with the premises demonstrates that the premises fail to support the conclusion.

Usually we can tell whether two statements are consistent simply by comparing the meanings of the two. Consider these two sentences:

Socrates is the husband of Xanthippe.
Socrates is childless.

Without knowing Socrates' biography, we can tell that both of these statements may be true: There is nothing about Socrates' being Xanthippe's husband from which it follows necessarily that Socrates has children; nor is there anything about Socrates' being childless from which it follows that he is not the husband of Xanthippe. All that is required for two statements to be *consistent* is this: that the truth of one statement *does not exclude* the truth of the other statement.

Consistency is thus a weak relationship between statements: Knowing that a statement is true does not enable one to infer that a statement consistent with it is also true. It may be the case that "Socrates is the husband of Xanthippe" is true but that "Socrates is childless" is false. Indeed, it may be the case that both statements are false. To say that two statements are consistent is only to say that there is nothing to prevent both statements from being true, as far as logic is concerned. Knowing that statements are consistent with each other does not enable one to pronounce any one of them to be true or all of them to be true; it only enables one to say that it is logically possible for all of them to be true. Since an argument asserts that its conclusion is true just because all its premises are true, every sound argument must have—as an indispensable minimum requirement—premises and conclusion whose statements are capable of all being true together. Whereas the consistency of statements does not alone make an argument sound, any inconsistency of its statements is a fatal flaw.

Inconsistency often arises in the combination of a number of statements. The inconsistency of just two statements is usually too obvious to go unrecognized; but when more than two statements are being asserted at the same time inconsistency may go undetected. This occurs because it is necessary to relate the meanings of a number of different statements to each other. Each statement taken singly may be consistent with each of the other statements, but when they are taken all together inconsistency may develop. For example, consider the following trio:

Socrates was the only husband of Xanthippe.
Xanthippe's husband died a natural death.
Socrates was executed in 399 B.C.

Any two of the above statements are consistent with each other, but the three statements taken all together are inconsistent. If it is true that Socrates was Xanthippe's only husband and that her husband died a natural death, it cannot be true that Socrates was executed. Or if it is true that Socrates was executed and that Xanthippe's husband died a natural death, it must be false that Socrates was Xanthippe's only husband. If it is true that Socrates was executed and that Socrates was Xanthippe's only husband, it must be false that Xanthippe's husband died a natural death. Thus *all three* statements cannot be true; the truth of any two of them requires that the third be false. When statements are inconsistent with one another, we cannot tell simply from the inconsistency which one (or more) is false, but we do know that they cannot all be true. Further information is needed to tell which statement is false.

In everyday reasoning inconsistency is frequently more subtle, turning on some strong factual connection between the statements as well as on a necessary connection of meanings. Consider this trio:

Plato is the same age as Xanthippe's son.
Socrates is Xanthippe's husband.
Socrates is childless.

Here we must suspect inconsistency between the three statements: If Xanthippe has a son and Xanthippe is Socrates' wife, then it is very likely that Socrates also has a son and is not childless. But before we can establish inconsistency in this case we need to rule out the possibility that Xanthippe's child was fathered by someone other than Socrates. Often common knowledge or truisms provide the information needed to show that a set of statements is inconsistent.

There are various ways in which a statement may be inconsistent with another. Consider the kind of inconsistency here:

Socrates is childless.
Socrates has two children.

Note that the truth of either statement excludes the truth of the other: If Socrates has two children, he surely cannot be childless; also if he is childless, he cannot have two children. However, it may happen that *both* statements are *false*—if Socrates has one child only. This kind of inconsistency has the special name of *contrariety*: Two inconsistent statements are *contraries* when both cannot be true but both may be false. Thus when two statements are contraries one may, from the truth of one alone, infer the falsity of the other. But one may not infer from the falsity of a statement that its contrary is true. For example, knowing that "Socrates has two children" is true, one may correctly infer the falsity of "Socrates is childless." But knowing only that "Socrates has two children" is false, one may not infer the truth of "Socrates is childless"—one needs further information. Contrariety is a special kind of inconsistency which only permits valid inference from the *truth* of one statement to the *falsity* of its contrary.

To determine whether two inconsistent statements are contraries, one must reflect on whether there are circumstances in which *both* statements may be false. Contrary statements are easiest to recognize when both statements speak of a subject in universal terms, such as *all* or *none,* or in comparatives, such as *most* or *few,* or attribute contrary characteristics, such as *rich* or *poor.* "Most professors are liberal" is the obvious contrary of "Few professors are liberal" as well as of "Most professors are conservatives." Many statements in ordinary language show inconsistency of this kind, in which both may possibly be false although both cannot be true.

In contrast, two statements are *contradictories* when they exhibit a more complete kind of inconsistency. In this case one may go from the truth of one to the falsity of the other and *also* from the falsity of one to the truth of the other. Every statement has a contradictory, obtained by negating the statement grammatically. The contradictory of "Socrates is childless" is "Socrates is not childless," for example. And of course, "Socrates is childless" is also the contradictory of "Socrates is not childless." For if it is true that Socrates is not childless, then it must be false that Socrates is childless, and if it is *false* that Socrates is *not* childless, then it must be true that Socrates *is* childless. Thus in order for a statement to be the contradictory of another it need not have a negative term. (Indeed, every statement is the contradictory of some other statement, which is its contradictory.) There are various strategies for obtaining the contradictory of a statement: One may add *not* to the main verb or one may use a negative term. "Socrates is a father" is the contradictory of "Socrates is childless," for example. Or one may simply preface the whole statement with a negating phrase such as "it is false that" or "it is not the case that" or "it is not true that."

These alternative ways of obtaining the contradictory of a given statement are important to keep in mind, for ambiguity often crops up when a statement is negated. "Xanthippe was not the shrewish wife of Socrates" is, for example, the contradictory of "Xanthippe was the shrewish wife of Socrates." But it is not clear in this case what is being negated: Are we to take it to mean that Xanthippe was not Socrates' wife at all, or that Xanthippe was his wife but not a shrew? We must be alert to the different possibilities, in that they may make a substantial difference in the content of the premises or conclusion of an argument.

It is particularly important, too, when assessing debates in which speakers apparently hold inconsistent views on a subject, to keep in mind the distinction between contradictory statements and contraries. In such disputes both speakers and hearers tend to believe that casting doubt on or disproving one side proves the rightness of the other side. But this only happens when the opposing theses are contradictories. It often happens that the theses are inconsistent but contraries, so that both may be false. The truth of the matter may lie in a third alternative, not even mentioned. For example, in a debate about whether a moderate increase in the property tax or one in the income tax is needed to balance the budget, it may be that neither will do, but a cut in expenditures is called for.

One frequently finds that apparently incompatible positions are really consistent. For example, one might say a shortage is caused by decreased supply or by the holding back of supplies from the market—both statements may be true and consistent with one another. In assessing arguments from which apparently incompatible conclusions are drawn, the first step is to determine whether the conclusions are indeed consistent or inconsistent. If they are inconsistent, we then ask whether they are contraries—in which case both may be false—or genuine contradictories. Remember that it is only in the case of genuine contradictories that proving the falsity of one statement is the equivalent of proving the truth of the other.

Fallacy of Special Pleading

A particular type of fallacy involving inconsistency is called the *fallacy of special pleading.* It sometimes happens that a speaker will assert or imply that a generalization is true but insist that a special case, which apparently falls under the generalization, is an exception not covered by the generalization. When the case is one in which the speaker for some reason has a special interest, one may suspect his or her pleading that this case is not an instance in which the generalization properly applies. For example, in a political campaign one candidate questioned the propriety of his opponent being entertained by a private industry at an expensive club on a golfing weekend. He thereby indicated that he accepted the general rule that elected officials should not accept favors from private industry. When reporters later called to his attention an occasion on which a private company had paid for his and his family's stay at a plush resort during his term as governor of his state, he claimed there was no impropriety in this instance, because at the time he was discussing a matter involving government business with the head of the private company. Here the question surely arises whether the candidate was inconsistent in not applying the general rule to his own case: whether his making an exception of his own acceptance of corporate hospitality is *special pleading,* and thereby fallacious.

This case illustrates a difficulty arising from many of the fallacies ordinarily listed in logic books—that of deciding in each case whether an argument is a genuine or only an apparent instance of the fallacy in question. Human affairs are sufficiently complex for us to recognize that there are justifiable exceptions even to well-grounded general rules. Therefore, we cannot immediately condemn a person for making an exception to a general rule even in a personal case. We need to listen to the special pleading itself in order to determine whether a legitimate case can be made for the exception. In the preceding case, the candidate defended the exception by arguing that his stay at the resort involved more than mere personal pleasure (as opposed to his opponent's situation), and that he convinced the company head to undertake conservation measures advantageous to the state. Do these circumstances suffice to exonerate the candidate of the charge of inconsistency? One might go on to question whether the discussion of government business excuses the acceptance of favors from a private company by an elected official, or whether the favorable outcome of the negotiations wipes out the impropriety. These are ethical questions which go beyond the question of inconsistency, and their solution calls for methods of reasoning we will take up in a later chapter. For the moment we simply note that labeling something a case of special pleading does not necessarily prove that a fallacy has been committed.

We must be alert to the fallacy of special pleading, for it is a human weakness to overlook the applicability of a general rule to a case in which one's own interests are involved. These interests, whether private, professional, or even public, may make it difficult for a person to see that his or her stand in a particular case is inconsistent with a general principle he or she acknowledges to be true. Inconsistency in our beliefs is not a trivial matter: It should lead us to suspect that at least one of our beliefs is false or needs qualification. We ought not to be complacent about holding false beliefs nor about acting on them.

Ferreting out inconsistency is an essential step in evaluating arguments. The presence of an inconsistency alerts us to weakness or outright falsity of some premise, or the illogicality of the conclusion in view of the premises offered. To remedy the situation some premise must be either entirely eliminated or qualified so as to avoid inconsistency, but this change in premises may weaken the whole argument. It is also possible that the conclusion may have to be qualified or reformulated, a move which may also make the argument less effective or interesting. Before dismissing an argument on grounds of inconsistency, however, one needs to determine whether it can be reformulated so as to avoid inconsistency and still retain its force.

EXERCISE 4A

1. Which of the numbered statements is the contrary of the lettered statement? Which is the contradictory? Which are consistent?

    a. All philosophers are atheists.
        1. Not all philosophers are atheists.
        2. No philosophers are atheists.
        3. Most philosophers are atheists.
        4. All atheists are philosophers.
        5. It is false that all philosophers are atheists.

    b. Socrates has courage.
        1. Socrates is a coward.
        2. Socrates is not courageous.
        3. It is false that Socrates is a coward.

      4. It is false that Socrates does not have courage.

      5. It is true that Socrates does not have courage.

  c. Most flowers smell sweet.

      1. Few flowers smell sweet.

      2. Most flowers do not smell sweet.

      3. Most flowers smell bad.

      4. Few flowers smell bad.

      5. Most flowers have no smell.

2. What inconsistencies can you detect in the following? Can an inconsistency be removed without affecting the argument? Is there any fallacious special pleading?

  a. A doctor engaged in fetal research defended experiments conducted on live fetuses still in the womb or survivors of surgical abortion as follows: "It is the business of medicine to promote the health of the human being throughout his whole lifetime. At present we can only do half the job, because we can only treat a human *after* he's born. But we cannot treat the human body before birth unless we engage in fetal research. Therefore research on live fetuses should not be prohibited but encouraged." The doctor also spoke in favor of legislation permitting abortion at any stage of pregnancy, including the most advanced.

  b. The federal government requires a warning to be printed on cigarette packages saying that cigarette smoking is dangerous to the health. But the agriculture department still subsidizes farmers for growing tobacco. Is it proper for the federal government to promote the use of substances it maintains to be dangerous to the health of its citizens? As leader of the "Stop Smoking Now" seminars, I call on the government either to remove the warning label on cigarettes or cut off subsidies to tobacco growers.

4B NECESSARY AND EMPIRICAL CONNECTIONS

The simplest type of argument is one consisting of exactly two statements, one of which is premise, the other, conclusion. Making an inference from the truth of a statement to the falsity of its contradictory or from the falsity of a statement to the truth of its contradictory are examples of such an argument. For example, one may infer directly from the truth of "Socrates is not childless" to the falsity of "Socrates is not a father", or from the falsity of "Socrates is not a father" to the truth of "Socrates is not childless." This kind of argument is called *immediate inference* since one is able to step immediately from just one premise to a conclusion without the intermediary of any additional premise. Such arguments occur frequently in everyday and scientific reasoning, both by themselves and in conjunction with longer pieces of reasoning. Immediate inferences may also proceed from the truth of one statement to the truth of another or from the falsity of one statement to the falsity of another. We will now take up some principles that will enable us to make immediate inferences which are valid arguments and to detect invalid inferences.

In general we can make a valid immediate inference when we know that there is some kind of *necessary connection* between two sentences. The term *necessary* has the same basic meaning in the phrase *necessary connection* as it has when we use it to distinguish necessary sentences from empirical sentences. There is a necessary connection between two different sentences when merely knowing the meanings of the two sentences suffices to tell us something definite about the truth-values of the two statements in relationship to each other. When one is true, the other must be false; or when one is true, the other must also be true; or when one is false, the other must also be false.

There is *no* necessary connection between two sentences when one needs to know *more* than the meanings of the two sentences to go from the truth or falsity of one to the truth or falsity of the other. Often there is some obvious connection between the truth-values of two sentences, but not a *necessary* one. Take these two statements:

> Socrates was convicted of impiety in 399 B.C.
> Socrates was executed in 399 B.C.

Here the statement that Socrates was convicted of impiety gives us a legal ground for believing he may have been executed, so that the truth of the first statement is relevant to the truth of the second. Yet there is no *necessary* connection between the two statements. It might well be true that Socrates was convicted but false that he was executed. He might have been punished by fine or exile or have escaped from prison without being executed at all; or he might have been executed, but on grounds of treason or murder, not impiety. Thus, we have to know more than the meanings of these two sentences; we also need to know the circumstances relating to Socrates' conviction and execution. In such cases we can say there is an *empirical connection* between the two statements.

In line with the previous distinction between necessary and empirical sentences, we can discriminate between sentences that have a *necessary connection* to each other and those that have an *empirical* (or *synthetic* or *contingent*) *connection*. In the case of an empirical connection between two sentences, one cannot go automatically from the truth-value of one sentence to the truth-value of the other. Whether one is justified in inferring something from one sentence about another will depend on the *strength* of the empirical connection. This strength is determined by what the facts are and by how much we can rely on the knowledge supporting those facts. In some cases the empirical connection is so strong that our confidence in it is as strong as it is for a necessary connection. For example, consider the empirical connection between these two sentences:

> Xanthippe is the mother of two sons.
> Therefore, Xanthippe is not a virgin.

Our knowledge of the physiology of reproduction is sufficiently firm that we would not hesitate to say that the truth of the first statement warrants our inferring the truth of the second. We would have some grounds for doubt in the case of these two statements:

> Xanthippe is the wife of Socrates.
> Hence, Xanthippe is not a virgin.

That Xanthippe is the wife of Socrates does give us grounds for inferring that she is not a virgin, of course. But there are cases of marriages not being consummated, so our confidence is a shade less than in the previous case. When we come to two statements like the following, our confidence is much weakened:

> Xanthippe is unmarried.
> Therefore, Xanthippe is a virgin.

When there is an empirical connection between two statements, the soundness of an inference is relative to the quality of our knowledge of the subject matter. To assess the validity of an immediate inference based on an empirical connection between two statements, we usually need to apply the principles of inductive reasoning, the subject of some later chapters. For the present, we will emphasize those kinds of necessary connections between sentences that enable us to arrive at principles for drawing immediate inferences, primarily of a deductive kind. Some of these principles we also commonly apply to empirical connections which have such a high degree of assurance that they can be considered matters of common knowledge, and which provide grounds for sound immediate inference as well.

The notion of necessary connection between statements permits us to formulate the distinctive feature of a deductive argument. In a *deductive argument* a necessary connection of the following kind is asserted between the premise(s) and conclusion of the argument: the premise(s) being true, the conclusion must also be true. The most common type of immediate inference, that based on a necessary connection between statements, is thus a deductive argument, containing just one premise.

EXERCISE 4B

1. Between which of the following pairs of statements is there a necessary connection?

    a. Socrates was born before Plato.
       Socrates died before Plato.
    b. Socrates' two children were of differing sex.
       Socrates had one daughter.
    c. Plato was the teacher of Aristotle.
       Aristotle taught Alexander the Great.
    d. A whole is equal to the sum of its parts.
       A whole is greater than the sum of its parts.
    e. The whole is greater than any of its parts.
       The half is lesser than the whole.

2. List five pairs of sentences containing some kind of necessary connection.

    a. Xanthippe was the wife of Socrates.
    b. Socrates was married.
    c. Socrates was short and snub-nosed.
    d. Xanthippe was Socrates' widow.
    e. Socrates was snub-nosed.
    f. Socrates was tall.
    g. Socrates was married twice.
    h. Socrates was tall and handsome.

4C   EQUIVALENCE AND IMPLICATION

To grasp the rules of argument that make an immediate inference valid or invalid we have to understand some different kinds of logical relationships among statements. We must be able to do two things: (1) tell when one statement bears a necessary connection to another statement and (2) determine the *exact kind* of necessary connection between the truth-values of the two statements. One statement's being true may be grounds for the other statement's being true; one statement's being true may be grounds for the other statement's being false; one statement's being false may be grounds for the other statement's being true; one statement's being false may be grounds for the other statement's being false. These are the four different possible necessary connections between the truth-values of two statements. We shall now distinguish two types of necessary connection between statements which are particularly useful in reasoning, namely, equivalence and implication.

Equivalence is one of the strongest of logical relationships between statements. When two statements are equivalent, they are necessarily the *same* in *truth-value;* that is, the facts that make one of them true coincide with the facts that make the other one true. A given statement is true when it corresponds to the facts; the facts that make a given statement true will also verify any other statement that is its equivalent. Similarly when a given statement is false, so that there exists no fact corresponding to it, any other statement equivalent to it is also false. Thus when two statements are equivalent, knowing that either one of them is true permits us to infer correctly that the other is also true; also, knowing that either one of the two is false permits us to infer validly that the other is false.

How can one know that two statements are equivalent? The following three equivalent statements illustrate the most common forms encountered in everyday reasoning:

1. Socrates praised Eros, the god of Love, at Agathon's banquet.
2. Eros, the Love god, was praised by Socrates at Agathon's feast.
3. An encomium to the god of Love, Eros, was delivered by Socrates during Agathon's banquet.

Statements 1 and 2 can easily be recognized as equivalent even though the subjects of the two sentences are different and the verb of 1 is active and the verb of 2 is passive. The differences between 1 and 2 exhibit alternative grammatical arrangements for asserting the same fact. Language provides a number of ways of organizing a sentence so as to present the same information in varying grammatical forms, all familiar to speakers of the language. The statement

4. Agathon praised Eros, the Love god, at Socrates' banquet.

is not equivalent to 1. It contains the same words, but the grammar of the sentence orders the terms logically in a very different way. 4 is also not equivalent to 2 or 3. Agathon's making a speech at Socrates' banquet is a different fact from Socrates' making a speech at Agathon's banquet.

A second way of obtaining an equivalent statement is to substitute a term with the same meaning for one or more terms in the original sentence. The resulting sentence is then equivalent to the original sentence. Since *feast* is a common synonym of *banquet*, it is easy to see the equivalence of 1 and 2. To one who realizes that an *encomium* is a conventional speech of praise, the equivalence of 3 with both 2 and 1 becomes clear.

Each of the three sentences may be interpreted as having a slightly different emphasis—1 focuses attention on what Socrates did, 2 on the subject discussed by him, and 3 on the kind of discourse made. But the facts that make one statement true also make the other statements true. There are typically a large number of ways for expressing the same facts in common speech. These enable us to express ourselves fluidly and also—through choice of words and word order—to direct attention to the facts in subtly different ways. But for the purposes of logic we must be aware of what is being asserted by the statement and alert to the equivalence or nonequivalence of statements we are examining. The equivalence of two statements hangs on what the facts must be for the statements to be true together and false together.

Implication is a less intimate relationship between statements than equivalence. The truth-values of equivalent statements are like a two-way street: Correct inferences may proceed in either direction. If any of its equivalents is true, a statement is true; if any of its equivalents is false, a statement is false; whenever a statement is true, all of its equivalents are also true; whenever a statement is false, all of its equivalents are false. But implication is like two one-way streets. One has to note in which direction the implication runs and mark the difference between the statement that does the implying (the implier) and the statement that is implied.

Consider the logical relationship between these two statements:

1. Socrates is the father of two sons.
2. Socrates is male.

Statement 1 implies 2, but statement 2 does not imply 1. If it is true that Socrates is the father of two sons, it follows *necessarily* that Socrates is male; but if it is true that Socrates is male, it does not follow necessarily that Socrates is the father of two sons, or any sons at all. Thus, in implication, it is essential to specify exactly which statement is the implier and which one is implied, in order to make correct inferences.

There is a necessary connection between 1 and 2 such that 1 implies 2 and 2 is implied by 1 because the term *father* includes *male* as part of its connotation. Thus that "Socrates is the father of two sons" is true automatically establishes the truth of the statement that Socrates is male. Sometimes it is said that the meaning of the statement *implied* is contained within the meaning of the implying statement. The image of a container reminds us that a container must be larger than what is contained within it; as one cannot reverse or exchange the container and its contents, so one cannot say that "Socrates is male" implies "Socrates is the father of two sons." When one statement implies another, whenever the implier statement is true the implied statement must also be true. But knowing only that the implied statement is true, one may not correctly infer that the implier statement is true. So, knowing it to be true that Socrates is male, one cannot infer merely from that knowledge alone that it is true that Socrates is the father of two sons. Further information is needed. In implication, the inference goes only from the truth of the implying statement to the truth of the implied statement, not back again.

In implication, however, there is a *reverse* flow from the *falsity* of the *implied* statement to the *falsity* of the *implier* statement. In our example, if it is false that Socrates is male, it follows necessarily that it is false that Socrates is the father of two sons. He cannot be a father at all unless he is a male. This kind of necessary connection, from the falsity of the implied statement to the falsity of the statement that implies it, is very important and useful in reasoning but often overlooked. One way to keep it in mind is to think of implication as a relationship between a greater statement (the implier) and a lesser (the implied) statement. The truth of the greater implies the truth of the lesser, obviously. But, just as obviously, it follows that if the lesser statement is *false,* the greater statement must also be false. Finally, the falsity of the greater statement does *not* mean that the lesser statement must be false. If it is false that Socrates has two sons, we cannot then infer that it is false that Socrates is male. The direction of inference also travels one way with respect to falsity—from the falsity of the implied statement to the falsity of the implier statement only.

The reader may already have deduced that when two statements are equivalent each statement implies the other, so that the truth of either one implies the truth of the other and the falsity of either one implies the falsity of the other. Since "Xanthippe is the wife of Socrates" is equivalent to "Socrates is the husband of Xanthippe," the two statements mutually imply each other.

It is usually more difficult to recognize implication between two statements. In general one needs to compare in detail the exact meanings of the terms and to delineate the interrelationships of the words and especially of qualifying phrases such as *all, some,* and *no.* Consider whether the circumstances that make one statement true also make the other statement true. For example, the fact that makes "Melissus is Plato's uncle" true also establishes the truth of "Melissus is male." Check to see whether the circumstances that make the *implied* statement *false* also make the *implier* statement false—as the fact that makes "Melissus is male" be false requires that "Melissus is Plato's uncle" be false too. Be careful to understand the direction of implication: "Melissus is Plato's uncle" implies "Melissus is male"; but "Melissus is male" does not imply "Melissus is Plato's uncle."

We also speak of equivalence and implication as holding between statements that have an empirical connection with each other so well established as not to be subject to practical doubts. Such cases may be described as instances of *empirical* equivalence and *empirical* implication, to indicate that the connection between the two statements is based on matters of fact rather than merely on language and logic. For example, a correlation already mentioned has been discovered between being a female human and possessing a matching set of XX chromosomes. On the basis of this correlation, true statements concerning female humans will also hold for statements concerning humans with matching XX chromosomes, and statements false of female humans will also be false for humans possessing matching XX chromosomes; in other words, statements about female humans are equivalent to statements about humans with a matching set of XX chromosomes.

Similarly with implication: We have learned that oil does not exist except where vegetation previously lived, so that "There is oil on the moon" implies "Vegetation has existed on the moon." We may thus infer from the falsity of "Vegetation has existed on the moon" the falsity of "There is oil on the moon."

We must, however, keep in mind the distinction between empirical equivalence and implication and logical equivalence and implication. For if an inference based on equivalence or implication of statements is challenged, or if we wish to question it, the ways in which we do so will differ. In cases of logical implication or equivalence we look only to the logical structures of the statements and the meanings of the terms; but in the case of empirical equivalence or implication, we need to search out the empirical evidence for the existence of a strong connection between the truth-values of the sentences.

In testing the soundness of an argument it is important to keep in mind what statements are equivalent to or implied by those statements that constitute the premises and conclusion of the argument. For if a statement equivalent to or implied by a statement of the argument is dubious or even known to be false, the same doubt or falsity applies to that statement of the argument. Suppose the following argument were presented:

The United States ought to explore the moon because there may be oil there and the United States needs oil.

Since "There is oil on the moon" implies "Vegetation has existed on the moon," and all the available evidence points to the falsity of the implied statement, the implier statement, "There may be oil on the moon," is very dubious. Since this statement is a major premise of the argument, a weakness of the argument is thereby exposed. Similarly, inconsistencies between the various statements often come to light when we reflect on the equivalents and implications of the statements made.

We add to our list of *rules of immediate inference* the following, based on the relationships of equivalence and implication:

1. When statements are equivalent: (a) one may infer from the truth of one to the truth of any of its equivalents; (b) one may infer from the falsity of one to the falsity of any of its equivalents.
2. When one statement implies another: (a) one may infer from the truth of the implier statement to the truth of the implied statement; (b) one may infer from the falsity of the implied statement to the falsity of the implier (implying) statement.

EXERCISE 4C

Apply the rules of immediate inference in the following exercises.

1. Suppose the statement "Socrates praised Eros at Agathon's banquet" is *true*. What can be inferred about the truth or falsity of each of the lettered statements?
   a. There were no speeches at Agathon's banquet.
   b. The husband of Xanthippe was one of the speakers who praised the god of love at Agathon's banquet.
   c. Socrates never spoke in favor of Eros.
   d. Someone discussed love at Agathon's banquet.
   e. Socrates' discourse at Agathon's banquet was an encomium.
   f. It is untrue that Socrates was silent at Agathon's banquet.
   g. At Agathon's feast, there was heavy drinking and one after-dinner talk.
   h. If anyone discussed love at Agathon's banquet, it was Socrates.
2. Suppose the statement "There is evidence of biological activity on Mars" is false. What may then be inferred about the truth or falsity of each of the lettered statements?
   a. No signs of life have been found on Mars.
   b. It is more than likely that there is life on Mars.
   c. It is unlikely that there is life on Mars.
   d. All physical processes so far discovered on Mars are non-biological.

    e. Little evidence of biological activity on Marx exists.

    f. Some biological processes have been found on Mars.

    g. It is unlikely there is oil on Mars.

3. List several statements equivalent to the following statement and several implied by it: "Smoking causes lung cancer."

Review Exercise For Chapter 4

Use the rules of immediate inference to expose inconsistent, false, or dubious statements in the following.

1. In a panel discussion on how decisions on the continuance of life-support devices should be made, a doctor maintained they should be left strictly to the medical profession. "It's the doctors who have the medical knowledge and are familiar with the facts of the case who should decide," he said. He maintained that a doctor should take into account not just the patient's condition and prognosis but also the effect of the patient's illness on the family's welfare and the cost to society of use of a hospital's resources. He recommended discontinuance of life-support equipment on the patient whose case had provoked the panel discussion subject, although the physicians on the case had ordered continuance.

2. An education expert criticizes the practice of teaching children to read by learning whole words first and the sounds of the language (phonics) afterwards, claiming it has led to functional illiteracy and declining verbal test scores. To illustrate the defectiveness of the "look-say" method, he lists "fifty common words" not taught by it at the end of the fourth grade.

3. In a campaign debate, candidate Gerald Ford argued: "Now Governor Carter complains about the deficits that this administration has had and yet he condemns the vetoes that I have made that have saved the taxpayers nine billion dollars and could have saved an additional thirteen billion dollars. Now he can't have it both ways."

chapter 5

The Logic
of Categorical Statements

5A THE FOUR TYPES
OF CATEGORICAL STATEMENTS

Many arguments involve as intermediate steps *immediate inferences* derived from some premise or a conclusion of the reasoning. Ambiguity in our ways of speaking sometimes makes the distinction between legitimate and illegitimate immediate inference a difficult task, not readily solved in a mechanical way. We shall now apply some principles of immediate inference to four basic types of sentences, called *categorical sentences,* in order to gain insight into some logical relationships among statements that justify immediate inferences. Categorical sentences were singled out for attention by Aristotle, who first formulated the principles of valid reasoning for arguments containing this type of sentence; these arguments are called *syllogisms* and are the subject of the following chapter.

Logicians distinguish four types of categorical statements, two of which are called *universal* statements, one kind being the *universal affirmative* and the second the *universal negative.* The statements we have called *generalizations* are examples of universal categorical statements: "All students are poor" is a universal affirmative categorical statement, which is also a generalization. "No students are poor" is a universal negative categorical statement, which is a generalization. "All the students in this room are brown-eyed" is a universal affirmative categorical statement, and "No students in this room are brown-eyed" is a universal negative categorical statement; both are *accidental* generalizations. In these two sentences the subject terms refer to a limited group of individuals, whereas the subject term of an *essential* generalization is a class with an indefinite number of members, such as the class of students.

The verbal sign for a universal affirmative categorical statement is a sentence beginning with the word *all*; the verbal sign for a universal negative statement is a sentence beginning with *no*. Sentences beginning with *every, each,* and *any* also signal universal affirmative statements, but by convention only a sentence of the exact form "All *S* are *P*" is a universal affirmative statement. Similarly, sentences beginning with *none, not any,* or *no one* also express universal negative categorical statements, but the conventional logical form is "No *S* are *P*." Sentences in ordinary language are easily reworded into one or the other of these logical forms: "None of the students in this room has blue eyes" will become "No students in this room are blue-eyed"; "Every student in this room has blue eyes" will read "All students in this room are blue-eyed."

A universal affirmative categorical sentence begins with the word *all*, followed by the words for the subject term (for example, "students in this room" in the sentence above), followed by the verb *are*, followed by the words that stand for the predicate term ("blue-eyed" in the sentence above): All *students in this room* are *blue-eyed.*

A universal negative categorical sentence begins with the word *no*, followed by the words for the subject term (for example, "students in this room"), followed by the verb *are*; followed by the words for the predicate term ("blue-eyed"). No *students in this room* are *blue-eyed.*

It is important to note that a sentence of the form "All *S* are not *P*" does not ordinarily express either a universal affirmative or a universal negative statement. A speaker who says, for example, "All students are not poor" is usually not making any kind of universal statement, but is *denying* the universal affirmative statement, "All students are poor." To deny that a statement is true is equivalent to saying that its contradictory is true, so that someone who says "All students are not poor" is affirming the contradictory of "All students are poor." The contradictory of "All students are poor" is a statement that is necessarily true in case "All students are poor" is false. If it is false that *all* students are poor, it must be the case that at least one student (and perhaps more than one) is not poor—it may be that few students are not poor or most students are not poor. To cover this variety of cases, we use the form of categorical statement called the *particular* categorical. A particular categorical statement has as its verbal sign the word *some*. Sentences in ordinary language speaking of at least one, a few, or most of a group must be translated into particular categorical form.

The *particular affirmative* categorical statement has the logical form

"Some *S* are *P.*" "Some students are poor" is the categorical statement that is the logical contradictory of the universal negative categorical statement, "No students are poor." If it is false that no students are poor, it must be true that there are one or more students who are poor. The *particular negative* statement, "Some students are not poor," is the contradictory of the universal affirmative statement, "All students are poor," as we just observed.

The word *some* in both particular affirmative and particular negative statements means simply "at least one or more." Thus the particular affirmative "Some *S* are *P*" does not exclude the possibility that "*All S are P*" and the particular negative "Some *S* are not *P*" leaves open the possibility that "*No S* are *P.*" In ordinary language when we want to be clear that we are using the word *some* in a strong exclusive sense, we usually say "Some, but not all" or "only some." A sentence of the form "Not all *S* are *P*" is often best interpreted as saying *both* "Some *S* are *P*" *and* "Some *S* are not *P.*"

The particular affirmative categorical statement begins with the word *some,* followed by the words for the subject term (for example, *students*), followed by the verb *are,* followed by the words for the predicate term (for example, *poor*): "Some *students* are *poor.*"

The particular negative categorical statement begins with the word *some,* followed by the words for the subject term (for example, *students*), followed by the verb *are not,* followed by the words for the predicate term (for example, *poor*): "Some *students* are not *poor.*"

The words *all, no,* and *some,* which begin a categorical statement, are called *quantifiers,* since they indicate how many of the things named by the subject term are spoken of in the categorical statement. The words *are* and *are not,* which join the subject term to the predicate term, are called the *copula* (a Latin term meaning *joiner*). Using the notions of quantifier, subject term, copula, and predicate term we may exhibit the logical form of the four types of categorical statements and their components:

	Quantifier	Subject Term	Copula	Predicate Term
Universal affirmative	All	*S*	are	*P*
Universal negative	No	*S*	are	*P*
Particular affirmative	Some	*S*	are	*P*
Particular negative	Some	*S*	are not	*P*

One can construct an exact equivalent for many of the statements in ordinary language in one or another of the four types of categorical statements. Having obtained an equivalent categorical statement, one may readily trace out its logical relationships with other categorical statements and distinguish valid immediate inferences from invalid inferences. In translating from ordinary language into categorical form, one must choose a form that preserves the full meaning of the original, neither adding nor leaving out anything contained in the original sentence, so far as possible. We shall now consider how this may be done.

A categorical statement, through its logical form, describes how the members of one group coincide or fail to coincide with the members of some other group. The two groups in question are designated by the words for the subject term and the words for the predicate term, respectively. Thus, if the meaning of a statement can be expressed as saying that two groups coincide or fail to coincide, then it is usually possible to find an exact categorical equivalent. If the statement asserts that one group falls wholly within a second group, it is translatable into a universal affirmative, All S are P. A statement that asserts that part of one group falls within a second group is translatable into a particular affirmative, Some S are P. When a sentence says that the whole of one group falls *outside* a second group, it has as its categorical equivalent the universal negative, No S are P. Lastly a sentence which says that part of one group falls outside a second group is equivalent to a particular negative, Some S are not P.

Statements in ordinary language which describe the properties possessed by the members of a limited group or class are most readily translated into categorical form, although a little tinkering with language may be needed. Take a sentence such as this:

To practice law in Maryland, one must pass the Maryland bar exam.

This sentence says that the whole group consisting of practicers of law in Maryland falls within the group of those who have passed the Maryland bar. It is equivalent to the universal affirmative categorical statement, "*All practicers of law in Maryland* are *passers of the Maryland bar examination.*" It would be wrong to translate it into the particular categorical, "Some practicers of law in Maryland are passers of the Maryland bar examination," for the latter statement is *weaker* than the original. Neither would "All passers of the Maryland bar examination are practicers of law in Maryland" be correct: It says something *different* from the original statement.

In translating a sentence into a universal affirmative, one must be careful to place the proper group into the subject term, as the preceding example illustrates. A statement like "Venus is the planet which rules over the destinies of those born in Taurus" can be translated as "All *persons born in Taurus* are *persons under the rule of Venus.*" But if we changed the subject term, and translated it into the different universal affirmative, "All *persons under the rule of Venus* are *persons born in Taurus,*" we would be making a different statement, one not in accordance with astrological lore, since Venus is the ruling planet for those in the sign of Libra as well as of those in Taurus.

Similarly, sentences of the form "Only X are Y," "None but X are Y," and "None except X are Y" regularly translate into universal affirmatives in which the group designated X, that is, the group immediately following the words *only*, *none except*, or *none but*, correctly goes into the *predicate* term. Thus a sentence such as "Only females are mothers" becomes the true statement, "All mothers are females," and not the false statement, "All females are mothers."

The presence of a negative term in phrases such as *none but* and *no one except* does not mean that sentences containing them translate into universal negative categorical statements. Negative universal statements *exclude* one whole group from another whole group: The negative term is usually unqualified, as in "No virgins are mothers," "No one under 35 is eligible to be President," or "None of the beans in this barrel is black." When a sentence is equivalent to a negative universal categorical, it does not matter which term is subject or predicate: "No mothers are virgins," "No persons eligible for President are persons under 35," and "No black beans are beans in this barrel" are equally good translations of the sentences previously mentioned. When *all* of one group fall outside of another group, it is clear that no members of the latter group will be found in the former one either, so it is a matter of convenience which term takes the subject or predicate position.

In the case of particular affirmative statements also, it does not matter which term is subject and which is predicate: "Some college students are handicapped" has the same logical content as "Some handicapped persons are college students." But we must exercise caution in translating sentences into particular negative categorical form, for here again the meaning of the statement depends on the position of the terms: "Some doctors are not psychiatrists" is a true statement, which is obviously not equivalent to the false statement, "Some psychiatrists are not doctors."

In handling statements containing negative terms, one must watch to see that translation preserves the original meaning and does not cancel or even reverse the sense: "Everyone who is not white belongs to a minority group" is equivalent to "All nonwhites are minority group members" but not to "No whites are members of minority groups" or "All minority group members are nonwhites."

Usually sentences that are flat negations are correctly translated into universal negatives. "Dead men don't lie" obviously means "No dead men are liars," and "Fetuses do not have human rights" translates into "No fetuses are beings with civil rights."

Empirical sentences that are generalizations made without quantifiers, like *all*, *no*, and *most*, sometimes raise questions about the proper categorical form. If a statement expresses a well-established empirical law, such as "Acids turn blue litmus red," translation into a universal form is correct; many empirical generalizations only have the logical force of "for the most part," however, and cannot be correctly rendered as universal statements. A sentence such as "College women nowadays prefer careers to motherhood" is not usually to be interpreted as a universal statement about all college women without exception; indeed the lack of specificity often reflects the speaker's unwillingness to go so far. In assessing an argument containing such a generalization, one must consider how much the force of the argument depends on interpreting the statement as a universal statement, and whether the speaker is fudging the issue by speaking in broad and vague terms.

Whenever it is clear that a sentence is not meant to cover every member of the group or class named in its subject term, then the sentence must be translated into either a particular affirmative categorical or a particular negative categorical. Since the quantifier *some* in particular categorical statements has the indefinite meaning, *one or more,* one cannot preserve the distinctions between *most, more,* or *few* in translating sentences from ordinary language into particular categorical form. Thus both "Most college women prefer careers to motherhood" and "Few college women prefer careers to motherhood" have to be rendered into the particular affirmative, "Some college women are women preferring careers to motherhood." In such cases we must simply recognize that the logic of categorical statements is not powerful enough to produce a full equivalent for these sentences. Arguments in which such distinctions are crucial cannot be fully assessed by the logic of categorical statements alone but require other techniques of reasoning.

In general, sentences that can correctly be classified as universal categorical statements are (1) statements about a limited group of people which can be verified by summing up a limited number of observations, such as "All the people in this room are over 12 years old"; (2) necessarily true statements, which can be confirmed by reflecting on the meanings of terms and their logical relationships, like "All mothers are females"; (3) well-established empirical generalizations or regulations, such as "No acids turn red litmus blue" and "All American Presidents are over 35 years old."

In general one should translate a sentence from ordinary language into a particular categorical form whenever (1) less than all the members of the subject term are spoken of and (2) a universal statement is denied— into a particular negative when a universal affirmative is denied and into a particular affirmative when a universal negative is denied. Thus, "It is false that all college women are career-oriented" should be translated into the particular negative, "Some college women are not career-oriented"; and "It is not true that no American Presidents are Catholics" will be correctly rendered by the particular affirmative, "Some American Presidents are Catholics."

EXERCISE 5A

1. Select the numbered statement which best translates each lettered statement. Say why it is better than the other numbered statements and whether it preserves the full meaning of the original.

    a. Psychologists do not have M.D. degrees.
        (1) No psychologists have M.D. degrees.
        (2) No psychologists are holders of M.D. degrees.
        (3) Some psychologists are not holders of M.D. degrees.
        (4) All psychologists are not M.D.s.
        (5) Some psychologists are holders of M.D.s.
    b. Only nonwhites belong to minority groups.
        (1) All nonwhites are members of minority groups.
        (2) All members of minority groups are not white.
        (3) Some nonwhites are members of minority groups.
        (4) No whites are members of minority groups.
        (5) All members of minority groups are nonwhite.
    c. All residents except minors may buy alcoholic beverages.
        (1) All who may buy alcoholic beverages are minors.
        (2) No minors may buy alcoholic beverages.
        (3) All residents who may buy alcoholic beverages are nonminors.
        (4) All nonminor residents may buy alcoholic beverages.
        (5) All nonminor residents are persons who may buy alcoholic beverages.

2. Translate each of the following sentences into a standard categorical form. Say whether the form preserves the full meaning of the original.

    a. Psychiatrists must have medical degrees.
    b. There are no psychiatrists who are not doctors.
    c. Most doctors are not psychiatrists.
    d. Lesbians are female homosexuals.
    e. Diamonds are the hardest natural substance.
    f. Only diamonds are able to scratch glass.
    g. None but incompetent doctors are poor.
    h. Anyone who tries can stop smoking.
    i. Few teenagers are good insurance risks.
    j. Heavy smokers are not good insurance risks.
    k. Heavy smokers are more likely to develop lung cancer than light smokers or nonsmokers.

5B IMMEDIATE INFERENCE BETWEEN CATEGORICAL STATEMENTS

Translating sentences from ordinary language into equivalents of categorical logical form is useful for the following reason: Once we obtain a categorical form of statement which fully preserves the meaning of the original statement, it is easy to see how its truth or falsity is related to that of other forms of categorical statements having the same subject and predicate terms. In this way, we may easily distinguish valid immediate inferences from invalid ones. Given a statement in categorical form, we can determine which categorical statement is its contradictory, whether it has a contrary, and what other categorical statements it is consistent with, implies, or is implied by.

If a statement is translatable into a universal affirmative categorical, such as "All students are poor," its contradictory is the particular negative categorical statement with the same subject and predicate terms, "Some students are not poor." Any statement correctly translated into the logical form of a particular negative categorical statement has as its contradictory the universal affirmative with the same subject and predicate term. Similarly, any statement correctly translated into universal negative categorical form, like "No students are poor," is the contradictory of a statement correctly translated into particular affirmative logical form, "Some students are poor."

One way of checking the truth or falsity of a given statement is to consider whether the contradictory of its categorical equivalent is clearly true or false. The greater our assurance that a statement is true, the more certain we should be that its contradictory is false. For example, if we are quite sure that some students are not poor, we must be equally certain that it is false that (the contradictory) all students are poor. If we know that some students are poor, we must also be able to say that it is not the case that no students are poor. Any statement that we can assert to be *false* must also enable us to say that its contradictory is *true*. If we know it to be false that some organic substances have been discovered on Mars, we also must know it to be true that no organic substances have been found on Mars.

When we operate with the categorical form of statement, the distinction between *contradictory statements* and *contraries* emerges clearly. Two sentences are contraries when the truth of one precludes the truth of the other, but it is still logically possible that neither statement is true (that is, they may both be false). A universal affirmative categorical statement is always the contrary of a universal negative categorical statement with the same subject and predicate terms. Thus "All students are poor" and "No students are poor" are contraries. If it were true that all students are poor, it would have to be false that no students are poor, and vice versa; but as we know, neither statement is in fact true. If we knew it to be the case that no unidentified flying objects are extraterrestrial vehicles, we could deny that all unidentified flying objects are extraterrestrial vehicles; but knowing the falsity of the latter does not enable us to pronounce the former to be true (whether "No unidentified flying objects are extraterrestrial vehicles" is true or false remains open).

Statements of particular categorical form with the same subject and predicate term are not logical contraries, however; rather they are always *consistent* with one another; that is, it is logically possible that both the particular affirmative and the particular negative with the same subject and predicate terms are true. It is logically possible, and in fact true, that some students are poor and also that some students are not poor. Similarly, the fact that "Some unidentified flying objects are not extraterrestrial vehicles" is true is consistent with the truth of the statement, "Some unidentified flying objects are extraterrestrial vehicles" (although, of course, it does not in any way prove it, or even imply it).

Note that "Most students are poor" is the logical contrary of "Few students are poor": If it is true that most students are poor it would have to be false that only a few are poor; but both statements are false in case there are about as many students who are poor as are not poor. Of course neither statement is of categorical logical form. As we observed in the preceding section, both would have to be translated into the particular affirmative, "Some students are poor," a translation which obviously does not preserve the full meaning of the original statements, and in which the contrariness of meaning involved in *most* and *few* is lost.

We can also illustrate an important type of *implication* by reference to categorical statements. The truth of a universal statement implies the truth of the corresponding particular with the same subject and predicate terms: "All UFOs are extraterrestrial vehicles" implies "Some UFOs are extraterrestrial vehicles"; "No UFOs are extraterrestrial vehicles" implies "Some UFOs are not extraterrestrial vehicles." Thus once we know the truth of a universal affirmative categorical statement, we may validly infer the truth of the particular affirmative categorical statement with the same subject and predicate terms; similarly the truth of a particular negative statement is validly inferred from the truth of the universal negative categorical with the same subject and predicate terms. The truth of the stronger universal claim enables us automatically to infer that the weaker particular claim is also true.

Moreover, if we know the weaker particular categorical, "Some UFOs are extraterrestrial vehicles," to be false, we can infer that the stronger corresponding universal categorical, "All UFOs are extraterrestrial vehicles," is also false; similarly, the falsity of a particular negative categorical, such as "Some UFOs are not extraterrestrial vehicles," enables us to say that the corresponding universal negative, "No UFOs are extraterrestrial vehicles," is likewise false. For if it is *false* that "Some *S* are not P," its contradictory, "All S are P," must be *true*; in which case, the contrary of "All S are P" must be *false*, and that contrary is the universal negative, "No S are P."

The relationships of contradiction, contrariety, and implication obtaining between categorical statements having the same subject and predicate terms can be graphically represented in The Square of Opposition:

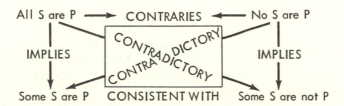

The universal categorical statements occupy the two upper corners of the square, with the affirmative universal on the left and the negative universal on the right. The particular categoricals occupy the bottom two corners of the square, with the affirmative again on the left and the negative on the right. The lines joining the various corners of the square indicate the logical relationships holding between the categorical statements occupying the respective corners. It shows for example that "All S are P" implies "Some S are P," is the contrary of "No S are P," and is the contradictory of "Some S are not P."

The Square of Opposition is a useful memory device. Keeping it in mind, the student can figure out, for any statement in ordinary language that has a full categorical equivalent, what other categorical statements having the same subject and predicate terms may be inferred from it, what other categorical statements it is consistent or inconsistent with, and whether the inconsistency is one of contradiction or contrariety. Translating the statement into categorical form makes apparent the logical commitments we make in asserting or denying it. By considering which categorical form correctly expresses what we or others mean to say, we can avoid or reveal ambiguous formulations in ordinary language that cover up loopholes in reasoning, disguise contraries as contradictories, or confuse consistency and inconsistency.

We must now single out a class of universal statements that pose a special hazard, that group whose subject terms name a class of things which may turn out not to have any instances. We sometimes make hypothetical statements concerning things we do not know to exist. For example, a man, X, may make a will and leave all his property to be divided equally among his children. He could do this quite reasonably even if he had no children or just one child. In this case he is asserting something expressible as a universal affirmative, "All children of mine are equal sharers of my estate." Analyzing this statement in accordance with the Square, we could infer the truth of the particular affirmative, "Some children of X are equal sharers of X's estate." Usually the particular statement is understood to assert that there do in fact exist beings to whom the subject term of the particular statement applies. Thus, in X's case we may be led to infer falsely that there do exist one or more children of X, who are equal heirs to his estate.

To avoid such false inferences, logicians distinguish two ways of interpreting the interrelationships among categorical statements:

1. The *existential interpretation* assumes that there do exist things to which the subject terms of categorical statements apply, so that all the interrelationships among categorical statements illustrated by the Square of Opposition hold.
2. The *hypothetical interpretation* does not assume that there exist things to which the subject terms of categorical statements apply; therefore, only the logical relationship of contradiction illustrated on the Square of Opposition holds.

The hypothetical interpretation is a very minimum one which leaves open the possibility that nothing exists in the group or class named by the subject term of categorical statements. This is the interpretation appropriate in the case of the presently childless man making a will which names his children as heirs to his estate. On the hypothetical interpretation, the universal affirmative means "All S (if there are any) are P," and the universal negative, "No S (if there are any) are P." Thus the universal affirmative no longer implies the particular affirmative, nor does the universal negative imply the particular affirmative, for the hypothetical interpretation does not claim that there are any things of the kind named by its subject term (nor does it deny this, of course). One cannot infer from the truth of "All children of X are heirs to X's estate" the truth of "There are one or more children of X, who are heirs to his estate." Similarly, on the hypothetical interpretation, the universal affirmative and the universal negative are no longer contraries: The truth of "All children of X are heirs to X's estate" does not falsify "No children of X are heirs to X's estate," just in case X has no children. The only relationship on the Square that continues to hold on the minimum hypothetical interpretation is that between contradictories: If it is true that all children of X are heirs of X (the universal affirmative), it is necessarily false that some children of X are not X's heirs (the particular negative), even if X has no children. Likewise, the truth of the universal negative, "No children of X are heirs of X," requires the falsity of "Some children of X are heirs of X," regardless of whether any children of X exist.

There are many cases in science and in law where the hypothetical interpretation is the proper one, and the existential interpretation is wrong. For example, a scientist who says "All organic substances on Mars are of exotic chemical makeup" should clearly be interpreted as speaking hypothetically, for he is speculating about the chemistry of Martian organic substances rather than asserting that they exist. When it is obvious that we do know that there are things to which the subject of a categorical statement applies, the existential interpretation is preferable; otherwise, we would not draw inferences that we are actually justified in making. In doubtful cases, it is best to adopt the minimum hypothetical interpretation, in line with our usual logical practice of only assuming what follows necessarily from the logical form of statements.

EXERCISE 5B

Assume that each numbered statement is true. What can be inferred by the rules of immediate inference about each lettered statement? Indicate any case requiring existential interpretation. Repeat, assuming each numbered statement to be false.

1. Some astronomers practice astrology.
    a. All astronomers practice astrology.
    b. Some who practice astrology are not astronomers.
    c. No astronomer practices astrology.
    d. Some who do not practice astrology are astronomers.
    e. Some astronomers do not practice astrology.

2. No fetuses have human rights.
    a. Anyone having human rights is not a fetus.
    b. Every fetus has human rights.
    c. Some fetuses have human rights.
    d. Some fetuses do not have human rights.
    e. All possessors of human rights are fetuses.

3. Some U.S. citizens are not native-born Americans.
    a. Every U.S. citizen is a native-born American.
    b. Every native-born American is a U.S. citizen.
    c. Some U.S. citizens are native-born Americans.
    d. No U.S. citizen is a native-born American.
    e. Some native-born Americans are not U.S. citizens.

4. All fallen angels are devils.
    a. Some fallen angels are devils.
    b. No fallen angels are devils.

    c. No angels are devils.

    d. Some fallen angels are not devils.

    e. Every devil was once an angel.

5C   CATEGORICAL EQUIVALENTS

In the previous exercise, the student may have reasoned that in some cases inferences could be drawn between categorical statements whose subject and predicate terms occurred in opposite positions; for example, from "Some astronomers are astrologers" to "Some astrologers are astronomers." We shall now study inferences between statements in categorical form which are justified because the statements are *equivalent*. Equivalent statements are statements which are necessarily true together and false together, so that knowing one statement's truth or falsity enables one to infer the corresponding truth or falsity of the other. As in the above two statements, if it is true that "Some astronomers are astrologers," it must likewise be true that "Some astrologers are astronomers," since the two statements, if it is true that "Some astronomers are astrologers," it statement true or false will also make the other true or false.

Converse Categorical Statements

These two statements are examples of *converse* categorical statements, the most familiar variation. Two categorical statements are converses when they are both the same type of categorical statement and contain exactly the same terms but in reverse order, the subject term of one being the predicate term of the other, and the predicate term of one being the subject term of the other.

Some *astronomers* are *astrologers.*

Some *astrologers* are *astronomers.*

Here the categorical form of both statements is particular affirmative: The subject term of the first statement, *astronomers*, is the predicate term of the second; the predicate term of the first, *astrologers,* is the subject term of the second.

Intuitively, it is easy to recognize these two statements as being equivalent. We shall, however, draw a diagram to demonstrate their equivalence, in preparation for dealing with other sorts of equivalences which are not so obvious. Let us make one circle, representing an area in which we imagine all astronomers to be included, and a second circle overlapping the first, in which we suppose all astrologers to be gathered.

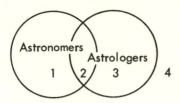

FIGURE 5.1 Area 1: Astronomers who are not also astrologers. Area 2: Those who are both astronomers and astrologers. Area 3: Astrologers who are not also astronomers. Area 4: Those neither astronomers nor astrologers.

The area within the left circle includes everyone who is an astronomer; it is divided into two sections, the one farther left (numbered 1) includes astronomers who are not astrologers, since it lies outside the right circle containing all the astrologers. Area 2 of the left circle also lies within the right circle, and thus is the place where all who are both astronomers and astrologists are included. The second area within the right circle contains astrologers who are not astronomers, since it is outside the left circle containing all the astronomers. The area outside both circles, containing beings who are neither astronomers nor astrologers, is numbered 4. On this diagram we are thus able to represent our knowledge concerning the relationships between those who are astronomers and those who are astrologers which categorical statements assert.

Particular categorical statements assert that there exist one or more members of the group named by the subject term who also are members of the group named by the predicate term. "Some astronomers are astrologers" says that one or more astronomers are also astrologers. We shall use an asterisk, or star, to represent the fact that something does exist within a given area. We can demonstrate the content of the particular categorical, "Some astronomers are astrologers," by placing a star in section 2, the area which falls within both circles, the circle of the astrologers and the circle of the astronomers (Figure 5.2).

To represent the information contained by the *converse* categorical, "Some astrologists are astronomers," we put a star in the very same area

FIGURE 5.2

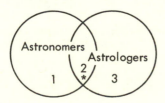

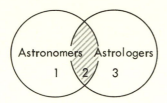

FIGURE 5.3

2, which also contains astrologers who are astronomers—graphic evidence of the logical equivalence of the two statements. In general the converses of particular affirmative categorical statements are equivalent.

Are the converses of the other three forms of categorical statements also logically equivalent? We can use the method of diagramming to discover whether this is so. Let us first examine the converses of universal negative categorical statements to determine whether they are equivalent, using the same two terms, *astronomers* and *astrologers*. Our two converse universal negative statements are then

No *astronomers* are *astrologers*.
No *astrologers* are *astronomers*.

The universal negative categorical statement maintains that no being who belongs to the group named by its subject term also belongs to the group named by its predicate term. We can represent this information on our diagram by showing that the area containing beings who belong to both groups is *empty*, that no one is to be found there. To show that an area is empty, we simply shade the whole area with diagonal lines (Figure 5.3).

This diagram gives the information contained in the universal categorical, "No astronomers are astrologers." What would the diagram of its converse, "No astrologers are astronomers," be? Clearly we would have to shade the very same area 2, which contains the astrologers who are also astronomers. Since the diagrams of both statements are identical, we have proof that the converses of universal negative statements are logically equivalent.

Many persons suppose that the converses of universal affirmative statements are also logically equivalent. Let us use the diagram method to determine whether it is generally the case that a statement of the form "All *S* are *P*" is equivalent to "All *P* are *S*." Using the same two terms, *astronomers* and *astrologers*, our two converse universal affirmatives are

All *astronomers* are *astrologers*.
All *astrologers* are *astronomers*.

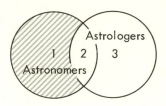

FIGURE 5.4

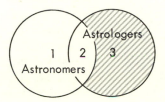

FIGURE 5.5

To represent "All astronomers are astrologers," we shade the whole of area 1, which would contain astronomers who are not astrologers, in order to show that there are none (Figure 5-4). To diagram a universal affirmative, one always shades the area of the subject term circle outside the predicate term circle.

But to diagram the converse universal affirmative, "All astrologers are astronomers," we need to shade out area 3, to show that there are no astrologers who are not also astronomers, as that statement claims (Figure 5.5).

Comparing the two diagrams, we see that they are not identical, and do not therefore contain the same information. In the diagram for "All astronomers are astrologers," area 1 is shaded, but in the diagram for "All astronomers are astrologers," area 1 is not shaded, indicating no evidence about this area. In the diagram for "All astrologers are astronomers," area 3 is shaded instead, showing the statement gives evidence about that area rather than area 1. The differing diagrams indicate that the facts that make one true do not necessarily make the other true also. This significant difference between the facts conveyed by the converses of universal affirmatives may be illustrated by the fact that "All mothers are females" is a true universal affirmative categorical statement, whereas its converse, "All females are mothers," is a false universal affirmative categorical statement. A common error in reasoning is the immediate inference from the truth of a statement of the logical form "All S are P" to the truth of its converse, "All P are S." But such an inference is not in general valid. If our evidence entitles us to say only that "All S are P," we cannot make the further immediate inference, "All P are S"; we need to have independent additional evidence for the truth of the latter statement, over and above the truth of "All *S* are *P*."

The temptation to make the inference from the truth of a universal affirmative to that of its converse arises in part from the fact that it sometimes happens that both statements are true. For example, in chemistry one learns that "All acids turn blue litmus paper red" and also that "All liquids turning blue litmus paper red are acids," and both facts tend to be weakly expressed by one universal affirmative of the form "All *S* are *P*." The case in which both a universal affirmative and its converse are true is exactly expressed by saying "All *and only S* are *P*." Condensed in this statement is the compound sentence, "All *S* are *P* and only *S* are *P*." But "only *S* are *P*" translates into the categorical statement "All *P* are *S*." Thus "All and only *S* are *P*" is equivalent to asserting both the universal affirmative, "All *S* are *P*," and its converse, "All *P* are *S*."

Particular negative statements do not have equivalent converses, as we can show by drawing a diagram for the particular negative categorical statement. A particular negative statement asserts that one or more of the members of the group named by its subject term are *excluded* from the group named by its predicate term. To represent this fact, one places an asterisk in the area of the circle for the subject term that lies *outside* the circle of the predicate term. Thus the particular negative, "Some astronomers are not astrologers," is represented in Figure 5.6a.

Its converse, "Some astrologers are not astronomers," is illustrated by Figure 5.6b, which shows an asterisk in the area of the astrologers' circle that falls outside the area of the astronomers' circle.

The two diagrams are clearly different, showing asterisks in different areas: Thus the two statements are not equivalent but represent

FIGURE 5.6a

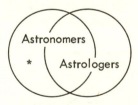

FIGURE 5.6b

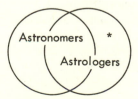

two different facts. In general, then, the converses of particular negative statements are not equivalent.

Contrapositive Categorical Equivalents

One cannot simply switch subject and predicate terms of universal affirmative or particular negative statements and obtain an equivalent statement. However, if one negates each term and also switches the position of subject and predicate terms, the result is an equivalent universal affirmative or particular negative statement, called the *contrapositive*. The contrapositive of "All astronomers are astrologers" will be "All *non*astrologers are *non*astronomers"; that of "Some astronomers are not astrologers" is "Some *non*astrologers are not *non*astronomers." It must be remembered that obtaining the contrapositive of a statement requires two different operations: (1) negating both the subject term and the predicate term and (2) switching the positions of subject and predicate terms. To prove that the contrapositives of universal affirmatives and particular negatives are equivalent, study the diagrams we have already made, in order to note that in both cases the same information is contained.

Obverse Categorical Equivalents

There is one variant of a categorical statement which provides equivalents for every type of categorical statement: It is called the *obverse,* and also consists of two operations. The first step is to change the type of statement from affirmative to negative or from negative to affirmative: A universal affirmative becomes a universal negative, a universal negative becomes a universal affirmative, and so on. Second, one negates the predicate term, P being changed to *non-P*. The four *obverses* are as follows:

All S are $P:$ ⟷ No S are non$P$.
No S are $P:$ ⟷ All S are non$P$.
Some S are $P:$ ⟷ Some S are not non$P$.
Some S are not $P:$ ⟷ Some S are non$P$.

Intuitively it is easy to recognize that there are obverse equivalents for each type of categorical statement: The two steps of obversion amount to a double negative, or negating of a negation, which returns one to a position equivalent to the original statement. Clearly, "All mothers are female" is equivalent to "No mothers are nonfemale"; "No males are mothers" is equivalent to "All males are nonmothers"; "Some females are mothers" is equivalent to "Some females are not nonmothers"; and "Some females are not mothers" to "Some females are nonmothers."

In constructing the obverse or contrapositive of a categorical statement, one must exercise care to use the true negation of any term. The best strategy is to preface the term by *non*, as in the foregoing examples we spoke of *nonastronomers*. It is wise to reserve the word *not* as the sign for the particular negative categorical statement only.

Incorrect inferences may result when the contrary of a term, rather than its negation or contradictory, is used. Just as every statement has a contradictory but not every statement has a contrary, so it is that every term has a contradictory but not every term has a contrary. A number of familiar terms are contraries: *hot* is the contrary of *cold; beautiful* of *ugly; male* of *female.* But many other terms have no contraries, such as *electromagnetic, desk,* and *table.* However, every term has a contradictory, which can be expressed by placing the prefix *non* in front of it. The contradictory of *beautiful* is *nonbeautiful*, a term which applies to anything not describable as beautiful; the nonbeautiful includes not only the ugly but also the aesthetically indifferent and properties unrelated to beauty altogether, such as electromagnetic.

We can thus distinguish between contrary terms and contradictory terms: Either a term or its contradictory must apply correctly to every kind of thing, whatever the thing is, just as either a statement or its contradictory must be true. Contrary terms cannot both apply correctly to the very same thing, but there are some things to which neither term applies. Analogously, contrary statements cannot both be true, but both may be false. Since *alive* and *dead* are contrary terms, anything properly described as alive cannot at the same time be properly described as dead; but some things are not properly described as either alive or dead— numbers, statements, inanimate objects in general. The contradictory of *alive* is *nonliving* or *inanimate.* False inferences arise frequently when one reasons from the inapplicability of a term to the applicability of its contrary instead of its contradictory; for example, from the fact that someone is not beautiful, to the fact that he or she is ugly, or that all who are not wise are therefore foolish or ignorant.

We called attention in the preceding section to the fact that universal statements in their interrelationships with other categorical statements may be interpreted in a more noncommittal sense—the hypothetical interpretation—and in a less noncommittal sense—the existential interpretation. The instructions given for diagramming universal statements illustrate the hypothetical interpretation, for they do not assume that any things in fact exist of the kind named by the subject term of the universal statements. In Figures 5.7a and 5.7b, representing "All astronomers are astrologers" and "No astronomers are astrologers," there is no assumption that any astronomers at all exist: The absence of either an asterisk or shading in an area of a diagram indicates that it is an open question whether or not that area is occupied.

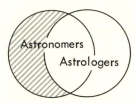

FIGURE 5.7a   All astronomers are astrologers. (Hypothetical interpretation)

FIGURE 5.7b   No astronomers are astrologers. (Hypothetical interpretation)

In both the diagrams one area of the circle for the subject term, *astronomers*, is shaded, indicating that no astronomers of the kind contained in that area actually exist; the other area contains neither shading nor asterisk, so that neither diagram embodies any assumption that any astronomers exist. The universal affirmative merely says: If there are any astronomers, all of them are also astrologers. The universal negative says: If there are any astronomers, none of them are also astrologers.

Since there are occasions when valid inferences can only be made by using the existential interpretation, we need to be able to draw a diagram suitable for that interpretation. We must include in it the information that astronomers do in fact exist. To present that information, we put in the diagram an asterisk in an appropriate place in the circle of the subject term, *astronomers*. We must be careful to put the asterisk in the correct place—it would be wrong to put it in any area of the circle that is already shaded, for shading means that an area is empty, that no beings are to be found there. In diagramming the existential interpretation, the first step is always to shade the area appropriate for that kind of universal statement, exactly as in the hypothetical interpretation. For the universal affirmative, one shades the area of the subject term falling outside the circle of the predicate term; for the universal negative, one shades the area of the subject term that overlaps the predicate term. The second step is simply to place an asterisk in the remaining unshaded area. The diagrams for the existential interpretation of the two kinds of universal statements are shown in Figures 5-8a and 5-8b.

The contrast between hypothetical and existential interpretations relates specifically to the subject term; of course it would be possible to

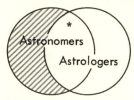

FIGURE 5.8a All astronomers are astrologers. (Existential interpretation)

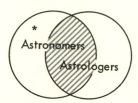

FIGURE 5.8b No astronomers are astrologers. (Existential interpretation)

make assumptions about the existence of things to which the predicate term applies, but doing so turns out not to be helpful in logic. It is essential to remember to use the existential interpretation only when there is evidence that there do exist things of the kind named by the subject term of the statement.

EXERCISE 5C

State whether each lettered sentence is an obverse, converse, contra-positive, or none of these of the numbered sentence. In which cases is the lettered sentence equivalent to the numbered sentence?

1. Some UFOs are not extraterrestrial objects.
   a. Some things of extraterrestrial origin are UFOs.
   b. Some terrestrial objects are UFOs.
   c. Some nonextraterrestrial objects are not UFOs.
   d. Some terrestrial objects are not UFOs.
   e. Some terrestrial objects are not things that are not UFOs.
   f. Some UFOs are terrestrial objects.

2. No Catholics are non-Christian.
   a. All Catholics are Christian.
   b. No non-Christians are Catholics.
   c. All non-Catholics are non-Christians.

    d. No Catholics are Moslems.

    e. All Christians are Catholics.

    f. Some Catholics are Christians.

3. Some plants are edible.

    a. Some plants are not edible.

    b. Some edible things are plants.

    c. Some nonedible things are plants.

    d. Some plants are not inedible.

    e. Only plants are edible.

    f. Some plants are safe to eat.

4. Only unemployed persons pay no income tax.

    a. All who pay no income tax are unemployed.

    b. All unemployed persons pay no income tax.

    c. All employed persons pay income tax.

    d. No unemployed persons pay income tax.

    e. Some unemployed persons do not pay income tax.

    f. Some who pay no income tax are unemployed.

Review Exercise For Chapter 5

1. Construct the converse, contrapositive, and obverse of each of the following sentences and say whether it is equivalent.

    a. All medical expenses are tax-deductible.

    b. Some money gifts are not tax-free.

    c. Some investment losses are tax-deductible.

    d. No dividends are tax-free.

    e. All vegetarians eat cheese.

    f. Some vegetarians do not eat eggs.

    g. Only nonvegetarians eat meat.

    h. No seafood lovers are vegetarians.

    i. Some vegetarians eat eggs.

2. Suppose each lettered sentence is true. What can be inferred about the truth or falsity of each numbered sentence? Suppose each lettered sentence is false. What can be inferred concerning the truth or falsity of each numbered sentence?

    a. All young people are romantic.

        (1) No young people are romantic.

        (2) Only the young are romantic.

        (3) All old people are unromantic.

        (4) No young people are unromantic.

        (5) Some young people are romantic.

(6) Some young people are unromantic.

(7) Some romantic people are young.

b. Some good things are not pleasant.

(1) No good things are pleasant.

(2) Some good things are pleasant.

(3) Some things that are not pleasant are not lacking in goodness.

(4) Not all good things are pleasant.

(5) No painful things are good.

(6) All good things are pleasant.

(7) All pleasant things are good.

c. No intellectuals are conservatives.

(1) All intellectuals are nonconservatives.

(2) Some intellectuals are not conservatives.

(3) Some conservatives are intellectuals.

(4) All intellectuals are radicals.

(5) No conservatives are intellectuals.

(6) Some conservatives are not intellectuals.

(7) All who are not conservatives are intellectuals.

d. Some socialists are communists.

(1) All socialists are communists.

(2) All communists are socialists.

(3) Some socialists are noncommunists.

(4) No socialists are communists.

(5) Some communists are not socialists.

(6) Some communists are socialists.

(7) Some noncommunists are nonsocialists.

3. Answer the following questions by constructing and analyzing a diagram for each statement. Indicate whenever the existential interpretation of a universal statement is needed.

a. Is "All astronomers are physicists" the contradictory of "Some physicists are not astronomers"?

b. Is "All magicians are chemists" the contrary of "No chemists are magicians"?

c. If "No doctors are illiterate" is true, can one infer that "Some illiterates are not doctors" is true?

d. If "All lawyers have passed the bar exam" is true, can one infer that "All who have passed the bar exam are lawyers" is also true? Can one infer that some passers of the bar exam are lawyers?

e. Assuming that it is true that no elves are over six inches tall, are we entitled to infer that some elves are not over six inches tall? May we infer that some beings over six inches tall are not elves?

May we infer that it is false that some elves are over six inches tall?

f. In what circumstances may we infer from a statement of the form "No X are Y" both that "Some X are not Y" and "Some Y are not X"? In what circumstances would the two inferences be incorrect?

chapter 6

Deductive Reasoning: The Syllogism

6A DEDUCTIVE REASONING AND EVERYDAY REASONING

A fundamental way of extending our knowledge is through deductive reasoning. In deductive reasoning we make inferences which are justified either by (1) the logical structure of the statements of the argument or (2) the relationships of meanings between the various terms in the statements. For example, the term *uncle* includes being *male* as part of its meaning: Thus we can deductively infer "Melissus is male" from "Melissus is Plato's uncle," without knowing anything else about Melissus. Such inferences are valid whenever one statement implies another statement because of the meanings possessed by the terms that describe the subject matter of the statements. Whether such deductive inferences are valid depends on the facts of linguistic usage, and in most cases, are readily settled; more difficult cases may need to be resolved by applying the rules for real and standard definition.

In this chapter and the one following, we shall study deductive inferences that are based on the logical structure of statements in the argument, quite apart from the meanings of the terms standing for the subject matter under discussion. For example, we have already noted in the section on immediate inference that any statement whose logical form is that of a universal affirmative categorical statement, that is, "All *S* are

P," is the contradictory of another statement whose logical form is that of a particular negative categorical statement, that is, "Some *S* are not *P*," no matter what meanings are assigned to the subject and predicate terms *S* and *P*, as long as the meanings of the *S* term and the *P* term are exactly the same in both statements. Thus, from the truth of "All vegetarians are eaters of bread," we may infer deductively that "Some vegetarians are not eaters of bread" is false, simply from examining the logical structures of the two sentences without any further observation of the eating habits of vegetarians. Since "Some vegetarians are not eaters of bread" is of the logical form "Some *S* are not *P*," it is the contradictory of "All vegetarians are eaters of bread," whose logical form is "All *S* are *P*." Therefore, without thinking at all about vegetarians or bread-eaters, but simply noting that one statement is a particular negative categorical sentence and the other is a universal affirmative sentence containing exactly the same subject and predicate terms, we may infer deductively that whenever one of the statements is true, the other must be false.

In everyday reasoning we seldom separate the logical form of a statement from its subject matter; following a course of reasoning involves attending to both at once. However, there are two ways in which our powers of reasoning are enhanced by concentrating on the logical forms of the statements in an argument and ignoring its subject matter. First, our awareness that there exists some kind of connection between the sorts of things designated by the terms that stand for the subject matter of the statements sometimes makes us leap to conclusions that are not warranted by the facts expressed in the statements. For example, many persons are likely to infer from these two premises

No American Presidents are members of the Communist Party.
All Communists are socialists.

the conclusion, "No American Presidents are socialists." Yet that conclusion does not follow logically from those premises. By concentrating on the logical form of the statements made in an argument, we can avoid making such mistakes in reasoning.

Second, we may gain knowledge of the truth of statements which follow necessarily from the facts already in our possession, as in the kind of deductive discoveries for which literary detectives are admired. Indeed, much of the utility of deductive reasoning lies in the fact that two or more statements in combination often imply statements that are not derivable from each one separately. Deductive reasoning enables us to elicit from our true statements true consequences that might otherwise escape notice. However, deductive reasoning cannot provide truths not latent in the combined premises of an argument. This fact is often expressed by saying that the conclusion of a valid deductive argument does not go beyond its premises; it is already contained in the premises: not in any one of the premises taken separately (except of course in the case of immediate inference), but in the premises *taken together*. Since most people are limited in their power to foresee the logical consequences of more than one true statement at a time, deductive reasoning is often needed to spell them out clearly. The more premises that are added, the more numerous and also the more complex the conclusions that can be inferred. Mathematics is a form of knowledge which uses deductive reasoning to weld chains of inferences into structures of great theoretical and practical importance. Everyday reasoning which involves the application of mathematics is a common form of deductive reasoning. If one's savings account contains $5,000 and a car will cost $4,000 and college tuition is $2,000, one infers deductively that one cannot both pay college tuition and buy a car out of one's savings.

In ordinary reasoning we also employ deductive reasoning of a nonmathematical kind. A woman who reads the sentence, "Only women who have given birth are able to use IUD contraceptive devices" and is aware that she herself has never borne a child, will readily infer that she cannot use this form of contraception. She is applying a generalization to an individual case, a common type of deductive reasoning. Another type is the derivation of a generalization from other generalizations. For example, from the generalizations that all union workers are upholders of collective bargaining and all upholders of collective bargaining demand the right to strike, it is an easy step to the deduction that all union workers will demand the right to strike.

Deductive reasoning can only prove statements whose truth is *necessarily* connected with the premises of the argument. That is, the conclusions which can be drawn by formal deductive reasoning are strictly limited to statements connected to the premises through the logical structures of the statements in the argument, quite independently of the subject matter. For example, the foregoing argument is valid *because* its premises are of the logical form,

All S (union workers) are M (believers in collective bargaining).
All M (believers . . .) are P (claimers of the right to strike).
And its conclusion is of the logical form,
All S (union workers) are P (claimers . . .).

No matter what terms are put in place of S, M, or P, as long as one is consistent in substituting the same term throughout the argument, an argument whose statements are of the preceding logical form is deductively valid. The *validity* of a deductive argument depends simply on whether the premises are of such a logical form that they imply a statement with the logical form of the conclusion. But as with any argument whatsoever, the actual premises of a deductive argument must be known to be true independently of the argument in question; the fact that a deductive argument is valid only shows that the premises do have a necessary connection to the conclusion; it does not show that the premises are themselves true. In the preceding example, the two premises, "All union workers are believers in collective bargaining" and "All believers in collective bargaining claim the right to strike," are empirical generalizations whose truth needs to be established by observation and known to us independently of this argument.

Whether the premises of a deductive argument are true or false is a separate matter from whether they have a necessary connection with the conclusion. When we evaluate an actual piece of deductive argument in ordinary reasoning, we must consider both matters. In order to distinguish the two clearly, we shall speak of the *validity* or *invalidity* of a deductive argument when we consider whether the premises do or do not imply the conclusion. When, in addition, we judge the truth or falsity, probability or improbability, of the premises of the argument, we will speak of the *soundness* of the argument. An argument may be deductively valid, but it may be unsound because of the doubtfulness or known falsity of some premise. However, in order to be sound, a deductive argument must *at least* be valid; that is, its premises must genuinely imply the conclusion for the argument to be worthy of acceptance.

It sometimes happens that the conclusion of a deductive argument is by itself quite plausible, even though it fails to have any necessary connection with the premises offered in the argument. This is the case with the argument previously cited, which drew the conclusion "No American Presidents are socialists" from the two premises, "No American Presidents are Communists" and "All Communists are socialists." Although the conclusion is plausible given the premises, the argument is an invalid deductive argument because these premises do not imply the conclusion logically: The conclusion does not follow *necessarily* from these premises *alone,* for the logical form of the premises leaves open the possibility that there could be an American President who was a socialist but not a Communist. Thus one is not entitled by the two statements offered as premises to conclude that "No American Presidents are socialists." The premises could be true, but the conclusion might still be false; that is, the falsity of the conclusion is *consistent* with the truth of the premises. It might be true that no American Presidents are socialists, but *this* argument does not demonstrate it. We need evidence other than what is presented in its premises to draw the conclusion correctly. If the reader does not intuitively see that this is so, he may be persuaded of the need to have in hand some principles for distinguishing valid syllogisms from invalid ones.

When a deductive argument is invalid, its premises do not allow one to infer *anything at all* about the conclusion, either that it is true or that it is false. Thus a valid deductive argument proves only that its conclusion must be true, *provided* its premises are true; an invalid deductive argument proves nothing whatsoever. Obviously deductive reasoning by itself is not capable of demonstrating to us all or even much of what we want or need to know; the truth of the premises of a deductive argument much of the time must be derived from some source other than deductive reasoning. Nonetheless, deductive reasoning is very useful, indeed indispensable, for both theoretical and practical purposes. Historically it is the first mode of reasoning developed systematically. By employing its techniques ancient thinkers achieved substantial insights on a great variety of subjects. The fruitfulness of deductive reasoning extends beyond merely showing the further consequences of what we already know to be true. It also reveals what other things have to be true in order for a given statement to be true; it enables us to sort out our beliefs into those which go together and those which are in conflict, a procedure essential in systematizing our knowledge of a subject matter.

Deductive reasoning also enables us to discover false assumptions. A conclusion derived by valid deductive reasoning must be true, provided the premises are true. When a deductively valid conclusion is known to be false independently of the reasoning in the argument, it must be the case that some premise of the reasoning is faulty. In this way, the principles of deductive reasoning act as a corrective to assumptions that are plausible but mistaken. For example, ancient thinkers deduced that the earth was not flat from observing that as a ship approaches the shore, the tops of its sails come first into view before the whole ship is visible. They reasoned deductively that if it were true that the earth is flat, then (because light travels in straight lines) the whole of the ship should appear at once, only much reduced in size, just as we see the whole figure of a person approaching on a plain. They thus inferred that what appears to be an empirical truth based on sense observation—that is, "The earth is flat"—must nevertheless be false. This argument is an example of another common form of deductive reasoning in which the statements that are premises and conclusion are not categorical statements (and to which we devote a subsequent chapter).

Some people have a great deal of intuitive skill in deductive reasoning, and most people are easily able to make the simpler steps. Its principles have been extensively codified, so that anyone able to read can learn some of them with a bit of application.

1. Which of the following are deductive arguments?

   a. This man claims to be my first cousin, but he must be lying, since both my mother and father had no siblings.

   b. Anyone who invests his savings in oil prospecting runs the risk of losing all he puts in. Only people of more than ample means can take such chances. Therefore people without a substantial income cannot afford to invest in oil prospecting.

   c. The income from municipal bonds is tax-free, but the interest rate is low. The income from industrial bonds is taxable, but the rate is higher, so it's better to invest in the latter.

   d. The dividends from blue-chip stocks are taxable, but dividends from municipal bonds are never taxed, so there cannot be any municipal bonds among the blue-chip stocks.

   e. Everyone who has blue eyes has either a mother or a father with blue eyes. This little boy has blue eyes, so either his mother or his father must have blue eyes.

2. Use deductive reasoning to discover the answer to the following riddle. Write down the premises which imply the conclusion.

   Brothers and sisters have I none,
   But that man's father is my father's son.
   Who am I?

6B THE STANDARD FORM OF A SYLLOGISM

A syllogism is a deductive argument whose premises consist of two categorical statements that contain one term in common. The conclusion of a syllogism is a categorical statement joining the two other terms contained in the premises. In one of the most common types of syllogism a generalization is derived from two other generalizations, as in this argument discussed earlier:

> All union workers are believers in collective bargaining. All believers in collective bargaining are claimers of the right to strike. Therefore, all union workers are claimers of the right to strike.

Here the common term contained in both premises is "believers in collective bargaining"; it is called the *middle term* of the syllogism. The conclusion joins the other two terms, "union workers" and "claimers of the right to strike," which are the *end terms* of the syllogism. One end term occurs in each premise together with the middle term; the premise that contains the end term that is the predicate term of the conclusion is called the *major premise;* the premise that contains the end term that is the subject term of the conclusion is called the *minor premise.*

To test whether a given syllogism is valid, we must determine whether the logical forms of the premise statements have a necessary connection with the logical form of the conclusion statement. Our first step is to note the logical forms of both premises and conclusion—whether universal affirmative, universal negative, particular affirmative, or particular negative. The second step is to observe the position of each of the three terms in the two premises and the conclusion. We expose the logical structure by marking each end term and schematizing the whole argument as follows, separating the premises from the conclusion with a straight line:

All *S* are *M*.	*S*—union workers
All *M* are *P*.	*M*—believers in collective bargaining
All *S* are *P*.	*P*—claimers of the right to strike

In this argument it is fairly easy to see that there is a necessary connection between the two premises and the conclusion: If everything that is *S* is also *M*, and everything that is *M* is in turn also *P*, then it must be the case that anything that is *S* is also *P*, no matter what *S, M,* or *P* may be. Any argument that can be translated into three universal affirmative categorical statements as premises and conclusion which combine middle and end terms, as illustrated, is a valid deductive argument.

To determine the logical form of a syllogism it is essential to translate both premises and the conclusion into one of the four logical forms of categorical statements. Students are often inclined to take short cuts, but the most common error in syllogistic reasoning arises from mistaking the logical form of one or more statements of the argument and thus not representing the logical form of the syllogism correctly.

A special problem of translation arises in connection with the second most common type of syllogism, in which a generalization is applied to derive an inference about a particular instance. An earlier argument can be expressed as a syllogism of this kind, once we translate it into categorical equivalents:

> Only women who have given birth are able to use IUD contraceptive devices. I have never given birth. Therefore, I cannot use IUD contraceptive devices.

The first step always is to identify the three terms of the syllogism. Note that in this case we cannot use the simple word *women*: One term must be "women who have given birth" and the other term "women able to use IUD contraceptive devices." The third term must represent a definite individual, the woman speaker who is the subject term of the syllogism. Logically, the conclusion and one premise speak of one definite thing, and are singular statements. Since categorical statements express facts about the relationships between groups of things, we must use an artificial logical device to turn the singular statement into a statement about a group. The following strategy enables us to obtain an exact categorical equivalent for a singular statement: (1) For the subject term, we use the phrase "things identical to . . ." the individual instance, and (2) translate the sentence into a universal categorical sentence, affirmative or negative, as appropriate.

For example, the singular statement, "Socrates is a philosopher," has as its categorical equivalent "All things identical to Socrates are philosophers." Since Socrates is the one and only thing identical to Socrates, the two statements express exactly the same fact. Similarly, "Socrates is not handsome" can be expressed by the universal negative, "No things identical to Socrates are handsome." In the argument we are considering, the third term of the syllogism may be expressed as "Women identical to me."

Having identified the three terms, we next put each premise into the correct categorical form. The sentence, "Only women who have given birth are women able to use IUD contraceptive devices," in accordance with a previously cited rule translates into a universal affirmative in which the term following the word *only* goes into the predicate: "All women able to use IUD contraceptive devices are women who have given birth." The sentence, "I am a woman who has never given birth," in accordance with the rule for translating statements with a singular subject term, must be put into a universal statement whose subject term is "women identical to me." Since the other term is "women who have given birth," the appropriate translation is the universal negative, "No women identical to me are women who have given birth." Never translate a sentence about a definite individual instance into particular categorical form, for the particular categorical speaks of an *indefinite* number, at least one or more, and is thus not the categorical equivalent of a singular statement.

The argument in categorical form now reads as follows:

All women able to use IUD contraceptive devices are women who have given birth. No women identical to me are women who have given birth. Therefore, no women identical to me are women who are able to use IUD contraceptive devices.

The middle term, appearing in both premises, is "women who have given birth"; the end terms are "women identical to me"—the subject end term–and "women able to use IUD devices"—the predicate end term. The logical form of the above argument is

All *P* are *M.*   *S*—women identical to me
No *S* are *M.*   *M*—women who have given birth
─────────   *P*—women able to use IUD contraceptive devices
No *S* are *P.*

Is there a necessary connection between premises of these two kinds and a conclusion of this kind? Yes, if everything that is *P* is also *M* but nothing that is an *S* is an *M*, it must follow that nothing that is an *S* can possibly be *P*. The logical form of this argument is one of the most common types of valid syllogism, and any argument with this sort of form is a valid deductive argument. The order of the premises does not matter, but the *kind* of premises and conclusion and the *position* of middle and end terms in each premise must be exactly the same.

There are several methods for determining whether a given syllogism is a valid deductive argument. Each one is simple, once the syllogism has been put into standard form. To put a syllogism into standard form, follow these two steps:

1. Identify the three different groups named by the subject term, the predicate term, and the middle term of the syllogism. Be sure not to use a positive term and its corresponding negative, like *Republicans* and *non-Republicans.*
2. Translate both premises and the conclusion into three categorical statements containing the three different terms as subject and predicate terms. Do not use more than one negative premise, if possible.

In order to put an argument into standard form, it may be necessary to use some of the principles of equivalence described in the preceding chapter. For example, the following argument as it stands contains four terms and two negative premises:

No conservatives are feminists, but there are no Catholics who are not conservatives. Therefore, there can be no Catholic feminists.

This argument speaks of four groups: Catholics, feminists, conservatives, and those who are not conservatives. The last two terms are logically related, the one term being the negation of the other, but one cannot use both a term and its negation in a syllogism. To eliminate one of the terms, use the principle of obversion when one of the problem terms occurs in the predicate position in its premise. For example, the second premise would ordinarily be translated, "No Catholics are nonconservatives." By obversion, we obtain the equivalent, "All Catholics are conservatives," eliminating the negation from the term *nonconservatives*. In so doing we also eliminate one of the negative premises in the original form of the argument, so that it now reads

No conservatives are feminists.
All Catholics are conservatives.
No Catholics are feminists.

S—Catholics
M—conservatives
P—feminists

Alternatively, we might make *nonconservatives* the third term. Then we would need to convert the premise, "No conservatives are feminists," into its converse equivalent, "No feminists are conservatives," in order to put the term *conservatives* into the predicate position. Then we change the latter statement into its obverse equivalent, "All feminists are nonconservatives." The resulting syllogism again contains just three terms and only one negative premise:

No Catholics are nonconservatives.
All feminists are nonconservatives.
No Catholics are feminists.

S—Catholics
M—nonconservatives
P—feminists

EXERCISE   6B

Put the following arguments into standard form. Identify the subject term, the predicate term, and the middle term of each syllogism. Which syllogisms appear to be valid?

1. Only famous Englishmen are buried in Westminster Abbey. Karl Marx was German, so even though he died in England, I don't believe he could be buried in Westminster Abbey.

2. No person could be elected President who did not believe in the free-enterprise system. All elected presidents have belonged to one of the major political parties. Therefore, the major American political parties must be upholders of free enterprise.

3. All capital punishment is cruel and unusual punishment. Since the Constitution bans all cruel and unusual punishment, it follows that capital punishment is unconstitutional.

4. Penicillin cannot cure colds, for colds are not bacterial but virus infections, and penicillin only cures bacterial diseases.

5. Some tumors are not malignant but benign. Since only malignancies require surgery, there are tumors which do not need to be removed.

6C   TESTING A SYLLOGISM
BY VENN DIAGRAM

In this section we shall practice a diagramming technique which will enable us to tell whether a given syllogism is valid or invalid, no matter what its logical form happens to be. The ability to construct a diagram to represent facts and to interpret the factual content of a diagram is in itself a useful intellectual competence, worthy of development. Furthermore, by diagramming various sorts of syllogisms we can see quite graphically how it is that two categorical statements will combine to produce a third categorical statement as a conclusion in a valid syllogism, and also how they fail to combine so as to produce any valid inference in an invalid argument.

Our technique, an extension of the one used to represent categorical statements in the previous chapter, is called the Venn diagram. Since a syllogism's three statements contain three different terms, we need to add a third circle, overlapping the other two circles, to represent the third term. It is essential to keep in mind exactly what things belong in each area of the three overlapping circles. It is helpful to outline each of the three circles in a different color, just at the start at least, to help keep straight what each area contains. In Figures 6.1a and 6.1b, the left circle represents the S term, the subject of the conclusion; the right circle stands for the P term, the predicate of the conclusion; and the middle circle, the middle term, which appears in both premises but not in the conclusion.

Now, let us review what things go in each area numbered on the diagram: Area 1 is included in all three circles, so it contains the things that are S, M, and P. Area 2 is inside the P circle and the S circle but outside the M circle, and thus contains things that are S and P but *not M*. Area 3 is inside the S circle, but outside both the M circle and the P circle: It contains things that are S, but neither M nor P, or things that are S, *not M*, and *not P*. Area 4 is inside the S circle and inside the M circle but outside the P circle; thus it contains the S that are M but *not P*. In area 5 of the middle circle, which lies outside both the S circle and the P circle, will be found things that are M, *not S*, and *not P*. Area 6 is within the M circle and the P circle, but outside the S circle, so contains things that are M and P but *not S*. Area 7 of the P circle lies outside both the S circle and the M circle and thus includes the P which are *not S* and *not M*.

To diagram a premise of the form, "All M are P," one shades the two

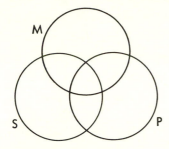

FIGURE 6.1a

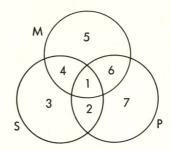

FIGURE 6.1b

areas of the M circle that lie outside the P circle; that is, areas 4 and 5. Similarly, to diagram "No M are P," both areas 1 and 6 need to be shaded. For the diagram of "All P are M," both areas 2 and 7 are shaded. In dieagramming a particular categorical premise, such as "Some M are P," an asterisk must go somewhere in the areas 1 or 6. For a particular negative, like "Some P are not M," an asterisk is placed somewhere in areas 2 or 7. But for the particular negative, "Some M are not P," the asterisk goes either in area 4 or 5.

We shall first list rules to follow in testing the validity of a syllogism by diagramming:

1. Translate both premises and conclusion into standard categorical form, if necessary.
2. Label the middle term of the syllogism M; label the end term that is the subject of the conclusion S; label the end term that is the predicate of the conclusion P.
3. Construct three overlapping circles, letting the middle circle represent the middle term M; the left circle, the S end term; and the right circle, the P end term.
4. Put into the diagram each of the two premises, shading or placing an asterisk as appropriate in the proper areas of the two circles involved in each premise.
5. Look to see whether the diagram contains shading or an asterisk in the areas required to represent the conclusion of the syllogism. If so, the syllogism is valid; if not, the syllogism is invalid.

To illustrate, let us diagram the syllogistic argument mentioned in the first section, which happens already to be in categorical form:

All Communists are socialists. No American Presidents are members of the Communist Party. Therefore, no American Presidents are socialists.

The middle term of this syllogism is *Communists; American Presidents* is the subject term; *socialists,* the predicate term. We now rewrite the syllogism, using *S, M,* and *P,* in order to expose its logical form:

All Communists are socialists.
No American Presidents are Communists.

No American Presidents are socialists.

All *M* are *P.*	*S*—American Presidents
No *S* are *M.*	*M*—Communists
No *S* are *P.*	*P*—socialists

Now we are ready to construct the three-circle diagram (Figures 6.2a and 6.2b), labeling each circle for one of the three terms as suggested. In diagramming each premise, it is helpful at first to trace with a pencil the two circles involved in each premise, one of which will always be the *M* circle; then note which areas in these two circles will need to be shaded or starred in accordance with the logical form of each premise. In the first premise of the preceding syllogism, "All *M* are *P,*" we work on the *M* circle and the *P* circle and ignore the *S* circle (block out the third circle, if need be). To diagram "All *M* are *P,*" we need to shade the areas of the *M* circle that lie outside the *P* circle, which are areas 4 and 5. To diagram the second premise, "No *S* are *M,*" we add onto this same diagram the shading needed to represent the second premise. Here both areas 4 and 1 will need to be shaded. Area 4 is already shaded, but it is wise to shade it over again, in order to remember that two areas must be shaded in diagramming any universal premise (Figure 6.2c).

Our diagram is now complete; we must now inspect the diagram to see whether the two premises do combine to produce the conclusion, "No *S* are *P.*" Thus we look at the *S* and *P* circles to see whether the areas which contain things that are both *S* (American Presidents) and *P* (socialists) are shaded, that is, areas 1 and 2. Area 1 is shaded but area 2 is

FIGURE 6.2a

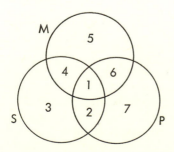

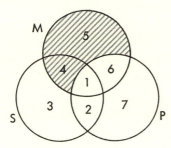

FIGURE 6.2b   Diagram of first premise: "All *M* are *P*."

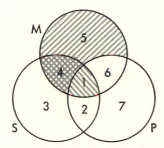

FIGURE 6.2c   Diagram containing both premises: "All *M* are *P*."
"No *S* are *M*."

not. Does the diagram say that no *S* are *P?* No. The diagram indicates that *it is possible* that something exists in area 2, since area 2 is not shaded—that is, that there may be American Presidents who are socialists but not Communists. Therefore, the diagram does not display the conclusion, "No *S* are *P*," and the argument diagrammed is invalid. The two premises do not combine so as to produce the conclusion; they only go part of the way toward establishing the conclusion. In deductive reasoning, part of the way is not enough; an argument either succeeds and is valid, or it fails and is invalid.

The diagramming of the argument does not show, however, that the conclusion, "No American Presidents are socialists," is false. To do that, the diagram would have to contain the contradictory of "No American Presidents are socialists," namely, the particular categorical, "Some American Presidents are socialists." In that case, the diagram would show an asterisk in area 1 or area 2, which it does not do. When an area has neither shading nor an asterisk, like area 2 in the diagram, the premises leave it an open question whether anything exists in that area or not. The conclusion, "No American Presidents are socialists," might indeed be true, as other premises or evidence may show. But the conclusion is not proved by deductive reasoning based merely on these two premises.

For contrast, let us diagram a valid deductive argument (Figures 6.3a, b, and c) to see how the two premises do combine to produce the

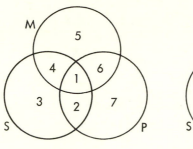

FIGURE 6.3a

FIGURE 6.3b Diagram of one premise: "All *M* are *P*."

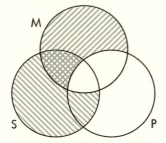

FIGURE 6.3c Diagram of both premises: "All *M* are *P*." "All *S* are *M*."

conclusion. Following the rules, we prepare to diagram the following syllogism by distinguishing and labeling its three terms:

> All union workers are payers of Social Security tax. All payers of Social Security tax are receivers of pensions at age 65. Therefore, all union workers are receivers of pensions at age 65.

All *M* are *P*.	*S*—union workers
<u>All *S* are *M*.</u>	*M*—payers of SS Tax
All *S* are *P*.	*P*—receivers of pensions at age 65

In the first step, we diagram the premise, "All *M* are *P*," shading the two areas of the *M* circle which lie outside the *P* circle, areas 4 and 5. In the second and last step we diagram the second premise, "All *S* are *M*," shading the two areas of the *S* circle which lie outside the *M* circle, areas 3 and 2. Now we inspect the diagram to see whether the conclusion, "All *S* are *P*," appears on it. For "All *S* are *P*," the areas of the *S* circle which lie outside the *P* circle must show shading, that is, areas 3 and 4. Both areas 3 and 4 are shaded in the diagram, area 4 being shaded by the first premise and area 3 by the second premise. In this way we see graphically illustrated how the two premises combine to establish the conclusion. Given the truth of the two premises, the truth of the conclusion necessarily follows from them. The diagram shows the syllogism to be a valid type of deductive argument.

So far we have considered syllogisms both of whose premises are universal statements. Now let us test for validity a syllogism with one particular premise, such as the following:

All those paying Social Security tax receive unemployment benefits. But there are some workers who do not receive unemployment benefits. Therefore, there must be some workers who do not pay Social Security tax.

We prepare for diagramming (Figures 6.4a, b, and c) by translating both premises and conclusion into standard categorical statements and labeling middle and end terms:

All payers of SS tax are receivers of unemployment benefits.
Some workers are not receivers of unemployment benefits.

Some workers are not payers of SS tax.

All *P* are *M*.   *S*—workers
Some *S* are not *M*.   *M*—receivers of unemployment benefits

Some *S* are not *P*.   *P*—payers of SS Tax

FIGURE 6.4a   FIGURE 6.4b   Diagram of one premise:
                                                               "All *P* are *M*."

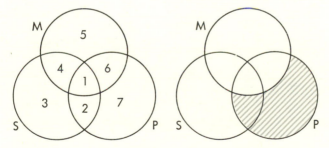

FIGURE 6.4c   Diagram of both premises: "All *P* are *M*." "Some *S* are not *M*."

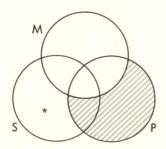

In diagramming a syllogism with one universal premise and one particular premise, the best strategy is always to diagram the universal premise first. The reason for this will soon be apparent. Diagramming the universal premise, "All *P* are *M*," we shade the two areas of the *P* circle that lie outside the *M* circle, areas 2 and 7. In the second step, we add to the diagram the second premise, "Some *S* are not *M*": we have to place an asterisk somewhere in the *S* circle that lies outside the *M* circle. Note there are two such areas, areas 2 and 3. But area 2 has already been shaded by the first universal premise, indicating that it is *empty.* Thus the only area that can take an asterisk is the remaining area, 3; accordingly, we place an asterisk there. The final step is to read the diagram to see whether it contains the conclusion, "Some *S* are not *P*." For it to do so, there must be an asterisk in some part of the *S* circle that lies outside the *P* circle. There is indeed an asterisk in area 3. Thus the two premises do combine to produce the conclusion, and the argument is valid.

In a three-circle diagram there will always be two different areas where an asterisk may be placed to represent the truth of a particular categorical statement, whether affirmative or negative. When the syllogism containing a particular premise yields a conclusion, the other premise is a universal premise which shades one of these two areas. Then only one area remains to take the asterisk required to represent the truth of the particular premise. And this second step places an asterisk in one of the two areas which represent the truth of a particular conclusion, as happens in the previous syllogism. (An asterisk in area 4 of this syllogism would also represent the truth of "Some *S* are not *P*"; but we only need to have an asterisk in one or the other of the areas, not in both.)

Some study of the diagram will reveal why a syllogism whose diagram works out in this way is valid. The universal affirmative premise *denies* that there is anyone who pays SS tax but does not receive unemployment benefits, so the two areas containing such persons are shaded. But the particular premise says that there *are* some persons who don't receive unemployment benefits and that these persons are workers. But these persons cannot be workers paying SS tax; they must be workers who are not payers of SS tax.

Observe how a problem arises in the diagramming of the particular premise, showing the syllogism is invalid. Consider the following argument:

> All workers paying SS tax receive pensions at age 65. But some workers do not pay SS tax. So there must be some who do not receive pensions at age 65.

As usual, we prepare to diagram by translating into categorical form both premises and the conclusion and by labeling middle and end terms:

All payers of SS tax are pension receivers at age 65.
Some workers are not payers of SS tax.
_____
Some workers are not pension receivers at age 65.

All *M* are *P.*   *S*—workers
Some *S* are not *M.*   *M*—payers of SS Tax
_____   *P*—pension receivers at age 65
Some *S* are not *P.*

Diagramming the universal premise first, we shade out the two areas
of the *M* circle that are outside the *P* circle, areas 4 and 5, as our first
step (Figures 6.5a and 6.5b). To diagram the particular premise, "Some *S*
are not *M*," we need to place an asterisk in an area of the *S* circle lying
outside the *M* circle. But in the above diagram there are two different
areas, 2 and 3, where an asterisk might be placed: In area 2 are workers
not covered by Social Security but still receiving pensions; in area 3 are

FIGURE 6.5a   FIGURE 6.5b   Diagram of one premise:
                                                  "All *M* are *P*."

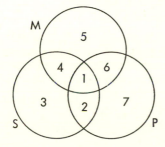

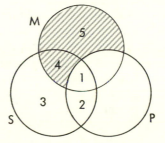

FIGURE 6.5c   Diagram of both premises: "All *M* are *P*."
              "Some *S* are not *M*."

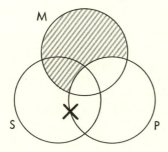

workers neither paying Social Security tax nor receiving pensions. The second premise by itself does not give us sufficient information to say whether there are workers in one area only or in both of these areas. In such a case it would be wrong to pick an area at random and place an asterisk there: Whicever one we choose, we shall be asserting more than the information given in the particular premise warrants. (Just as knowing that someone is a resident of New York or any other particular state.) In such a situation we have to find a way to express the particular premise in the diagram without going beyond what it says. One way to do this is to put an X exactly on the boundary arc separating the two areas. We then understand an X on a boundary arc as indicating that something exists in one or the other of the areas, but we cannot say exactly where.

Now let us read the diagram to discover whether it contains the conclusion, "Some S are not P." To do so, there must be an asterisk in area 3 or 4, the two areas of the S circle lying outside the P circle. But area 4 is shaded and surely cannot have an asterisk. The X on the boundary arc between areas 2 and 3 tells us there are S either inside the P circle or outside the P circle; that is, there are workers who may or may not receive pensions at age 65. But for a deductive argument to be valid, the conclusion must follow *necessarily*, not just *possibly*, from the premises. If one reflects, one can easily tell how the premises may be true without the conclusion being true: in case workers not paying SS tax receive pensions from some source other than the federal government—from private or state pension systems, for example. That is exactly the possibility the diagram allows. It is always a clue to the invalidity of a syllogism when diagramming the universal premise first still leaves two possible areas in which to place the asterisk for the particular premise.

In the arguments we have tested so far, we have used the hypo-thetical interpretation of universal categorical statements; that is, we have not indicated in the diagram that there do exist things corresponding to the subject term of the universal premises. Since American Presidents, union workers, socialists, and Communists obviously do exist, we also could have diagrammed the existentialist interpretation of universal premises containing subject terms referring to them, placing an asterisk in some unshaded part of the circle representing the subject term. But this is an extra step, superfluous in any argument whose premises and conclu-sion are all universal, or which contains just one particular premise. It is only when a syllogism has a particular conclusion, but both its premises are universal, that it is necessary to diagram the existential interpretation of universal premises. But it is essential to remember that the existential interpretation is permissible only when there is no doubt that there exist things named by the subject term; whenever there is ground for doubt, for example, when the subject term is *Martian organisms* or *immortal souls*,

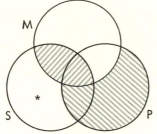

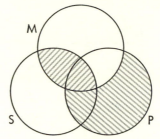

FIGURE 6.6a Existential interpretation of "No S
are M."

FIGURE 6.6b Hypothetical interpretation of "No S
are M."

there is no option—the hypothetical interpretation of the universal premise is required.

Here is a case in which the existential interpretation is legitimate and where the validity of the argument may not be recognized unless it is diagrammed (Figures 6.6a and 6.6b):

All who pay union dues are union members. Since no lawyers belong to unions, some lawyers do not pay union dues.

All *P* are *M*.	*S*—lawyers
No *S* are *M*.	*M*—union members
Some *S* are not *P*.	*P*—payers of union dues

In the diagram using the hypothetical interpretation, the conclusion, "Some *S* are not *P*," does not appear, since there is no asterisk in the unshaded part of the *S* circle. Because lawyers clearly do exist, we can put an asterisk in the one remaining open area of the *S* circle, lawyers, in diagramming the premise, "No *S* are *M*," and the conclusion is now apparent in the diagram. However, even under the hypothetical inter-pretation, a little reasoning will enable us to derive this same conclusion. In the diagram using the hypothetical interpretation, the conclusion, "No lawyers are payers of union dues," appears on the diagram since areas 1 and 2 of the diagram are shaded. According to the principles of immediate inference, the truth of this universal negative implies the truth of the corresponding particular negative, "Some lawyers are not payers of union dues," whenever we know that the subject term of the universal negative categorical names existing things.

In diagramming the existential interpretation, however, we must be certain that the "existence assumption" is in accordance with our knowl-edge, or weird results ensue. Consider the following syllogism, as dia-grammed according to the existential interpretation of one of its universal premises (Figures 6.7a and 6.7b):

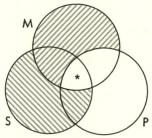

FIGURE 6.7a Premises diagrammed with existential interpretation of "All *S* are *M*."

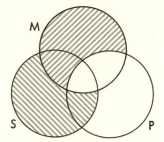

FIGURE 6.7b Premises diagrammed with hypothetical interpretation of "All *S* are *M*."

All UFO crew members are visitors from other planets.
All visitors from other planets are intelligent beings.

Some UFO crew members are intelligent beings.

All *S* are *M*.   *S*—UFO crew members
All *M* are *P*.   *M*—visitors from other planets

Some *S* are *P*.   *P*—intelligent beings

According to the diagram of the existential interpretation, we can take it as proved that there exist UFO crew members who are intelligent beings from the stated and plausible premises. However, a little reflection will convince us that we are not justified in assuming the existence of UFO crew members. The correct way to diagram the argument is by using the hypothetical interpretation; as shown, the premises no longer produce the particular conclusion. The conclusion, "All UFO crew members are intelligent beings," does appear on the diagram; but on the hypothetical interpretation, it means simply, "All UFO crew members, *if there are any*, are intelligent beings."

EXERCISE 6C

Put the following arguments into standard syllogistic form and test for validity by the diagramming method.

1. All acids turn blue litmus red. But this liquid does not, so it cannot be an acid.

2. Anything that is not an acid is a base. Since soap is not an acid substance, it must be a base.

3. If all angels are winged creatures, and all seraphim are angels, some winged creatures must be seraphim.

4. All earthlike organisms must have water to survive. But no organisms on Mars would find enough water to survive. Therefore some Martian organisms must be quite unlike earth organisms.

5. If there are intelligent beings on other planets, they are capable of doing mathematics; if there are some beings on other planets capable of doing mathematics, we can communicate with them by a number code. Therefore, the beings on other planets we can communicate with by a number code will have to be intelligent beings.

6. Not all fanatics are dangerous. Therefore, even though there are some religious fanatics, religious people are not dangerous.

7. Only wars fought to defend one's country are just. Since some wars are defensive wars, there are just wars.

6D   TESTING A SYLLOGISM BY RULES

A second way of testing a syllogism is by seeing whether it follows a certain set of rules. Two of these make use of a logical notion called *distribution,* so we must discuss distribution before we can state the rules for testing syllogisms.

A categorical statement is said to *distribute* its subject or predicate term whenever its logical form is such that the statement *necessarily* speaks of *every kind* of thing referred to by the subject term or the predicate term.

The subject terms of the two universal categoricals are distributed, for they are preceded by the two *universal* quantifiers, *all* and *no*: "All *S*" means "*all kinds of S*"; "No *S*" means "*no kinds of* S."

The subject terms of particular categorical statements are not distributed: "Some *S*" means only "*some kinds* of S." The predicate terms of affirmative categorical statements are also undistributed. "Some *S* are *P*" is equivalent to "*Some kinds* of S are *some kinds* of P." The fact that converses of particular affirmative form are equivalent illustrates the following: "Some kinds of *S* are some kinds of *P*" makes the same claim as "Some kinds of *P* are some kinds of *S*."

Similarly, the predicate term of a universal affirmative categorical is undistributed: "All *S* are *P*" says "All kinds of *S* are *some kind of P*." Since the subject term of the universal affirmative is distributed but the predicate term is undistributed, the converses of universal affirmative form are not equivalent: "All kinds of *S* are some kind of *P*" says something quite different from "All kinds of *P* are some kind of *S*."

The predicate terms of the two negative categorical statements are distributed. A negative categorical says that some or all kinds of the subject term S are excluded from *every kind of P*—the exclusion is total. In saying "No S are P," we say that no P's are included among the S's as well as that no S's are to be found among the P's. "No S are P" is then equivalent to "No P are S."

In the particular negative categorical, "Some S are not P," the subject term is undistributed (as indicated in "Some S") but the predicate term is distributed: "Some kind of S are *no kind of P*." Remember that in the diagram for a particular negative, the asterisk goes in an area of the subject term circle outside the circle containing all kinds of the predicate-term group.

In summary, we show the distributed terms in each type of categorical by underlining: All $\underline{S}$ are P; No $\underline{S}$ are $\underline{P}$; Some S are P; Some S are not $\underline{P}$.

In a valid deductive argument the conclusion does not go beyond the information contained in its premises. The reasoning in a syllogism goes as follows: The conclusion says that the S group and the P group are related to each other because of the way each of them is related to the middle-term group by the two premises. No relationship can be established between the S group and the P group unless a premise connects them by speaking about the whole of the middle-term group. The first rule for a valid syllogism is this: *The middle term is distributed in one premise.*

The second rule requires that *an end term distributed in the conclusion must also be distributed in its premise.* If a term is distributed in the conclusion but not in its premise, the conclusion says something about every kind of thing named by the end term, whereas the premise does not. Therefore, the conclusion goes beyond the information contained in the premises, and the argument is invalid. Thus, the second step in applying the rules of the syllogism is to inspect the *conclusion* to see whether its subject term or predicate term is distributed: The subject term of a universal conclusion is distributed, and the predicate term of a negative conclusion is also distributed. Then check to see whether any end term distributed in the conclusion is also distributed in its premise.

The other two rules of a valid syllogism concern the presence of negative statements in the argument. The third rule states that *no valid syllogism has two negative premises.* If a syllogism has two negative premises, no necessary connection is made between the two end-term groups, since both premises will exclude part or all of one end-term group from part or all of the middle-term group. For example, suppose we try to combine the two true negative premises:

No cannibals are vegetarians.	S —cannibals
No vegetarians are meat-eaters.	M —vegetarians
? cannibals ? meat-eaters.	P —meat-eaters

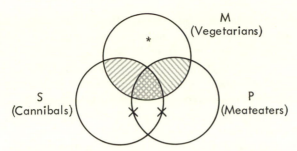

FIGURE 6.8 Diagram of premises, both with existential interpretation

Here it is tempting to suppose that one could obtain the conclusion, "All cannibals are meat-eaters." But even if we diagram the existential interpretation of the two true premises, it is clear that no conclusion, universal or affirmative, particular or negative, can validly be inferred from the relation of the S and P terms (Figure 6.8).

The final rule requires a syllogism with one negative premise to have a negative conclusion. In such a syllogism, the relationship established between the two end terms via the middle term is one of exclusion; thus the conclusion must also exclude part or all of the subject-term group from the predicate-term group. Conversely, a syllogism with a negative conclusion must also be matched with a negative premise if it is to be valid. Thus the fourth rule states that a valid syllogism matches a negative premise with a negative conclusion: *A valid syllogism has a negative conclusion if and only if it has a negative premise.*

The foregoing rules enable one to determine the validity or invalidity of any syllogism, including those valid under the existential interpretation of universal premises. Any syllogism which satisfies all four rules is valid; a syllogism which violates any one of the four rules is invalid.

However, in testing by these rules a syllogism with universal premises but a particular conclusion, we need in addition to examine the facts to see whether the existential interpretation of the universal premises is reasonable—recall that one cannot infer a particular categorical from a universal categorical under the hypothetical interpretation. For example, let us test this argument by the rules:

All Marxists are materialists. But no one who believes in the immortality of the soul is a materialist. Hence, some Marxists do not believe in the immortality of the soul.

As usual we put the syllogism in standard form:

All Marxists are materialists. S—Marxists
No materialists are believers in immortality. M—materialists
_____ P—believers in
Some Marxists are not believers in   immortality
    immortality.

First we apply the two rules of distribution: The middle term, "materialists," is distributed in the second premise, satisfying the first rule. The predicate term, "believers in immortality," is distributed in the conclusion, being the predicate of a negative statement. It is also distributed in the second premise, where it is again the predicate of a negative statement, thus satisfying the second rule. It also satisfies both rules concerning negative statements: It has just one negative premise, and it has a negative conclusion.

However, since the conclusion is particular and the premises are universal, we must be sure that an existential interpretation of "All Marxists are materialists" is justified. May we presuppose that Marxists exist? Clearly we may, for we know very well that Marxists do exist. The syllogism is valid, since it satisfies all rules as well.

Whenever the existential interpretation of the universal premises is not reasonable, a syllogism with universal premises but particular conclusion cannot be pronounced valid, as the following example shows:

All warlocks are male.	S—males
All warlocks are beings with magical powers.	M—warlocks
Some males are beings with magical powers.	P—beings with magical powers

The above syllogism satisfies all four rules; but because it has universal premises and a particular conclusion, we need to examine the facts of the universal premises. Clearly, the existence of warlocks is dubious, as well as that of beings with magical powers; only the hypothetical interpretation is reasonable.

The Four Rules of a Valid Syllogism

1. The middle term is distributed in one premise.

2. An end term distributed in the conclusion is also distributed in its premise.

3. No valid syllogism has two negative premises.

4. If a syllogism has a negative premise, it has a negative conclusion; and if a syllogism has a negative conclusion, it has a negative premise.

EXERCISE 6D

Put the following arguments into standard syllogistic form and test for validity by applying the preceding four rules.

1. Anyone who believes in the sanctity of life opposes capital punishment, and all who oppose abortion believe in the sanctity of life. Therefore, anyone who opposes abortion should also oppose capital punishment.

2. Only three-year-olds run in the Kentucky Derby, and any colt who runs in the Derby is eligible to run in the Preakness. So all the horses who run in the Preakness must be three-year-olds too.

3. Some persons with driver's licenses are not of legal drinking age, for anyone with a driver's license is over sixteen, but some persons over sixteen are not of legal drinking age.

4. Drivers under twenty-five pay additional premiums for insurance because they are more accident-prone, and more accident-prone drivers must pay a higher insurance rate.

5. Air-conditioned buildings are great energy-consumers, but they are comfortable in the summer. Thus only buildings that are great energy-consumers are comfortable in the summer.

6E TESTING A SYLLOGISM BY INSPECTION

In this section we present a method for determining whether a syllogism is valid or invalid that involves simply inspecting its logical form. Every syllogism, valid or invalid, asserts a claim about how three different groups of things—those named by the subject, predicate, and middle terms of the syllogism—are related to each other. Whether or not a syllogism is valid depends on whether the two group relationships asserted by the premises will necessarily produce the group relationship expressed by the conclusion.

Logicians have calculated that there are 256 possible types of syllogisms, combining 64 possible sets of premises of the 4 different kinds of categorical statements. Of this large number, only 24 different types of syllogisms are valid. But even this number is too large to keep in mind. We may reduce the 24 valid forms of syllogisms to a more manageable number of 8, once we recognize two facts about the logic of a syllogism:

1. The subject and predicate terms of a universal negative or particular affirmative premise are interchangeable, since each has an equivalent converse. The following four syllogisms, for example, make exactly the same logical claim:

Some S are M.   Some S are M.
No M are P.   No P are M.
-----------------   -----------------
Some S are not P.   Some S are not P.

Some *M* are *S*.   Some *M* are *S*.
No *P* are *M*.   No *M* are *P*.
————————————   ————————————
Some *S* are not *P*.   Some *S* are not *P*.

2. It is not necessary to recognize as distinct valid syllogistic forms arguments containing universal premises but a particular conclusion, such as the following:

All *S* are *M*.
No *M* are *P*.
————————————
Some *S* are not *P*.

The so-called *weakened* forms are valid only if the facts of the subject matter make the existential interpretation of a universal premise reasonable. Whenever the facts do justify the existential interpretation of a universal statement, one may always infer a corresponding particular categorical with the same terms. Our strategy for dealing with syllogisms having two universal premises and a particular conclusion is this: See whether the facts permit immediate inference from one of the universal premises of a particular categorical of the kind occuring in one of the basic valid syllogism types for the particular conclusion. If so, the syllogism is valid; if not, invalid. In the case of our sample syllogism, if the existential interpretation of "All *S* are *M*" accords with the facts, we may infer from it that "Some *S* are *M*" and substitute that as one premise of the syllogism, thereby obtaining one of the basic valid syllogisms yielding a particular negative conclusion.

    This strategy has two advantages: (1) It emphasizes the fact that the validity of the traditional weakened forms depends on factual considerations, not just the logical form of the syllogism. (2) It limits the basic valid syllogisms to those whose validity follows from the logical form of the statements of the argument, regardless of the subject matter.

    The logical form of a syllogism depends on the categorical form of premises and conclusion and the positions of its three terms in these statements. The order in which premises are listed does not matter. Since the interrelation of the three groups of the syllogism is more apparent when the premise containing the *S* term, the subject of the conclusion, is written first, we follow that practice. What does matter is being consistent in distinguishing the groups named by the three different terms: When a premise or conclusion is universal affirmative or particular negative, the validity of a syllogism hangs on which end term is the *S* group and which is the *P* group.

    The eight basic valid syllogism forms are displayed in the table on page 125: there is one form only for the universal affirmative conclusion; two forms for the particular affirmative conclusion; two for the universal

TABLE OF BASIC
VALID SYLLOGISMS

Universal

(A)
All S are M
All M are P
———
All S are P

(E)
All S are M
No P are M
———
No S are P

(G)
No S are M
All P are M
———
No S are P

Particular

(B)
Some S are M
All M are P
———
Some S are P

(C)
All M are S
Some M are P
———
Some S are P

(D)
All M are S
Some M are not P
———
Some S are not P

(F)
Some S are M
No P are M
———
Some S are not P

(H)
Some S are not M
All P are M
———
Some S are not P

The traditional valid syllogisms may be expressed in the basic valid syllogisms as follows: (A) AAA1; (B) AII1, AII3, AAI1, AAI3; (C) IAI3, IAI4; AAI4; (D) OAO3; (E) EAE1, EAE2; (F) EIO1, 2, 3, 4, EAO1, 2, 3, 4; (G) AEE2, AEE4; (H) AOO2, AEO2, AEO4.

negative conclusion; and three forms yield a particular negative conclusion. A syllogism is valid if and only if it may be expressed in a valid form appearing on the table. These eight forms may be easily memorized, since they fall into a regular pattern consisting of four analogous pairs, as displayed in the table: Each of three basic valid syllogisms yielding a particular conclusion is below the syllogism yielding a universal conclusion to which it is analogous, that is, A and B, E and F, G and H. The remaining two analogous forms, both yielding a particular conclusion, are side by side, C and D.

There is only one basic valid syllogism for the universal affirmative conclusion, A: It is a regular progression of universal affirmatives, the S group being included in the M group, and the M group in the P group.

Of the two basic syllogisms for the particular affirmative conclusion, B is like A except that "Some $S \ldots$" replaces "All $S \ldots$" in one premise and the conclusion. In examining the logical form of a syllogism with a particular affirmative conclusion, remember that the converses of particular affirmatives are equivalent, so that one may replace "Some M are S" with "Some S are M" to obtain the basic valid form B.

The second basic valid syllogism for the particular affirmative conclusion, C, is analogous to one of the basic valid syllogisms for the particular negative conclusion, D: Each has as one premise "All M are S." Each has a particular premise: "Some M are P," the particular affirmative, in the case of the syllogism for the particular affirmative conclusion; "Some M are not P," the particular negative, in the case of the syllogism for the particular negative conclusion.

There are two basic valid syllogisms—E and G—leading to the universal negative conclusion, but they are quite comparable: In each case, one premise is universal negative, the other, universal affirmative. The universal affirmative premise says that all of one end-term group is included in the middle-term group; the universal negative excludes the other end-term group from the middle-term group. Here, remember that the converses of universal negative statements are equivalent: Thus, to obtain the correct logical form, one may substitute "No P are M" for "No M are P," or "No S are M" for "No M are S."

Each of these two basic syllogisms producing a universal negative conclusion has its counterpart producing a particular negative conclusion, F and H. The counterpart replaces the universal premise containing the subject term with the corresponding particular premise. In the case of syllogisms yielding a particular negative conclusion, remember that the converses of particular negative statements are not logically equivalent: Thus a premise reading "Some M are not S" may not take the place of the premise "Some S are not M," occuring in H.

Once one knows these eight basic valid syllogism forms, one may determine whether or not a syllogism is valid by seeing whether its arguments can correctly be expressed in one of them. One may need to switch the terms of a universal negative or particular affirmative premise in order to achieve one of the forms listed. If an argument is expressible in one of the eight basic valid syllogism types, it is valid; if not, it is invalid.

Here is an argument to test by inspection:

All unemployed persons make no contribution to the economy; but not all unemployed persons are housewives. Therefore, there are some persons who make no contribution to the economy who are not housewives.

As usual put the argument in standard form, labeling the subject, predicate and middle terms of the syllogism:

All M are S. S—non-contributors to the economy
Some M are not P. M—unemployed persons
Some S are not P. P—housewives

Since the conclusion is particular negative, "Some S are not P," the argument must be one of form D, F or H, the three forms of syllogism yielding a particular negative conclusion. Checking the Table of Basic Valid Syllogisms we see the argument is an instance of D. Thus the argument is valid.

Now let us test the validity of an argument reaching a universal negative conclusion:

All Marxists are materialists. Since no materialists are believers in the immortality of the soul, it's obvious that no Marxists believe that the soul is immortal.

As usual, we put the syllogism in standard form, labeling the subject, predicate and middle terms:

All S are M. S—Marxists
No M are P. M—materialists
No S are P. P—believers in the soul's immortality

The conclusion being universal negative, the syllogism must be an instance of E or G to be valid. Its first premise is exactly like E, but its second reads "No M are P" rather than "No P are M." Since these two statements are logically equivalent, we may substitute "No P are M" for "No M are P," thus obtaining form E. Therefore, the argument is valid.

Let us inspect the following argument, whose logical form may appear similar to the preceding:

All materialists are philosophers. Since no materialists are religious, it follows that no philosophers are religious.

All *M* are *S*.   *S*—philosophers
No *M* are *P*.   *M*—materialists
─────────────
No *S* are *P*.   *P*—religious people

Here the first premise says "All *M* are *S*" instead of "All *S* are *M*," of form *E* in the Table. However, there is no way of altering the premise to make the argument conform to *E*, since "All *M* are *S*" is not logically equivalent to "All *S* are *M*." Since the syllogism is neither of form *E* nor of form *G*, it is invalid.

In dealing with an argument containing two universal premises and a particular conclusion, remember that one needs to consider the facts to see whether the existential interpretation of the universal premises is reasonable. If so, see whether one may obtain a particular statement by immediate inference from one of the universal premises that will be the exact kind needed in the appropriate basic valid syllogism. It may be necessary to make more than one inference to obtain the exact premise needed, as happens in a syllogism of this form:

No *M* are *S*.   → No *S* are *M*.   → Some *S* are not *M*.
All *P* are *M*.   All *P* are *M*.   All *P* are *M*.
─────────   ─────────   ─────────
Some *S* are not *P*.   Some *S* are not *P*.   Some *S* are not *P*.

Here we first infer the converse equivalent "No *S* are *M*" from "No *M* are *S*." If the evidence indicates that things of kind *S* do indeed exist, we may then infer the particular negative, "Some *S* are not *M*." Substituting this premise for the original "No *M* are *S*" produces the basic valid syllogism *H*, showing that the original syllogism is valid, providing the existential interpretation of the universal statements is reasonable.

EXERCISE 6E

Put each argument into standard form; determine its validity by inspecting its logical form.

1. A diabetic is not a good health risk, and only those who are good health risks can buy life insurance cheaply. So a diabetic cannot buy cheap life insurance.

2. All self-employed persons are gainfully employed, but some self-employed workers do not pay income tax. Therefore some payers of income tax are not gainfully employed.

3. All earthlike planets can support life. Some satellites of sunlike stars are

earthlike in nature. Therefore, there must be satellites of sunlike stars capable of supporting life.

4. No socialists are opposed to communism, but all capitalists are. Thus, no socialists are capitalists.

5. Since some housewives are authors, and authors are self-employed, some housewives must be classified as self-employed.

6. No unemployed workers are gainfully employed, and none of them pay SS tax either, so no gainfully employed persons pay SS tax.

7. All self-employed persons are classified as being gainfully employed, and all authors are classified as self-employed. Therefore, some authors are gainfully employed.

8. Rock stars make big money and are much admired by teenagers. So it is not true that teenagers never admire moneymakers.

6F SYLLOGISMS IN EVERYDAY REASONING

Complete syllogistic arguments, such as those in the previous sections, sometimes occur in everyday reasoning, principally when the syllogism derives a generalization about a group from other generalizations involving that group. The presence of a syllogistic inference is signaled by such words or phrases as:

> hence; therefore; it must be the case; from these premises it follows that . . .; it necessarily follows . . .; if X is true and Y is true, then Z must be true.

Very often all that is needed is a translation of the premises and conclusion into categorical equivalents; then the validity of the reasoning may be tested by one of the methods of the previous section. But particularly in syllogistic reasoning it is not unusual to find arguments that are elliptical; that is, some essential premise or even the conclusion is left unstated. Usually the omitted premise is some obvious truth or some generalization that can readily be filled in from the remaining statements of the argument, or it involves the application of a generalization to the instance under discussion. However, fallacious or unsound reasoning is less obvious when crucial statements of a syllogistic argument are left unsaid. Before we can test an elliptical syllogistic argument (called an *enthymeme* by logicians), we must be able to reconstruct the whole argument.

The most common kind of enthymeme leaves out one of the premises and consists of just one premise and the conclusion, as in the following example:

Any being of advanced intelligence on another planet should be able to do mathematics. Therefore, we can communicate with them by a number code.

Here the conclusion can be expressed as a universal affirmative:

All beings of advanced intelligence on other planets are beings we can communicate with by a number code.

We arrive at the subject term of this conclusion by spelling out the "them" in the elliptical conclusion, which refers us back to the one premise of the argument. It is easily translated into the universal affirmative,

All beings of advanced intelligence on other planets are beings capable of doing mathematics.

This premise gives us one of the end terms of the syllogism and the syllogism's middle term. Here the end term is "beings of advanced intelligence on other planets," the group referred to in the conclusion as "them"; it is, as we see, the S term of the syllogism. The P term from our expanded conclusion is "beings we can communicate with by a number code." The middle term is the other term in the premise, "beings capable of doing mathematics."

Once one identifies the three terms, it is a simple matter to reconstruct the missing premise: It will be a categorical statement joining the middle term from the stated premise with the other end term that occurs in the conclusion but not in the stated premise. In this case the missing premise must join the middle term, "beings capable of doing mathematics," with the term "beings communicated with by a number code." The form of the premise should be a categorical statement of such a kind as to produce the conclusion in combination with the stated premise, if the argument is to be a valid one. To be fair to an elliptical argument, one must look for a plausible premise which will do this. In this case, the universal affirmative premise, "All beings capable of doing mathematics are beings communicable with by a number code," will produce the conclusion by a valid form of argument and is plausible. The converse of this universal affirmative, "All beings communicable with by a number code are beings capable of doing mathematics," is even more plausible, but it would not yield the conclusion in a valid argument. Once one fills in the missing premise, one tests the syllogism in any of the usual ways.

It happens more rarely that the conclusion is left unexpressed. But suppose a speaker were to say

A politician running for office always is in need of campaign funds, and anyone needing campaign funds will be responsive to special-interest groups.

Obviously the speaker expects one to draw some conclusion from these two premises. In filling out the argument, we again begin by identifying the three terms. The middle term appears in both premises: In this case it is "politician needing campaign funds"; the end terms are the two other terms, "politicians running for office" and "politicians responsive to special-interest groups." The unstated conclusion should join these two terms in some kind of categorical statement which may be validly inferred from the two premises. We need, then, to put the premises into standard categorical form as follows:

> All politicians running for office are politicians needing campaign funds.
> All politicians needing campaign funds are responsive to special-interest groups.

The two premises are of the logical form, universal affirmative, and in the second premise, the middle term appears as the subject term. If we make "politicians running for office" the subject end term of the whole syllogism, and make the conclusion universal affirmative, we come out with a valid syllogism, whose conclusion will be: "All politicians running for office are responsive to special-interest groups." This clearly is the conclusion we are expected to draw from the two stated premises.

It is characteristic of common speech to vary phrases from one sentence to the next, and this frequently happens in syllogistic-type reasoning. As long as the denotation and connotation of the terms of the syllogism remain roughly the same, so that the variation does not affect the logical course of the argument, it is logic-chopping to find fault with the argument even though the phrases used for the various terms are not strictly synonymous. For example, the last argument might well have been phrased thus:

> A politician running for office always needs campaign funds; any politician looking for campaign contributions will be responsive to special-interest groups.

The terms "politician needing campaign funds" and "politician looking for campaign contributions" are not strictly synonymous, but the difference between them is not enough to render the argument invalid for that reason.

It frequently happens that a premise will name as subject term a group of broader extension than the group that is the subject term of the conclusion. The first elliptical argument we discussed might have been put as follows:

> Any advanced intelligent being should be able to do mathematics. So we should be able to communicate with intelligent beings on other planets by a number code.

If we filled out this argument, we would have, strictly speaking, the S term in the premise, "advanced intelligent beings," and in the conclusion, "intelligent beings on other planets." In such a case we must be sure that the group in the conclusion is a genuine subgroup of the group named in the premise; that being so, if the universal premise is true of the whole group, it will also be true of the subgroup. If one considers the drift of the whole argument, any intelligent being with whom we could communicate across vast distances of space would have to be of advanced intelligence. Since "advanced intelligent beings on other planets" is a proper subgroup of "advanced intelligent beings," the change in the subject term does not affect the validity of the argument.

Sometimes considerable juggling may be needed before we can expose the syllogistic structure of an argument and consider its validity. Consider the following bit of reasoning:

> I say it's impossible for a Catholic to be a feminist, for no one who upholds traditional family values can be called a feminist, and no genuine Catholic rejects traditional family values.

The reader can surely sense that this argument contains some kind of syllogistic reasoning. However, we cannot take it simply as it stands and put it into a syllogism. Both premises are negative as stated, and we cannot construct a valid syllogism from two negative premises. Also there are four terms here, "feminists," "Catholics," "upholders of traditional family values," "rejecters of traditional family values." There is an obvious logical connection between the latter two terms, for they are *contrary* terms; it would be possible to neither uphold nor reject traditional family values but to be indifferent to them. In a syllogism contrary terms have to be counted as two different terms (so do contradictory terms, of course). There is a simple strategy that can always be applied to statements containing contrary and contradictory terms: Take one of the terms as the basic term, and eliminate the contradictory term by finding some categorical equivalent of the statement in which it appears. For example, a statement like "All Catholics are nonfeminists" can be obverted to obtain the equivalent, "No Catholics are feminists." In the case of contrary terms, one must first convert the contrary term into the contradictory of one's basic term. For example, one can take "upholders of traditional family values" as the basic term and substitute "nonupholders of traditional family values" (the contradictory term) for the contrary, "rejecters of traditional family values." In doing this we do not obtain a term which is the full logical equivalent of "rejecters of traditional family values" but a weaker term implied by it. However, this loss is not enough to weaken the argument, and we gain from being able to apply the syllogistic technique to it. Following this strategy one can usually obtain two premises containing three terms, as illustrated in this case:

No upholders of traditional values are feminists.
No Catholics are nonupholders of traditional family values.

Now it is an easy step to use *obversion* to translate the second premise into an affirmative equivalent, "All Catholics are upholders of traditional family values." We can now formulate the argument as a standard syllogism, which the reader should be able to recognize as having a valid logical form:

No upholders of traditional family values are feminists.
All Catholics are upholders of traditional family values.
No Catholics are feminists.

When an argument in ordinary language contains two negative premises, it should not be rejected as invalid for that reason. First an attempt should be made to reformulate one of the negative premises into an affirmative equivalent. This can always be accomplished by *obversion,* the process of inference by which an affirmative statement becomes a negative one, and vice versa. *Contraposition* can be used to remove negative terms or obtain them in the cases of universal affirmatives and particular negatives. *Conversion* enables one to switch the position of subject and predicate terms in universal negatives and particular affirmatives. By using the various techniques of immediate inference, it is often possible to translate statements in ordinary language into categorical equivalents containing just three terms and one negative premise, so that deductive testing techniques may be applied to the argument when the original argument contains contrary or contradictory terms. However, one must remember that only universal affirmatives and particular negatives have equivalent contrapositives; and only universal negatives and particular affirmatives have equivalent converses.

EXERCISE 6F

Use the techniques described to translate each of the following arguments into standard form and test its validity.

1. Cancer studies indicate that eating saccharin promotes cancer, so young children should not be encouraged to drink diet sodas.

2. Jones jogs ten miles before breakfast every morning; he must be some kind of health nut.

3. All feminists are man-haters and all nymphomaniacs are man-lovers, so there can be no nymphomaniac feminists.

4. Since lesbians are not fond of sexual intercourse with men, they are not likely to have children.

5. Only social policies based on the equal dignity of all men are acceptable to the United States. But no apartheid policy acknowledges the equality of blacks and whites. Since South Africa's policy is clearly apartheid, the United States government finds its social policy unacceptable.

6. A four-cylinder car uses less gas than a six-cylinder car. Most foreign cars are four-cylinder, whereas American-made cars have six cylinders or more. So, most cars that are not gas-guzzlers are foreign cars.

7. Many soccer players also play lacrosse, and a few hockey players play lacrosse, so it must be the case that some soccer players are also hockey players.

6G   PROVING CONSISTENCY
AND INCONSISTENCY

An important use of the syllogism is in proving that a statement is inconsistent with other statements. Whenever a set of statements can be translated into categorical equivalents expressing the interrelationships among three groups of things, it may happen that the relationships asserted by two of the statements will *exclude* the possibility that the third statement is true, because of the logical form of the three statements. In this case the three statements will be inconsistent with each other—one or other of them must be false. Detecting inconsistencies between statements is a standard part of reasoning in many situations. For example, this kind of argument is familiar:

> Jones can't possibly be the gold-toothed burglar. He was in jail during November, when the gold-toothed burglar is alleged to have committed two bank robberies.

This reasoning can be expressed in the following valid syllogism:

No persons in jail during November are persons committing robberies in November.

All persons identical to the gold-toothed burglar are persons committing robberies in November.

No persons in jail during November are persons identical to the gold-toothed robber.

The truth of the two premises excludes the possibility that Jones, who was in jail during November, could be the gold-toothed burglar, for that statement will be inconsistent with the truth of the premises. In case we are quite sure those two premises are true, we could go on to infer that it is indeed false that Jones is the gold-toothed bandit. However, the inconsistency could also be accounted for by one of the premises being false—for example, suppose a person to be in jail but on outside work privileges or on a weekend pass, as in some penal systems. Then the premise, "No persons in jail during November are persons committing robberies in November," might be the false statement. In such a case it might be true that Jones is the gold-toothed burglar after all.

Syllogisms can be used to prove the inconsistency of three categorical statements containing three terms by constructing a valid syllogism containing two of the statements as premises and the *contradictory* of the third statement as the conclusion.

An important use of this technique is in exposing the inconsistency in beliefs which may be held simultaneously. In the last section a valid syllogism revealed that it is illogical for a person to be both a Catholic and a feminist because the two positions involve contradictory stands on the same issue, that is, the importance of traditional family values. It is not uncommon for persons to be unaware of the presence of inconsistency, because they do not take account of the implications of each belief. It is of course psychologically possible for a person to hold inconsistent beliefs knowingly, but anyone who respects and desires the truth ought not to be complacent about such behavior. Furthermore, inconsistency in beliefs on some subjects may carry with it conflicting emotions and attitudes, leading to frustration, indecisiveness, or even irrational action.

Phrases such as the following often indicate an argument that attempts to prove the inconsistency of a statement or belief with other statements or beliefs:

It cannot possibly be the case that . . . ; since you believe X, you cannot say Y; if you say X is true, you must admit that Y is . . . ; anyone who thinks X cannot possibly believe Y; you can't say both X and Y; everyone who says X must agree that Y is false.

A syllogism can even be used to prove the *consistency* of a statement or belief with other beliefs: Construct a valid syllogism in which the statement is shown to be obtainable as the conclusion of an argument in which the other belief is a premise. Any statement that is implied by another statement must be consistent with it. To illustrate, in a radio interview a speaker expressed surprise at hearing the vice-presidential candidate of the Libertarian Party, a woman, claim that she was also a feminist. He reasoned the inconsistency of a woman being both as follows:

> All members of the Libertarian Party oppose government intervention in the lives of citizens, wanting to dispense with many social welfare programs. But feminists, far from opposing such programs, want the government to provide day-care centers, abortion clinics, and so on.

The lady in question argued the consistency of her own position as follows:

> All feminists desire the liberation of women from male oppression. Intervention of the government in the lives of women, even in a supportive way, only subjects women further to male oppression. Not only is it consistent to be both a Libertarian and a feminist, but all feminists should be Libertarians if they truly wish to be free of male oppression.

This argument is a chain argument, in which the conclusion of one syllogism becomes the premise of a second syllogism to yield the final conclusion that "All Libertarians are feminists":

> All persons opposing government intervention in the lives of citizens are promoters of female liberation.
> All Libertarians oppose government intervention in the lives of citizens.
> ___
> All Libertarians are promoters of female liberation.
> All promoters of female liberation are feminists.
> ___
> All Libertarians are feminists.

This conclusion is the *contrary* of "No Libertarians are feminists" and supports the woman's contention that feminism is compatible with being a Libertarian. In such a case, where different valid deductive arguments reach opposing conclusions, we need to review the premises of each argument. Since the two opposing conclusions are contraries, we may suspect that both are false, indicating the presence of one or more false premises.

It is not unusual in everyday reasoning to employ chains of two or more syllogisms in order to reach a given conclusion. They often occur when a generalization is derived from other generalizations, as happens above. Frequently a generalization is inferred and its conclusion applied to an individual case, as illustrated in the reasoning about the gold-toothed bandit, which is completed as follows:

> No persons in jail during November are identical to the gold-toothed bandit.
> All persons identical to Jones are persons in jail during November.
> _____
> No persons identical to Jones are identical to the gold-toothed bandit.

So long as each syllogism in the chain argument is valid, the whole argument is valid; but if even one syllogism is invalid, the argument fails. Very often one needs to supply an unexpressed premise or intermediate conclusion, using the techniques already described.

Proving that a statement is consistent with other statements is not of course equivalent to proving that a statement is true. In much practical reasoning it does, however, provide some grounds for believing the statement to be true, especially when the statement in question appears to be the only available one that is consistent with the other known true statements. The following phrases often indicate an argument designed to prove the consistency of a statement with other statements:

> It is possible that both X and Y . . . ; one can believe X without denying Y; although X is true, Y is also true; X is true in spite of Y being true; if X is the case, Y may nevertheless be true.

The larger the number of true statements on a subject that are known, the greater is the likelihood that a new statement on the subject will be inconsistent with the accepted truths. Thus the fact that a statement is consistent with a large number of other true statements on the subject suggests that the statement is also true. There is even a philosophical conception of truth, called the *consistency theory,* which explains the truth of a statement in terms of its consistency with other statements: A statement is true, according to this view, if it is consistent with a large body of other statements that form a comprehensive system of knowledge. Particularly in theoretical work, when a systematic organization of the subject matter is desirable, determining the consistency of statements with each other is essential, and the processes of deductive reasoning often indispensable.

EXERCISE 6G

Use syllogistic reasoning to determine whether there is consistency or inconsistency as alleged in each of the following arguments:

1. It doesn't make sense to say that animals such as chickens or dogs have rights. Only persons possess rights, and only human beings can be persons.

2. If a person says that animals have rights, he must admit that the human fetus has rights: For although a fetus may not be a person, it surely is an animal.

3. I insist that anyone who promotes animal rights should be a vegetarian. It is undeniable that animals raised for human consumption are treated in an inhumane way, and no promoter of animal rights can eat the meat of such animals with a clear conscience.

4. It is quite possible to be a believer in animal rights without also being a vegetarian. Game animals and seafood are harvested humanely, so that a promoter of animal rights may eat them with good conscience.

Review Exercise for Chapter 6

Use appropriate techniques to put the following arguments into standard form. Comment on the soundness as well as the validity of the argument.

1. The use of aerosols disrupts the ozone layer of the atmosphere. This poses a serious threat to health because it subjects human beings to deadly radiation. Therefore, the use of aerosols ought to be banned.

2. Those who oppose abortion maintain the sanctity of life, and those who oppose the death penalty also insist upon the sanctity of life. So why don't those who oppose the death penalty also oppose abortion?

3. If Episcopalians and Catholics truly believed that women are fully human, they would permit women to be ordained as priests.

4. Jones claims he is a conservationist, but still he does not oppose nuclear power plants, even though they pose the greatest threat of all to the environment.

5. Some states of fever are best treated by immersion in cold water. Every state of fever is some state of fever. Therefore all fevers are best treated by immersion in cold water.

6. How could the former CIA agent have shot himself when his fingers showed no trace of gunpowder?

chapter 7

Deductive Reasoning: Truth-Functions

7A TRUTH-FUNCTIONS AND EVERYDAY REASONING

Syllogisms are only one of the forms of deductive argument that occur in everyday reasoning. Another form is based on statements called *truth-functions*. Its principles, formulated in ancient times not long after syllogisms were, have recently been extended and become the basis of a powerful logical technique used in computer programming. Once again, however, we shall consider only as much of the subject as may usefully be applied to ordinary reasoning. A truth-function is a kind of compound statement. A compound statement is one that consists of two or more statements joined by one or more of the parts of speech called *connectives*, words such as *and, but, if, nor, although*. For example, "It is snowing and the temperature has fallen" is a compound statement; its component statements are "it is snowing" and "the temperature has fallen," and they are connected by the word *and*. The sentence, "It is snowing and the temperature has fallen," is also a truth-function, because in order to know whether the whole compound statement is true or false all we need to know is whether its component statements are true or false. "It is snowing and the temperature has fallen" is true only if both its component statements are true. It is false whenever any one or both of its components are false.

Not every compound statement is a truth-function. For example, the compound statement, "It is snowing because the temperature has fallen," is not. It contains the same component statements, "it is snowing" and "the temperature has fallen," but knowing that both components are true does not enable us to say whether the whole compound statement, "It is snowing because the temperature has fallen," is true. The connective *because* connects the component statements in a more complicated way than the connective *and,* so that the truth of the whole compound statement does not depend solely on the truth-values of the component statements. We need to know in addition that the falling of the temperature has *caused* the falling of the snow. (Knowing this to be the case involves problems of reasoning we will treat later when we discuss causation.) A compound statement whose truth or falsity depends on additional factors, other than the truth or falsity of its component statements, is not a truth-function.

Some compound statements are of such logical complexity that they cannot be handled at all in truth-functional logic. In the case of some compound statements, such as the preceding one, part of their meaning may be preserved by transposing them into truth-functional statements; the logic of truth-functions may then be fruitfully applied to them to yield some kinds of valid inference. For example, the sentence, "Although it has turned cold, it is not snowing," is not a truth-functional compound statement. Its truth does not depend solely on the truth of the statements, "it has turned cold" and "it is not snowing," but on whether it is unusual that both these things have occurred. The closest truth-function into which we can transpose it is the simple *conjunction,* "It has turned cold and it is not snowing." This transposition preserves only that part of the sentence that asserts the joint truth of the two statements, but it leaves out all that relates to how it happens that they are both true. No kind of truth-function commits itself to saying anything at all about how or why or whether the facts expressed by its component statements are connected.

In fact, the subject matter of the component statements of a truth-function may be completely unconnected without affecting its logic in any way whatsoever: "It is raining and twice two makes four" is a respectable truth-functional sentence which is true only if both its component statements are true. In ordinary reasoning, of course, the truth-functional statements we make are usually ones in which the subject matters of the component statements are closely related. But the deductive inferences we make by truth-functional logic are not based on the subject matter of the component statements but on the logical structure of the whole compound statement, which depends on the kind of connective joining its component statements. Just as in syllogistic reasoning we learned to recognize which kinds of categorical statements are validly derived from two categorical premises containing three terms, so we will learn to recognize what assertions about component statements may validly be inferred from various types of truth-functional premises. In order to keep in mind that our reasoning is based on the logical form of the truth-functional statement, and not be distracted by considerations relating to the facts expressed by its component statements, it is customary to substitute a different capital letter for each component statement of a truth-function instead of operating with the actual words of the statements.

The first step in dealing with truth-functional arguments is always to identify every component statement of the truth-functional premises of the argument and label each with a different capital letter. Given the truth-functional premise, "It is raining and the temperature has fallen," for example, we could choose R to stand for "it is raining" and T for "the temperature has fallen."

We shall distinguish four different types of truth-functional compound statements: *negations, conjunctions, disjunctions,* and *conditional statements.* For each type there is a corresponding special connective and one or more valid types of truth-functional argument. We shall now study how to recognize statements in ordinary language which have the logical form of these four types, and to distinguish valid and invalid forms of argument in which they may appear as premises.

A component statement of a truth-function need not be short but may be of some length or complexity. The sentence, "It has been raining cats and dogs all over the world for forty days and forty nights since Noah set sail in the ark," might serve as a component statement of a truth-function just as well as "it is raining." To correctly identify the component statements of an argument, observe the statements that are the additional premises or the conclusion of the argument. Component statements often appear by themselves as additional premises or the conclusion of the argument; sometimes they appear as component statements of other truth-functions which are the premises or conclusion of that argument.

Negations

Like any statement whatsoever, each component statement of a truth-function is capable of being true or false. In a truth-functional argument it is essential to distinguish a premise or conclusion that asserts the truth of a component statement from one that asserts its falsity. To say that a component statement is false is of course the same as saying that its contradictory is true. By convention, the contradictory of a component statement is classified as a special kind of truth-function called a *negation.* Thus, assume "it is raining" is a component statement of a truth-function. Its contradictory will be the statement, "It is not raining." Judging by grammar alone, we can see that "it is not raining" is not a compound statement at all. However, it is equivalent to a sentence such as "It is false that it is raining," a complex sentence which we can think of as a statement containing the component statement, "it is raining." Such a statement is called a *negation*: It is a truth-functional statement which asserts that its component statement is *false*. A negation has the logical form, "It is false that . . . S . . . ," where S may stand for any statement whatsoever. A negation possesses the essential logical characteristic of a truth-function, for the truth or falsity of the whole negation statement depends entirely on the truth-value of its component statement. The whole negation statement is true whenever its component statement is false; and the whole negation is false whenever its component statement is true.

Alternatively one could select a sentence like "It is not raining" as the component statement of a truth-function; its negation would be "It is false that it is not raining," or more briefly, "It is raining." It does not matter which sentence one chooses as component statement, as long as one is consistent in expressing both the component statement and its negation in other statements of the argument.

The negation of a statement is commonly expressed by the word *not* inside the sentence near a verb form, as in "it is not raining." But it is also signified by phrases placed before or sometimes after the statement being contradicted, such as the following:

It is false that . . .; it is not true that . . .; it is not the case that . . .; I deny that . . .; S is false.

To symbolize the negation of a component statement of a truth-function it is convenient to use the word *Not* followed by a hyphen, followed by the capital letter that stands for the component statement. If R stands for the component statement, "it is raining"; then *Not-R* will be the negation of R. To symbolize the negation of a whole truth-functional compound statement, we will use a capitalized *Not*, followed by a set of parentheses surrounding the whole compound statement. If the truth-functional compound statement is, "It is raining and it is cold," its negation will be "It is false that it is raining and cold." This is symbolized as: "Not (it is raining and it is cold)." This device is useful in eliminating ambiguity as to whether the whole compound statement is being negated or just one of its component statements.

The immediate inference from the truth of a statement to the falsity of its negation or contradictory we shall now call *negative argument*. We may express it in symbolic form as follows:

$$\frac{S}{\text{Not (Not-}S)} \qquad \frac{\text{Not (Not-}S)}{S}$$

In words, the first form says: "Statement S is true. Therefore, Not-S is false." The second form says: "Not-S is false. Therefore, S is true."

EXERCISE 7A

Choose a letter to represent each statement, and symbolize its negation. What statement can be inferred in each case by negative argument?

1. I am always happy when the sun shines.
2. It is not raining hard at present.
3. Jones became unhappy after his wife died.
4. Cigarettes cause lung cancer.
5. Drinking wine is not unpleasant.

7B CONJUNCTIONS AND CONJUNCTIVE ARGUMENT

A conjunction, as we have already mentioned, is a compound statement which asserts that all of its component statements without exception are true. In ordinary language statements connected by words such as *and, also, both . . . and, neither . . . nor* are conjunctions.

A conjunction may contain any number of component statements, but for brevity we will confine ourselves in our examples to conjunctions with two or three component statements. We will use the capitalized word *And* between statements to represent any conjunction. Suppose R stands for "it is raining," C for "it is cold," and W for "the wind blows." Then "R And C And W" stands for the conjunction, "It is raining and cold and the wind is blowing."

The sentence, "Neither is it raining nor is it cold," is a conjunction also, but it *denies* the component statements, "it is raining" and "it is cold" (that is, it asserts their negations). In symbolizing sentences containing "neither . . . nor," one must take care to be consistent in representing the two negations. If one takes as components R for "it is raining" and C for "it is cold," the conjunction will read: "Not-R and Not-C." But if R is made to stand for "it is not raining" and C for "it is not cold," the conjunction must read "R And C."

The order of the components of a truth-functional conjunction should not matter, for "R And C" is equivalent to "C And R." In transposing from ordinary language, we must deal carefully with compound sentences in which the order of the component statements alters the sense of the whole. For example, "He took a running jump and leaped off the diving board" is a compound sentence in which the order of the statements affects the meaning of the whole. In such cases one must be sure to state the conjunction in such a way that its truth-value does not depend on the order of its component statements.

A conjunction is only true when every one of its component statements is true. It is false whenever *any one* of its component statements is false. Whenever a conjunction is true, an obvious kind of immediate inference which we call *conjunctive argument*, is always valid. If a conjunction is asserted to be true, one can validly infer that any one of its component statements is also true. We can symbolize it as follows, using R for "it is raining" and W for "the wind blows":

R And W It is raining and the wind blows. Therefore, it is raining.
R

Not-R And Not-W Neither is it raining nor is the wind blowing.
Not-W Therefore, the wind is not blowing.

Conjunctive arguments may seem too trivial to be worth mentioning, yet they are often useful, especially as intermediate inferences and in combination with other forms of reasoning.

EXERCISE 7B

1. Say whether or not each of the following statements is a truth-function. Symbolize each truth-function, choosing a different capital letter for each component statement.

    a. I get blue whenever it rains.
    b. I am blue because it is raining.
    c. It's raining but I am not blue.
    d. It is not raining and I am not blue.
    e. It is raining yet it's not cold.
    f. It started to rain and I got cold.
    g. Although it's raining it is warm.
    h. It's false that I feel blue when it rains.

2. What inferences can one draw from the following statements by negative argument or conjunctive argument?

    a. The sun is shining but a storm is coming.
    b. It's not true that the storm is over.

   c. Neither is the sun shining nor is the storm over.

   d. The storm is not over.

   e. The sun is not yet out although the storm is over.

7C DISJUNCTIONS AND DISJUNCTIVE ARGUMENT

A third kind of truth-function, called a *disjunction*, frequently appears in everyday reasoning. Usually indicated by the presence of the word *or* between two or more statements, it asserts that at least one of a number of alternative statements is true. We shall use the capitalized word *Or*, set between two capital letters representing component statements, as the abbreviation for a disjunction. For example, the disjunctive statement, "Either the temperature has fallen or it is raining," will read "*T* Or *R*," where *R* stands for "it is raining" and *T* for "the temperature has fallen."

As with conjunctions, a disjunction may have any number of component statements, which we represent by stringing on as many *Or*'s and different capital letters for each component as are required. For example, "*R* Or *T* Or *S* Or *W*" will stand for "Either it is raining or the temperature has fallen or it is snowing or the wind is blowing."

A disjunction is true whenever at least one of its components is true, no matter how many component statements it contains. It is also true when more than one of its component statements is true and even when all of its components are true. It is often assumed that a statement like "*R* or *S*" is true only when one of its components is true and the other is false. But seldom, even in ordinary speech, do we assign such a restricted meaning to statements expressed as disjunctions. For example, when a waitress says "There is pie or ice cream for dessert," she does not mean to exclude the customer from having the one if he or she chooses the other. From the logical point of view, it is always safest to take the minimum meaning, making only those assumptions to which one is entitled by the strict wording of the statement.

On the occasions when the words "Either ... or" have a stronger sense which permits only one of the component statements to be true, it is usually the subject matter that prevents one from supposing that both components might be true. This is the case in the statement, "Either John is married to Jane or he is married to Mary." This kind of statement has a more complicated logic which is not expressed by a simple disjunction and is more accurately spelled out by the sentence, "Either he is married to Jane or he is married to Mary, *but not both.*" As the word *both* indicates, the sentence is best expressed as a *conjunction* which has two components. One component is the disjunction, "Either John is married to Jane or he is married to Mary"; the other component is the negation of a conjunction with the same components, "It is false that he is both married to Jane and married to Mary." This is a fairly complicated truth-function in that it has other truth-functions as its component statements, but we can easily symbolize it using our notation. Letting J stand for "John is married to Jane" and M for "John is married to Mary," we represent it as follows, using parentheses to indicate components of the conjunction:

$(J$ Or $M)$ And Not $(J$ And $M)$.

In words this would read, "Either John is married to Jane or he is married to Mary, and it is false that he is both married to Jane and married to Mary." In ordinary language, when we want to stress that only one alternative is possible and when the subject matter does not make this clear, we usually add some phrase such as "but only one" or "but not both." Whenever this strong exclusive sense of *or* attaches to a statement it should not be rendered as a simple disjunction, but as a conjunction, in which one component is the disjunction of the basic statements, and the other component is the negation of their conjunction.

A disjunction is true as long as at least one of its components is true; it is false only when every one of its components is false. On the basis of these facts we form a type of valid inference called *disjunctive argument*. Given a disjunction as a premise, one can never make an immediate inference to any one of its component statements. It is necessary to have a second premise if one is to make any valid inference by disjunctive argument. Suppose one asserts the premise, "Either the temperature has fallen or it is raining," then adds a second premise stating that one of the components of the disjunction is false, such as "It is not raining." Now, in order for the whole disjunction to be true when one of its two components is false, its other component must be true. Thus, we infer that "the temperature has fallen" is true. We may schematize the argument as follows:

T: the temperature has fallen; R: it is raining

T Or R	Either the temperature has fallen or it is raining.
Not-R	It is not raining.
T	Therefore, the temperature has fallen.

Suppose one has as premise a disjunction with more than two component statements, such as "Either it is raining or snowing or the temperature has fallen." In such a case, the addition of a premise that asserts the falsity of only one component will merely permit one to infer the truth of the *disjunction* of the remaining components, as follows:

T: the temperature has fallen; *R*: it is raining; *S*: it is snowing

R Or *S* Or *T*	It is raining or snowing or the temperature has fallen.
Not-*R*	It is not raining.
T Or *S*	Either the temperature has fallen or it is snowing.

If on the other hand the second premise negates all the components but one of the first premise disjunction, one may then infer the truth of the one remaining component. To illustrate:

R Or *S* Or *T*	It is raining or snowing or the temperature has fallen.
Not-*T* And Not-*S*	It is not snowing and the temperature has not fallen.
R	It is raining.

In general a valid disjunctive argument has the following form:

1. One premise is a disjunction.
2. The second premise negates one or more of the components of the disjunction.
3. The conclusion is the truth of the one remaining component or the disjunction of the remaining components.

FORMS OF DISJUNCTIVE ARGUMENT

R Or *S*	*R* Or *S*	*R* Or *S* Or *T*	*R* Or *S* Or *T*
Not-*R*	Not-*S*	Not-*R*	Not-*R* And Not-*S*
S	*R*	*S* Or *T*	*T*

Suppose an argument has a disjunction as one premise and a second premise which asserts that one component of the disjunction is true. May one infer that the other component is false? For example, from the two premises, "Either it is raining or the temperature has fallen" and "It is raining," can one conclude that it is false that the temperature has fallen? The answer is no, such an inference is not *deductively* valid; that is, it does not follow from the logical structure of the two premises. A disjunction is true when more than one of its components is true and even when all of its components are true. If one is to have a valid disjunctive argument, the second premise must *negate* one or more of the components of the disjunctive premise. When the second premise affirms the truth of one of the components of the disjunction, no inference may be drawn, either that the remaining component is true or that it is false. Arguments that draw an invalid conclusion from a disjunctive premise together with a premise that affirms one of the components of the disjunction are said to commit the *fallacy of affirming a disjunct.*

Translate statements of the arguments into disjunctions, component statements, or negations. Which are valid disjunctive arguments?

1. Sally is either unwell or in love. From her behavior, I'd say she is in love. So she can't be sick.

2. Joe is indifferent to Sally or angry at her for some reason. Since he surely is not indifferent, he must be angry.

3. These are Jones' alternatives: He can go to Europe for a year or go to college. He would not be so foolish as to waste money on a holiday. Therefore, he must be going to college.

4. Either the temperature reads 70 degrees or the thermostat clicks on. I don't hear the thermostat clicking, so it's 70 degrees.

5. The mechanic says either the fuel pump doesn't work or the car is out of gas. I suspect the tank is empty. It follows that the pump is working.

6. No one could spend money like Jones without an income or being engaged in some illegal business. I'm positive he has no independent income—he's got to be in some shady business.

7. A married man like myself ought either to have life insurance or to save part of his salary regularly. Since I do save part of each check I don't need life insurance.

7D NEGATIONS AND EQUIVALENTS OF CONJUNCTIONS AND DISJUNCTIONS

Like any statement, a conjunction or a disjunction has a contradictory or negation, to use the truth-functional term. We deny that a conjunction or a disjunction is true, that is, assert that it is false, in words such as these:

> It's false that it is neither raining nor cold.
> It's not the case that it is both raining and cold.
> It's not true that it is going to rain and turn cold.
> It's impossible that it will both rain and be warm.
> No one supposes that neither of the two favorites will win the Derby.
> I can't believe that one of the two favorites won't win the Derby.

The negation of a truth-function can always be expressed simply by putting *Not* in front of the whole truth-function and enclosing the truth-function in parentheses. The second statement above would read as

follows, using R for "it is raining" and C for "it is cold": "Not $(R$ And $C)$."
The parentheses are essential for indicating that the negation is of the
whole conjunction, not just of its first component, R.

In order to be clear about what is being asserted when a conjunction
or disjunction is denied, we need to analyze what is being said about the
truth or falsity of each component statement. First, let us consider what is
being asserted in the negation of the disjunction: "It is false that either it
rains or it is cold." A disjunction is false in only one case, when every one
of its component statements is false. Thus, in the preceding case, both "it
is raining" and "it is cold" are said to be *false*; stated in ordinary language,
this would read, "It is neither true that it is raining nor that it is cold."
The negation of a disjunction is a *conjunction* whose component statements are the negations of each component of the disjunction. The
negation of a disjunction is *not* another disjunction, as one might hastily
suppose. Ordinary language faithfully expresses this fact, for the negation
or denial of an "either . . . or" statement is a "neither . . . nor" statement;
and a "neither . . . nor" statement is a conjunction of the negations of the
contained statements. In general then, "Not $(R$ Or $C)$" is equivalent to
"Not-R And Not-C."

Similarly, the negation of a conjunction is not another conjunction,
but a disjunction: To contradict or negate a conjunction is to say that at
least one of its component statements is false. Thus, "It is false that it is
both raining and cold" is equivalent to saying "Either it is false that it is
raining or it is false that it is cold." Putting that statement into a truth-
function, we turn it into a disjunction, "Either it is not raining or it is not
cold"; or schematically, "Not-R Or Not-C."

Many are tempted to say that the negation of a conjunction is also a
conjunction, one whose components are the negations of the component
statements of the conjunction. But is a conjunction false only when all its
component statements are false? No—a conjunction is false when any one
of its components is false, not just when all its components are false. Thus
the conjunction "Not-R And Not-C" is not necessarily true whenever "R
And C" is false—it is only one case among others, and so is not its genuine
contradictory. "Not-R And Not-C" only implies "Not $(R$ And $C)$"; it is not
equivalent to it as the negation of the negation of "R And C" would be. On
the other hand, the disjunction "Not-R Or Not-C" will always be true
whenever "R And C" is false, and so is the true negation or contradictory
of "R And C." "R and C" is false in three different cases: (1) whenever R is
false, (2) whenever C is false, (3) whenever both R and C are false. In each
of these three cases, "Not-R Or Not-C" is *true,* just as the contradictory or
negation of "R And C" should be. To prove that a conjunction is false, one
is not required to show that each one of its component statements is false,
only to show that some one or other of its component statements is false.

To summarize, one may *contradict* or *negate a conjunction, "R* And *S,"* in two ways:

1. by placing the negation sign *Not* in front of the *whole* conjunction, after putting a set of parentheses around the conjunction; that is, the *negation* of the conjunction "*R* And *S*" is "Not *R* And *S*)";
2. by a disjunction whose component statements are the negations of the component statements of the conjucntion; that is, the *negation* of the conjunction "*R* and *S*" is the disjunction "Not-*R* Or Not-*S*."

One may express the *negation* of a *disjunction,* "*R Or S,*" in two ways also:

1. by placing a negation sign in front of the whole disjunction, after putting a set of parentheses around the disjunction; that is, the *negation of "R Or S"* is "Not (*R* Or *S*)";
2. by a conjunction whose component statements are the negations of the component statements of the disjunction; that is, the *negation* of "*R* Or *S*" is "Not-*R* And Not-*S*."

In obtaining the negation of either a conjunction or disjunction in the second way, two steps are involved. First, each component statement must be negated; second, the conjunction must be transformed into a disjunction or vice versa.

It is crucial to distinguish the *equivalent* of a statement from its *negation.* The equivalent of a statement always has exactly the same truth-value, being true when the statement is true, and false when it is false. But the negation or contradictory of a statement is always opposite in truth-value, being true when the statement is false, and false when it is true. By negative argument, negating the negation of any statement is equivalent to saying that the statement is true. To negate a statement that is itself a negation, such as "Not (*R* and *S*)," one simply removes the negation sign—the negation of "Not (*R* And *S*)" is simply "*R* And *S*."

Keeping the rule of negative argument in mind, we can easily obtain an equivalent for any disjunction by negating the conjunction which is its negation. For example, starting with the disjunction, "*R* Or *S*," we express its negation by the conjunction, "Not-*R* And Not-*S*." Negating "Not-*R* And Not-*S*" gives us "Not (Not-*R* And Not-*S*)," which is the equivalent of "*R* Or *S*." To put this in words, suppose one starts with the disjunction, "Either it is raining or it is snowing." This statement is the equivalent of the negation of a conjunction, "It's false that it is neither raining nor snowing."

Similarly, the equivalent of any conjunction is the negation of the disjunction of its component statements' negations. Starting with the conjunction, "*R* And *S*," we obtain its negation, "Not-*R* Or Not-*S*." Negating that disjunction gives "Not (Not-*R* Or Not-*S*)," which by negative argument is equivalent to "*R* and *S*." In words, "It is both raining and snowing" is equivalent to "It is false that it is either not raining or not snowing."

In obtaining equivalents for conjunctions or disjunctions in this manner, it is again important to take care when a component is already a negation. The equivalent of "Not-*R* Or *S*" is "Not (*R* And Not-*S*)," for example; the equivalent of "Not-*S* And Not-*T*" is "Not (*S* Or *T*)."

We can formulate these two rules for obtaining the equivalent of a conjunction or disjunction:

1. *To obtain the equivalent of a disjunction: Write down the conjunction which is its negation; then place a negation sign before the whole conjunction.*

2. *To obtain the equivalent of a conjunction: Write down the disjunction which is its negation; then place a negation sign before the whole disjunction.*

These rules enable us to handle arguments that contain as a premise the negation of a conjunction or the negation of a disjunction. If a premise is the negation of a conjunction, simply translate the statement into its equivalent disjunction; then proceed by the rules of disjunctive argument. If a premise is the negation of a disjunction, translate the premise into the equivalent conjunction, and proceed by conjunctive argument. For example, consider the following argument:

My father says he won't both send me to college next year and pay for a trip to Europe this summer. Since I want to go to college next year, I'll have to finance my own way to Europe.

Let *C* stand for "My father pays my college expenses" and *T* for "My father pays for travel expenses." The first premise will read "Not (*C* And *T*)," a statement form to which we can apply neither conjunctive argument nor negative argument. By applying our rules for equivalence, we can translate "Not (*C* And *T*)" into its equivalent disjunction, "Not-*C* Or Not-*T*," and apply the rules for disjunctive argument.

EXERCISE 7D

1. Translate each of the following into a disjunction or conjunction, using *F* for "The fuel pump works" and *G* for "The car has gas." Write out the negations and equivalents of each.

    a. The car has gas and the fuel pump works.
    b. Either the fuel pump is not working or the car is out of gas.
    c. The fuel pump is not working and the car is out of gas.
    d. There is gas in the car but the fuel pump doesn't work.
    e. Either the car has gas or the fuel pump works.

2. Test the validity of the following arguments, using equivalents when necessary.

    a. Either Jones has divorced Jane or he is still married to her. Since this newspaper account lists her as his wife, he can't have divorced her.
    b. It is possible to reduce inflation or unemployment but not both at once. Thus, either we accept continued inflation or we must expect increased unemployment.
    c. It is not true that the government can reduce taxes and also increase social services. Having decided to increase social services, the government cannot cut taxes.
    d. The Supreme Court did not deny that race could be a criterion for admission or the legality of affirmative action plans. Therefore, it supported the principle of affirmative action.
    e. The city cannot both avoid an increase in the property tax and raise the salaries of municipal employees. Since the tax rate is staying the same, the city workers may get a raise.

7E CONDITIONAL STATEMENTS

Many arguments in everyday reasoning employ a conditional statement as a basic premise. We will now study in detail the logic of truth-functional conditional statements, since much mistaken reasoning involves a failure to understand the claims made in a conditional statement. A conditional statement most commonly appears in the form of a sentence containing two separate statements, one prefaced by the word *if*, the other by the word *then*; for example, "If it rains on the Fourth of July, then there are no fireworks." The statement following the *if* is called the *antecedent statement;* the one following the *then* is called the *consequent statement*. It is essential to be clear about which statement is antecedent and which is consequent, for the exact logical claim made by the conditional statement turns on this fact. Unlike disjunctions or conjunctions, the order of the component statements in a conditional statement cannot be altered without changing the meaning of the statement. For the purposes of analysis, we abbreviate the conditional statement by the word *if*, followed by the capital letter standing for the antecedent statement, followed by the word *then*, followed by the capital letter standing for the consequent statement. Letting R stand for "it rains on the Fourth of July" and F for "there are fireworks on the Fourth," the preceding conditional statement takes the form, "If R, then Not-F."

A conditional statement is so called because it makes the claim that the truth of the consequent statement follows from the truth of the antecedent statement. The whole conditional statement asserts that there is a connection between the truth of the antecedent statement and that of the consequent statement such that the antecedent statement cannot be true unless the consequent statement is also true. In the preceding example, the conditional asserts that when "it rains on the Fourth of July" is true, the statement "there are no fireworks on the Fourth," is also true. To put the matter negatively, in terms of falsity, the whole conditional statement claims that whenever the consequent statement is *false*—that is, in case there *are* fireworks on the Fourth—the antecedent statement is also *false*—that is, it is *not* raining on the Fourth of July.

The conditional statement asserts neither that its antecedent statement is true nor that its consequent statement is true. In our example, the conditional neither claims for a fact that it rains on the Fourth of July nor denies the existence of fireworks on that day. The conditional makes no flat truth claim about its component statements individually; it only makes a hypothetical claim about what would be the case in the event that its antecedent statement happened to be true. This claim, made by the whole conditional statement, is capable of being true or false just like the claim made by any other statement. Whether a conditional statement is true or false is determined by the relevant evidence in each case. Given our knowledge about the circumstances in which fireworks can be set off, the conditional statement, "If there is rain on the Fourth of July, then there are no fireworks," is one we would readily accept as true. On the other hand, we would doubt the conditional statement, "If there is rain on the Fourth of July, then there are fireworks on the Fourth."

A conditional statement is false, if the facts indicate its antecedent statement may be true, when its consequent statement is false. In the latter conditional statement, we have reason to suppose that when the antecedent statement, "there is rain on the Fourth of July," is true, the consequent statement, "there are fireworks on the Fourth," is more likely to be false than true; consequently we are ready to deny the truth of the whole conditional statement, "If there is rain on the Fourth of July, then there are fireworks."

The negation, or contradictory, of a conditional statement is a *conjunction*, one component of which is the antecedent statement of the conditional, whereas the other component is the negation of the consequent statement. The *negation* of "If there is rain on the Fourth of July, then there are *no* fireworks on the Fourth" is a conjunction, "There is rain on the Fourth of July and there are fireworks." In order to question the truth of a conditional statement, one needs to consider whether the conjunction—consisting of the antecedent and the negation of the consequent of the conditional—is likely to be true. If the negation of the conditional is likely to be true, the conditional itself is unlikely to be true.

In a conditional statement, the order of its component statements has a crucial effect on the truth or falsity of the whole conditional statement. Two conditional statements with the same component statements in reverse order (the antecedent of one being the consequent of the other) are called *converses*; a conditional statement is *not* the equivalent of its converse. For example, the conditional, "If there are no fireworks on the Fourth, there is rain on the Fourth of July," is not true under exactly the same circumstances as its converse, "If there is rain on the Fourth of July, there are no fireworks on the Fourth." Whereas, given common knowledge, we readily accept the latter conditional, we could not similarly say that its converse is true. We can easily posit circumstances in which the antecedent of the converse conditional, "there are no fireworks," would be true but its consequent, "there is rain on the Fourth of July," would nevertheless be false—fireworks may be illegal or too expensive or unsafe or unavailable, regardless of the weather conditions.

Thus it is extremely important in reasoning that employs conditional premises to identify correctly, in accordance with the facts being expressed, the statement that belongs in the antecedent position and that which belongs in the consequent position. One of the most common errors in reasoning is the misstatement or misinterpretation of the facts which results when the antecedent and consequent are not properly placed in the conditional statement which connects the two facts. Therefore we shall first list rules on how to interpret sentences in ordinary language so as to be able to place the antecedent and consequent components correctly in the conditional statement.

Statements that follow these words or phrases regularly go in the *antecedent* position of the conditional:

> if . . . ; provided . . . ; whenever . . . ; assuming that . . . ; in case . . . ;
> should it be the case that . . . ; it being true that . . . ; supposing
> that . . . ; on the condition that . . . ; in the circumstance that. . . .

Statements that go in the *consequent* position often occur at the beginning of a sentence without any index phrases at all; for example, "There are no fireworks, if it rains on the Fourth of July." The word *then* is the most frequent index phrase—the statement following the *then* belongs in the consequent position. Often one can identify the consequent statement by inserting a *then* in front of a likely candidate. Phrases such as the following may also signal the consequent of a conditional:

it follows that . . . ; it will be the case that . . . ; it will also happen that . . . ; the result will be . . . ; the consequence is. . . .

Whereas the statement following plain *if* in a sentence regularly belongs in the antecedent of the conditional, two statements joined by *only if* obey a quite different rule: Here the statement *immediately* following *only if* is always the *consequent* of the conditional. Consider these two sentences:

There are fireworks on the Fourth only if it does not rain.
Only if it does not rain are there fireworks on the Fourth.

Both these sentences translate into the conditional:

If there are fireworks on the Fourth, then it does not rain on the Fourth.

When the *only if* comes between the two statements, as in the first sentence above, the statement that comes directly *before* the *only if* is always the antecedent; the statement directly *after* the *only if* is always the consequent. When the words *only if* begin the sentence, as in the second instance, the statement immediately after *only if* is still the consequent, and the antecedent component comes at the end of the sentence.

A sentence containing two statements connected by the word *unless* is always a conditional statement. The connective *unless* all by itself is logically equivalent to *if not*. Thus the statement immediately following *unless* should be negated and placed in the antecedent. Consider these two statements:

There will be fireworks on the Fourth of July unless it rains.
Unless it rains, there will be fireworks on the Fourth of July.

Both of these sentences are correctly translated into

If it does not rain, then there will be fireworks on the Fourth of July.

Note that when the *unless* occurs in the middle of the sentence, as in the first example, the statement just before *unless* is always the consequent, and the *negation* of the statement just after the *unless* is the antecedent. When *unless* begins the sentence, as in the second case, once again the negation of the statement just following *unless* is the antecedent, and the statement at the end of the sentence is the consequent.

One can apply another rule when the statement not governed by *unless* is *also* a negation—that is, when sentences are of the form "Not-*P*, unless *Q*" or "Unless *Q*, Not-*P*":

There will not be fireworks unless the weather clears.
Unless it clears, there will be no fireworks.

Remember that a conditional statement asserts that its *antecedent* statement is *not* true *unless* its *consequent* statement is also true. Obviously "Not-*P* unless *Q*" expresses exactly the same connection of facts as "If *P*, then *Q*." Thus, the statement following the *unless* may be put into the *consequent* just as it stands; the other statement has its negation sign *removed* (that is, we negate the negation) and goes into the antecedent. The preceding two statements are then expressed by the conditional:

If there are fireworks, then the weather is clear.

One may use this rule, however, only when the ordinary language sentence is of the form "Not-*P*, unless *Q*,"—that is, when both component statements are negated—since *unless* is equivalent to *if not*. Whenever the statement is simply of the form "*P* unless *Q*," it is advisable to translate the *unless* as *if not*, and the conditional will be of the form "If Not-*Q*, then *P*."

One may also use the rule for *unless* alone, even with statements of the form "Not-*P* unless *Q*." In this case, one will end up with a different but equivalent conditional: "If Not-*Q* then Not-*P*" instead of "If *P* then *Q*." Note that the component statements of these two conditionals are *negations* of each other and *switched in position*:

If *P*, then *Q*.
If Not-*Q*, then Not-*P*.

Two such conditionals are called *contrapositives*, and they are equivalent. Recall that a conditional claims that its antecedent is true only if its consequent is true. Should the consequent then be false, the antecedent must also be false, according to that very claim. This is exactly what the contrapositive of a conditional says. For example, following the *unless* rule, "There are no fireworks unless the weather clears" translates into "If the weather does not clear, then there are no fireworks." This statement makes exactly the same truth claim as its contrapositive: "If there are fireworks, then the weather does clear." Do not confuse the converse of a conditional with its contrapositive: The converse of a conditional contains exactly the same component statements with the positions of antecedent and consequent reversed; converse conditionals are not equivalent to each other. But the contrapositive of a conditional contains the *negations* of the same components, with the positions of antecedent and consequent reversed; a conditional and its contrapositive are equivalent.

It is important to learn the rules for translating sentences in ordinary language containing *unless* and *only if* into standard "*if . . . then*" conditional statements; for these terms are commonly used when the speaker is being careful in pointing out the exact connection of facts. Suppose the instructor of your course says, "You will pass this course only if you turn in every assignment." This statement is correctly translated into the conditional, "If you pass this course, then you have turned in all the assignments." It is not correctly translated into the converse of the preceding conditional: "If you turn in all the assignments, then you pass the course." The instructor's original statement does not promise that turning in all the assignments will result in passing the course, as the last-mentioned converse does; rather it threatens that not turning in every assignment will result in not passing the course, a very different state of affairs.

It sometimes happens in ordinary speech that a conditional expressed simply with the word *if* amounts to very much the same thing as its converse conditional. When a speaker says, "I'll go if you go," he often also means to assert, "If you don't go, I won't go." When this is the case, the speaker is making a much stronger claim than the one expressed by the conditional "If you go, then I go," for he is also asserting its converse, "If I go, then you go." The latter statement is the contrapositive equivalent of "If you don't go, then I don't go," which is a different conditional from "If you go, then I go." In such cases, the statement is not properly translated as a single conditional; rather it is a conjunction whose component statements are two converse conditionals:

(If I go then you go) And (If you go then I go).

Such a conjunction of a conditional and its converse is sometimes called a *biconditional*; it is expressed in ordinary language by the words *if and only if*. It is easy to see that "P if and only if *Q*" expresses a conjunction of conditionals, for it says "*P if Q and P* only if *Q.*" In accordance with our rules, "*P* if *Q*" becomes the conditional, "If *Q* then *P*," and "*P* only if *Q*" becomes its converse, "If *P* then *Q*." When a speaker's intention is to assert "*P* if and only if *Q*" rather than merely "*P* if *Q*," the statement should not be translated into a simple conditional, but into a conjunction of the conditional and its converse, that is, the biconditional.

Occasionally the subject matter of the statement is such that both the conditional and its converse, that is, the biconditional, may be asserted, because the antecedent and the consequent statements turn out to be equivalent. For example, the statement, "If today is Tuesday, then tomorrow is Wednesday," is equivalent to its converse, "If tomorrow is Wednesday, then today is Tuesday." It is only in such exceptional cases, however, that reversing the positions of antecedent and consequent statements is legitimate.

Conditional statements are frequently used to express facts about causes and effects, or about the results of certain conditions; for example, "If one smokes heavily, one is likely to develop lung cancer." Often the fact asserted in the consequent statement takes place later than the fact asserted by the antecedent, as in "If it rains today, I'll cut the grass tomorrow." However, one must guard against assuming that the antecedent always refers to a cause or something occurring before the consequent. Suppose a doctor says, "If the patient breaks out in a rash tomorrow, he has measles." In such a case it is not correct to say that the fact expressed in the consequent statement occurs after the one expressed in the antecedent: Breaking out in a rash is not being cited as the cause of measles, but as a symptom. In drawing inferences from conditional statements by truth-functional deductive reasoning, we must avoid being influenced by considerations of cause or time that may be suggested by the subject matter. Inferences based on causal connections must be assessed by reasoning techniques other than deductive forms of argument. A truth-functional conditional statement preserves only that part of the meaning of a conditional statement which relates to the logical connection between the truth-values of its component statements expressed by the *If . . . then* form of the statement.

As with other kinds of truth-functions, there need be no connection in subject matter between the antecedent and consequent of the truth-functional conditional. In ordinary talk we sometimes assert conditionals containing statements whose subject matter is disconnected: "If she's thirty, I'm a monkey's uncle" is an example. Here we are meant to infer from the falsity of the consequent that the antecedent statement is false. In truth-functional deductive reasoning we limit ourselves to what follows necessarily from the very form of the words *if* and *then* in *all* cases of the conditional, omitting whatever may be implied by the subject matter of the statements joined by *if* and *then*. For this purpose, it is desirable always to substitute capital letters for the component statements of the conditional.

The reader may have noted some variation in the wording used to express the identical component of a conditional. The sentence, "You will pass this course only if you turn in every assignment," was, for example, translated into the conditional: "If you pass this course, then you have turned in every assignment." Here, "you turn in every assignment" in the original is reworded as "you have turned in every assignment." Such rewording is often needed to smooth out the grammar; but one must be sure that any change in wording does not alter the actual connection of facts. Using capital letters instead of the actual wording eliminates this awkwardness, but one must guard against substituting new or different facts in transposing back into ordinary language.

In the conditional statements we have mentioned hitherto, the component statements were all simple statements. However, we frequently make conditional statements whose antecedent or consequent is a compound statement, a conjunction, a disjunction, or even another conditional; for example, "If it is neither raining nor cold on the Fourth of July, we shall either go on a picnic or go to the fireworks." Here the antecedent is a conjunction of two negations, and the consequent is a disjunction. Using R for "it is rainy," C for "it is cold," P for "we go on a picnic," and F for "we go to the fireworks," we can symbolize the conditional as follows: "If (Not-R And Not-C) then (P Or F)." When the antecedent or the consequent of a conditional is also a truth-function, it is essential to use parentheses to separate the whole antecedent from the whole consequent in an unambiguous way.

EXERCISE 7E

Put each statement into *if... then* conditional form. Say which of the lettered statements is the equivalent, the converse, or the contrapositive of the numbered statement above it.

1. Jones will not buy a foreign car unless it costs under $8,000.

    a. If Jones buys a foreign car, it costs under $8,000.
    b. If Jones does not buy a foreign car, it does not cost under $8,000.
    c. If a foreign car costs under $8,000, Jones will buy it.
    d. Jones will buy a foreign car only if it costs under $8,000.
    e. If a foreign car does not cost under $8,000, Jones will not buy it.

2. The ERA amendment will become part of the Constitution if and only if it is ratified by 38 states.

    a. If the ERA amendment becomes part of the Constitution, it has been ratified by 38 states.
    b. If the ERA amendment is ratified by 38 states, it becomes part of the Constitution.
    c. If the ERA amendment is ratified by 38 states, it becomes part of the Constitution, but if it is not ratified by 38 states, it does not.
    d. The ERA amendment will become part of the Constitution provided it is ratified by 38 states; it will not become part of the Constitution unless ratified by 38 states.

e. The ERA amendment will become part of the Constitution only if it is ratified by 38 states.

3. If I win the lottery, I'll buy a car or take a cruise.
   a. If I don't win the lottery, I'll neither buy a car nor take a cruise.
   b. If I neither buy a car nor take a cruise, then I won't have won the lottery.
   c. I'll buy a car or take a cruise only if I win the lottery.
   d. If I buy a car or take a cruise I've won the lottery.

7F   VALID AND INVALID FORMS OF CONDITIONAL ARGUMENT

Once one understands those connections between the truth-values of the antecedent and consequent statements which a conditional statement asserts, it is easy to distinguish a valid conditional argument from an invalid one. To review, the conditional statement maintains that whenever its antecedent statement is true it follows that its consequent statement is also true; and that whenever its consequent statement is false its antecedent statement must also be false. Thus, the conditional asserts that its antecedent statement *implies* its consequent statement, with the antecedent playing the role of the *implying* statement and the consequent that of the statement *implied*. The relation of implication between two statements always has a direction, enabling one to infer from the truth of the implying (antecedent) statement the truth of the implied (consequent) statement. The reverse direction of implication goes from the falsity of the implied (consequent) statement to the falsity of the implying (antecedent) statement.

The two main types of valid conditional argument are based on the preceding facts. The first step in analyzing a conditional argument is to identify the conclusion, which must be one of the components (either the antecedent or the consequent) of the conditional statement. The second step is to translate the conditional into a standard *If . . . then* statement, substituting different capital letters for each component statement. It is extremely important to place statements correctly in the antecedent or consequent position in accordance with the rules formulated in the previous section, for the deductive validity or invalidity of the conditional argument turns on this point. One type of valid conditional argument starts with a conditional statement as one premise. The second premise asserts that the antecedent statement of the conditional is true. Clearly, we are entitled to infer that the consequent statement of the conditional is also true. For example, suppose the family cook says, "If it is hot today, there will be crabmeat salad for supper"—a conditional premise. The temperature climbs into the nineties, enabling one to assert the truth of the antecedent of the conditional premise, "it is hot today." Then, believing in the cook's truthfulness, we may infer the consequent statement of the conditional, "there will be crabmeat salad for supper." Any argument of this type is valid and is called *affirming the antecedent.* This phrase refers to an argument whose second premise asserts that the antecedent statement of the conditional premise is true, thus permitting one to infer the truth of the consequent statement of the conditional premise. We may schematize this kind of conditional argument as follows:

AFFIRMING THE ANTECEDENT

If A, then C	Premise 1, a conditional statement
A	Premise 2, asserts antecedent to be true
C	Conclusion that the consequent is true

The second type of valid conditional argument is called *denying the consequent.* This argument rests on the fact that the falsity of the consequent of a true conditional statement requires that the antecedent also be false. Suppose we have the same conditional premise, "If it is hot today there will be crabmeat salad for supper." Looking at the daily menu, we find that crabmeat salad is not listed. Again trusting the cook's veracity, we must infer that the antecedent of the conditional is also false, and conclude, "It is not hot today." Any argument of this type, in which a conditional premise is joined with a second premise denying the truth of the consequent of the conditional, entitles one to infer that the antecedent of the conditional premise is also false. Its form is as follows:

DENYING THE CONSEQUENT

If A then C	Premise 1, a conditional statement
Not-C	Premise 2, denying the truth of the consequent
Not-A	Conclusion that antecedent is false

Affirming the antecedent and *denying the consequent* are the only valid types of conditional argument containing just two premises, one a conditional premise, the other a premise affirming or denying the truth of one of the components of the conditional premise. There are two other logical possibilities for the form of the second premise, but they do not combine with the conditional premise to produce a valid deductive argument—one might have a second premise, which either denies the antecedent or affirms the truth of the consequent. Let us examine why they fail to produce any conclusion that would follow necessarily from two such premises. Let us take the same conditional premise, "If it is hot today, there will be crabmeat salad for supper." That day there is indeed crabmeat salad on the table (the consequent of the conditional turns out to be true). *Must* it also be the case that the antecedent of the conditional is true? No, the conditional only speaks of *one* circumstance (that is, it is hot) which will make crabmeat appear on the menu. It doesn't say that this is the *only* circumstance under which crabmeat might appear on the menu. Perhaps crabmeat will also be on the menu if the price is low, if someone has gone crabbing, or if the crabmeat on hand will spoil unless used immediately. In such cases the conditional premise will be true, as will its consequent, but its antecedent statement is not *required* to be true. Thus from an argument in which one premise is a conditional statement, and the second premise asserts that the consequent of the conditional is true, we can draw no inference whatsoever about the truth or the falsity of the antecedent statement—it may be true or it may be false. If we do infer that the antecedent premise is true, we are going beyond what the logical form of the argument justifies—we are committing the *deductive* fallacy known as *affirming the consequent*. In this fallacy a conclusion is invalidly deduced from a premise which affirms the consequent of the conditional premise to be true.

In the fourth possible type of conditional argument, the second premise denies the truth of the antecedent of the conditional premise, and thus commits the deductive fallacy appropriately called *denying the antecedent*. Take the same conditional premise, "If it is hot today, there will be crabmeat salad for supper." Join with it a second premise denying the truth of the antecedent, such as, "It is not hot today." May one conclude from these two premises that the consequent statement is also false, that is, "There will not be crabmeat salad for supper"? Many are tempted to do so, but it does not follow from the logical form of the statements of the argument alone. We might think it *likely* that the consequent statement is false too, but that hunch is not enough to allow us to justify the conclusion by deductive reasoning alone. The truth of the conditional premise requires only that the consequent be true whenever the antecedent is true, and the antecedent false whenever the consequent is false. The conditional statement does not make any claim about what must be the case when its antecedent is false. Just as in the other case, we can draw no valid deductive inference—either that the consequent is false or that it is true—from two such premises. Thus any deductive argument in which the antecedent of a conditional premise is said to be false or the consequent of the conditional premise is said to be true, is one which leaves the truth or falsity of the other component open to question: To make any inference about the other component is to take a step not justified by deductive reasoning alone.

Now that we have worked out the valid and invalid forms of conditional argument, it should be apparent why it is so crucial to place the antecedent and consequent statements correctly in the conditional premise. Since a valid argument can be obtained only with a second premise which asserts the truth of the antecedent or denies the consequent, the order of the statements in the conditional premise determines the validity or invalidity of the argument in question. Consider the following argument:

> There will be peace in the Middle East only if Sadat remains in power in Egypt. Sadat is firmly in control in Egypt and will surely remain so. Therefore, peace in the Middle East is assured.

We can analyze this argument in accordance with the rules given as follows:

P—There is peace in the Middle East; *S*—Sadat remains in power in Egypt.

If *P*, then *S*	Premise 1, conditional
S	Premise 2, affirms consequent of conditional premise
P	Conclusion, fallacy of affirming the consequent

The analysis shows the argument to be an instance of a deductive fallacy, the conclusion not following necessarily from the premises. To say that peace in the Middle East *requires* that Sadat remain in power by no means *guarantees* that there will be peace in the Middle East with Sadat in power. The conditional premise only says there will not be peace unless Sadat is in power, not that there *will* be peace if Sadat is in power.

But suppose the conditional premise, "There will be peace in the Middle East only if Sadat remains in power in Egypt," were carelessly transposed into this conditional: "If Sadat remains in power in Egypt, there will be peace in the Middle East." Then the whole argument would have this form:

If *S*, then *P*	Premise 1, conditional
S	Premise 2, affirms antecedent of conditional
P	Conclusion that consequent is true: VALID FORM.

In this case, the argument turns out to be valid, because the mistranslation of the conditional premise changes the logical form of the argument. This kind of error is one of the most common committed in everyday reasoning. It is insidious because it is very easy, through haste or carelessness, to reverse the proper order of the antecedent and consequent of conditional statements. Such an error can lead one to believe an argument to be valid when it is not. The opposite can also occur—a valid argument can be turned into an invalid one.

Which of the following conditional arguments are valid?

1. Sally cannot be pregnant if she is a virgin. Since she's certainly not pregnant, she must be a virgin.
2. Boys' Latin will not win the lacrosse championship unless St. Paul's loses its last game. Has St. Paul won? Then Boys' Latin misses the championship.
3. If the north side gets sun a few hours a day, a dogwood tree will grow there. I've just observed that the sun is there an hour or two in the morning and late afternoon. So a dogwood should flourish there.
4. Dad said we would go to Europe this summer only if we could join an economical tour. Because Mom said this morning we will go abroad this summer, they must have found a tour at last.
5. If my sore throat is not caused by a bacterial infection, an antibiotic will not help it. The doctor says it is a virus infection; thus there is no point in prescribing an antibiotic.
6. If motorists top off their tanks, there will be long lines at the pump this summer. The new regulation will stop topping off. Therefore, there will not be long lines for gas.
7. If airline passengers believe the DC-10 is a safe plane, they will continue to fly in them. But passengers are canceling their reservations on DC-10s. That's proof they do not trust them.
8. If there is a gas shortage, mobile home sales will drop. Since oil supplies will be tight for a while, mobile homes will be hard to sell.
9. Americans will not buy smaller cars unless a gas shortage threatens. Small-car sales are up, indicating there is a threat of gas shortage.

7G CONDITIONAL CHAIN ARGUMENTS

Very familiar in everyday and scientific reasoning is a conditional chain argument. It consists of a number of premises, all of them conditional in form:

> If there is water on Mars, there may be life on Mars; if there is life on Mars, there will be decayed organic matter; wherever decayed organic matter is present, oil may be found. If there is oil on Mars, it may be fairly abundant. If there is a substantial reserve of oil, it

would definitely be worthwhile to send a manned mission to Mars for oil exploration. Therefore, if there turns out to be water on Mars, it would be reasonable for us to send a manned mission there.

The point of chain arguments such as the preceding one is not so much that they reach definite conclusions as that they spin out the implications of plausible connections of facts. Such an argument typically consists of a string of conditional statements that lead to a conclusion which often sounds farfetched but which may also point up possibilities that are not otherwise apparent. Whether this kind of argument is *deductively* valid depends on the logical form of its premises and conclusion. A valid conditional chain argument has the following form: (1) The conditional premises must form an unbroken chain, in which each succeeding conditional has as its antecedent the consequent of the preceding conditional. (2) The conclusion of the argument must be a conditional whose antecedent is the same as the antecedent of the first premise and whose consequent is the same as the consequent of the last premise. We may schematize the logical form of a chain argument as follows:

VALID CONDITIONAL CHAIN ARGUMENT

> If A then B
> If B, then C
> _____
> If A, then C

In an argument taking this form, each component statement from the first conditional onward, implies the succeeding component statement, so that one may infer that the first component statement implies the last component statement. The conclusion drawn in a valid chain argument is not simply the last consequent statement in the chain; it must be a conditional statement linking the first antecedent of the chain with the last consequent in the chain (for the conclusion is always a *hypothetical* claim, which must be expressed as a conditional statement). The most common error in conditional chain reasoning is to infer the last consequent statement, leaping beyond what is implied by the conditional premises. In the argument cited, this error would be committed if the conclusion were simply, "It is worthwhile to send a manned mission to Mars." Note that the conclusion is the much more tentative statement, "If there turns out to be water on Mars, it would be reasonable for us to send a manned mission there." In order to test the deductive validity of a conditional chain argument, one simply schematizes the argument in the usual way and then inspects it to see whether it has the required logical form. For example, the preceding argument has the following form:

If W, then L	W: there is water on Mars; L: there is life on Mars
If L, then D	D: there is decayed organic matter on Mars
If D, then O	O: there is oil on Mars; S: there is substantial oil on Mars
If O, then S	M: it is worthwhile to send a manned mission to Mars
If S, then M	
If W, then M	

The argument does satisfy the two conditions for a valid conditional chain argument: The antecedent of each conditional premise (after the first) is the consequent of the preceding conditional premise; and the conclusion is a conditional statement joining the antecedent of the first conditional premise with the consequent of the last stated conditional premise. In saying that this argument is deductively valid, however, we only indicate that the logical form of the premises is such that a statement of the logical form of the conclusion necessarily follows from it. To assess the general *soundness* of the argument, one must determine whether there is sufficient evidence for the truth of each conditional premise, as in the case of any deductive argument. If any one of the conditional premises in the chain turns out to be false or highly dubious, the chain argument collapses, and the argument fails because all its premises are not true.

Schematizing the preceding argument makes clear how much has to be assumed to be true if we are to reach even the conditional conclusion, and reveals why we rightly tend to be leery of such arguments. For instance, there is enough evidence for the first two premises for them to be credible, although one might doubt whether the amount of water on Mars is sufficient to sustain life forms. But the last three conditional premises, especially the next to last, are highly dubious. Thus, even though the argument has a valid logical form, the limited credibility of so many of its premises makes the argument unsound.

The longer the chain of premises in a conditional chain argument, the more premises there are whose truth claims are required to be believable. A chain argument is rightly viewed with skepticism when it contains even one dubious premise, for the weakness of that premise tends to undermine the succeeding conditional premises and to neutralize the preceding ones. An argument containing more than one dubious premise may be dismissed, for the defect of each doubtful premise is magnified by the piling of dubious hypotheses one upon the other. If we wish to draw a conclusion consisting of the consequent statement of the last premise—to infer simply, "It is worthwhile to send a manned mission to Mars," for example, in the preceding argument—we would have to assume the truth of a vast array of premises. We would have to know not only that all the conditional premises were true, but also that each antecedent of each separate conditional premise was true.

A conditional chain argument which is not deductively valid does not usually merit serious consideration. It is, however, often worth the effort to see whether one can obtain a deductively valid argument by modifying some premise or even the conclusion. And in the case of a deductively valid argument with an unsound premise, one should attempt to produce a more plausible premise to see whether the argument can be reconstructed and still retain its deductive validity. Suppose we altered the highly dubious penultimate premise of our illustration to read, "If there is oil on Mars, there may be little or a large quantity." This is a stronger, more believable premise than "If there is oil on Mars, it may be fairly abundant." However, with this more believable premise, the argument is no longer deductively valid; its consequent is a disjunction, "Either there is a little oil on Mars or a large quantity." This disjunction is a very different statement from the antecedent of the succeeding conditional premise, "If there is a large quantify of oil on Mars, it is worthwhile to send a manned mission to Mars for oil exploration." In order to keep the argument's deductive validity, we would have to change the antecedent of this premise to the same disjunction as the preceding consequent: "If there is a little oil or a large quantity of oil on Mars, it is worthwhile to send a manned mission to Mars for oil exploration." However, this conditional premise is much less plausible than the original one, so that although the deductive validity of the argument is restored, the weakness of the new premise again shows the lack of soundness in the whole argument. Occasionally, however, this technique will show that an argument only needs to be more carefully phrased to be deductively valid. In other cases one discovers that the premise needed for a deductively valid argument is less believable than that actually offered, and one thereby uncovers the loophole covered by the original set of premises.

A conditional chain argument is not *sound*—worthy of belief—when it contains one or more dubious conditional premises, even if it is deductively valid. For a conditional chain argument to be sound it must be both deductively valid and all its premises must be true or highly probable.

EXERCISE 7G

Analyze the logical form of the following chain arguments to determine whether they are deductively valid. How may the premises of the invalid arguments be changed to obtain a valid argument? Review the plausibility of each premise to assess the soundness of each deductively valid argument.

1. If an oil shortage threatens, larger cars will not sell. If so, the market for smaller cars will improve. Thus the market for smaller cars will be favorable only if the threat of an oil shortage continues.

2. If quasars, very bright points of light seen through the largest telescopes since 1963, are one-half billion or more light years away, as indicated by their red shifted light, then a single quasar puts out as much light as 100 billion suns. If it burns at such a tremendous rate, it would burn itself out in about 100 million years. But if a quasar's life span is only about 100 million years, it would have ceased to exist by the time its light reaches earth at least one-half billion years later. So the quasars presently observed by astronomers no longer exist.

3. If banks give interest on checking account balances, customers will leave more money in them. If so, bank customers will put less money into long-term bank notes. If that happens, there is an increased likelihood of bank failures. Thus, if banks are permitted to give interest on checking balances, bank failures are more likely.

4. If consumers believe inflation will continue, they make major purchases immediately to beat the price rise. In doing so they increase consumer demand. As consumer demand grows, prices go ever higher. So the inflation rate will soar upward unless steps are taken to give consumers confidence that inflation will not continue at a high rate.

7H   COMPLEX TRUTH-FUNCTIONAL INFERENCE

By combining several premises consisting of various kinds of truth-functions containing some of the same component statements, one can generate longer and more complicated deductive arguments. Suppose an argument consists of the following premises: "If P then $(R$ and $S)$"—a conditional; "P Or Not-Q"—a disjunction; and Q the simple component statement. From these premises we can easily infer the conclusion, R, by an argument combining different rules of valid truth-functional inference. By disjunctive argument we can combine the premise, "P Or Not-Q," with Q to conclude P. Then we can use this conclusion with the conditional premise, "If P then $(R$ And $S)$," to obtain the conjunction, "R And S," by the valid conditional argument, affirming the antecedent. From "R And S" we infer R by conjunctive argument. We may represent this series of truth-functional inferences schematically as follows:

1. If P then $(R$ And $S)$ Conditional premise
2. P Or Not-Q Disjunctive premise
3. Q Premise
4. P Disjunctive argument, premises 2 and 3
5. R And S Conditional argument, 4 and premise 1
6. R Conjunctive argument, 5

As long as each step in an argument is justified by a rule of valid truth-functional inference, the whole argument is deductively valid. Examples of valid rules of truth-functional inference are the three rules of conditional argument (affirming the antecedent, denying the consequent, and chain argument) and the rule of disjunctive argument. Also, any statement derived from a previous line of the argument by immediate inference (equivalence, implication, conjunctive inference). Thus in the preceding argument, line 6 is derived from line 5 by immediate inference. The contrapositive of line 1, "If Not $(R$ And $S)$ then Not-P" might have been inferred, if useful in the argument, by the principle of equivalence.

Furthermore, one may infer any statement implied by a premise or previously derived statement of an argument. If, for example, the statement S occurs as a line in the argument, the disjunction, "S Or T", whose truth follows from S, may be derived from it; for "S or T" will necessarily be true, whatever T stands for, because S is true, and a disjunction is true whenever just one of its components is true. Similarly, given that P is true, the conditional "If Q then P" is also true, whatever Q may be. If this seems strange, recollect that the flat assertion that P is true is a stronger claim than the merely hypothetical claim made by "If Q then P." Similarly, the conjunction "R And S" implies the disjunction "R Or S."

In any truth-functional argument, one may also add as needed any truth-functional tautology, that is, a truth-functional statement which is necessarily true because of its logical form, independent of its subject matter. The following three tautologies express the three laws of thought, applied to truth-functional statements:

1. law of identity: If P then P.
2. law of excluded middle: P Or Not-P
3. law of noncontradiction: Not $(P$ And Not-$P)$.

Arguments combining various kinds of truth-functional inferences are common in logic and mathematics, and basic to the techniques of computer programming. There they are often combined with more advanced logical principles of inference which enable one to symbolize a larger variety of statements. Working out problems in truth-functional logic is an excellent way to familiarize oneself with the logic of truth-functional statements, as they demonstrate the exact claims made by each kind of truth-function and their implications when in conjunction with other statements. Doing such problems will help the student to become more precise in expressing facts in an unambiguous way, and in correctly interpreting the claims made by statements that exhibit the logical form of truth-functions.

Dilemmas

A special kind of truth-functional argument that involves a particular combination of conditional and disjunctive premises is the *dilemma*. Since dilemmas are a kind of argument used in everyday reasoning, we shall take special note of how to assess this logical form of argument. In a dilemma there are typically two conditional premises and a third premise which is a disjunction, one which affirms or denies the antecedents or consequents of the conditional premises. The conclusion either affirms or denies the other two components of the conditional premises in a disjunction.

Here is an example of a dilemma:

If President Carter insists on a human rights policy, he offends the Russians; but if he abandons it, he will offend his own American people. Since Carter must either carry through or abandon human rights as an issue, he must either offend the Russians or his own people.

The nature of a dilemma is that regardless of what happens or fails to happen, what is done or fails to be done, equally unacceptable or unfavorable consequences follow. The situation is, it is claimed, a "no-win" situation. In assessing a dilemma, two quite different sorts of considerations must be kept in mind. First we must ask whether the dilemma is a valid deductive argument—whether the conclusion follows necessarily from the stated premises. A valid dilemma follows the pattern for a valid conditional argument: The disjunctive premise either affirms the antecedents or denies the consequents of the two conditional premises. An invalid dilemma follows the pattern of an invalid conditional argument: Its disjunctive premise either affirms the two consequents or negates the two antecedents of the conditional premises. The dilemma cited is an example of a valid dilemma that follows the pattern of affirming the antecedent, as can readily be seen:

P—Carter insists on human rights Q—Carter abandons human rights
R—Carter offends Russians S—Carter offends Americans

If P then R	Conditional premise 1
If Q then S	Conditional premise 2
P Or Q	Disjunctive premise affirming antecedents of 1 and 2
R Or S	Conclusion affirms disjunction of consequents of 1 and 2: VALID DILEMMA

The second type of valid dilemma follows the pattern of denying the consequent, and thus has this form:

If *P* then *R*	Conditional premise 1
If *Q* then *S*	Conditional premise 2
Not-*R* Or Not-*S*	Disjunction of negations of consequents of 1 and 2
Not-*P* Or Not-*Q*	Conclusion is disjunction of negation of antecedents of 1 and 2: VALID DILEMMA

Curiously enough, one can challenge a valid dilemma of one kind by constructing a valid dilemma whose conditional premises point out favorable rather than unfavorable consequences. We could respond to the dilemma with another, as follows:

If Carter insists on human rights, he pleases Americans.
If Carter abandons human rights, he pleases Russians.
Either Carter insists on or abandons human rights.

Either Carter pleases Americans or pleases Russians.

However, an answering dilemma of the following kind is fallacious, committing the error of denying the antecedents:

If Carter insists on human rights, he offends the Russians.
If Carter abandons human rights, he offends Americans.
Either Carter does not insist on human rights or does not abandon the issue.

Either Carter does not offend Russians or does not offend Americans.

The two kinds of *invalid dilemmas* have the following forms:

INVALID: FALLACY OF DENYING ANTECEDENTS	INVALID: FALLACY OF AFFIRMING CONSEQUENTS
If *P* then *R*	If *P* then *R*
If *Q* then *S*	If *Q* then *S*
Not-*P* Or Not-*Q*	*R* Or *S*
Not-*R* Or Not-*S*	*P* Or *Q*

A dilemma having a logical form that is invalid, such as one of the two preceding, may be rejected on grounds of its deductive invalidity. However, since it is often possible to construct an opposing dilemma even for one which is deductively valid, it is obvious that rules of deductive reasoning alone will not enable us to deal with dilemmatic reasoning. Thus a second step in assessing a dilemma is to see whether it can be turned around, in the preceding manner. If so, one is in a position to balance the favorable consequences against the unfavorable ones. In so doing, we are no longer engaging in deductive reasoning, for each argument is deductively valid on its own, but are comparing the favorable consequences pointed out by one conclusion with the unfavorable ones expressed by the conclusion of the opposite dilemma. Such a comparative estimate involves us in a type of nondeductive reasoning whose rules we consider in a subsequent chapter.

A dilemma, although deductively valid in its logical form, may be unsound because its premises fail to be true, just like any deductive argument. In the case of a dilemma, common sense suggests that we review the credibility of the premises by asking whether they represent a correct reading of the situation. Is there a third alternative or a way of proceeding other than that mentioned in the premises? Finding some plausible alternative other than those mentioned is called *slipping between the horns of the dilemma*—the horns being the two mentioned unacceptable consequences. Thus the dilemma, even when deductively valid, may involve unsound reasoning because its premises neglect to mention a possible resolution of the problem it poses. For example, the President may find a way to handle the human rights issue without offending anyone—say, by dealing with it through private diplomatic channels rather than through public confrontation.

EXERCISE 7H

1. Construct a valid truth-functional argument from the premises written above the line to the conclusion written below the line. Indicate the rule of truth-functional inference which justifies each step of your argument.

a. If R then Not-S
 S Or Q
 Not-Q
 _____
 Not-R

b. P And T
 If T then S
 _____
 S

c. If S then R
 If T then S
 Q Or Not-R
 Not-Q
 _____
 Not-T

d. If $(R$ Or $S)$ then P
 If Not-R then S
 Not-S
 _____
 P

2. Are the following dilemmas deductively valid? Is there some way of slipping between the horns of the dilemma?

a. If a woman is to have sexual intercourse without becoming pregnant, she must use a contraceptive or take the pill. But using devices spoils the spontaneity of sex and the pill has possibly

serious side effects. It's clear nature has doomed the female sex—
women can't enjoy sex with safety and peace of mind.

b. The government can't keep down inflation and also unemployment. If there is inflation, the hardworking taxpayer is robbed of
real income by higher prices; but if unemployment is high, young
people who can't find work will resort to crime. Either way, the
hardworking taxpayer is robbed.

71   NECESSARY AND SUFFICIENT CONDITIONS

Truth-functions are useful in other ways than in argument: They enable us
to specify important connections between things in an unequivocal way.
One function served by the conditional statement is that of saying that one
thing is a necessary condition for something else. To do this, we ordinarily
use the form of sentence "*P* only if *Q*" and "Not-*P* unless *Q*," in which the
fact expressed by component statement Q represents the necessary condition. According to our rules, in sentences of this kind the statement
Q always goes into the consequent of the standard conditional of the form
"If *P* then *Q*." Thus the fact that one thing, *Q*, is a necessary condition for
something else, *P*, may be expressed by sentences of this form:

P only if *Q*; Not-*P* unless *Q*; If *P* then *Q*.

Thus if the electric company sends a notice saying, "You will not
receive electrical service after the 25th of August unless your bill is paid in
full by the 15th of August" or "You will continue to receive electrical service
after the 25th of August only if your bill is paid in full by August 15th," they
are telling you that paying your bill in full by August 15th is a necessary
condition for having electrical service after the 25th of August. This fact
and its consequence are indicated in the conditional,

If you receive electrical service after August 25th, then your bill has
been paid in full by August 15th;

as well as by the contrapositive equivalent:

If you do not pay your bill in full by August 15th, then you will not have
electrical service after August 25th.

It is useful to distinguish the case of one thing being a *necessary
condition* for another from that of one thing being a *sufficient condition* for
another. The latter case is expressed by the fact that is reported in the

antecedent of a standard conditional and in sentences like "*Q* if *P*," "*Q* provided *P*," "If *P* then *Q*." Suppose someone says, "If I win the lottery, I will buy a new car." Here the fact in the antecedent, "I win the lottery," indicates *one* circumstance in which the fact named in the consequent, "I will buy a new car," will also occur. The conditional, "If I win the lottery, I will buy a new car," does not say that winning the lottery is a necessary condition for buying a new car, but rather that buying a new car is a necessary condition of the truth that one has won the lottery. The truth of "If I win the lottery, I will buy a new car" is consistent with "If I earn enough money this summer, I will buy a new car" and "If I can swing a bank loan, I will buy a new car this summer." In each of these cases, the fact named in the antecedent of the conditional indicates one circumstance—a sufficient condition for the fact named in the consequent of the conditional. Being a sufficient condition must not be confused with being the *only* condition for something else's being true. There may be a number of sufficient conditions for the same thing, no one of which is also a necessary condition.

In general, then, the fact named in the antecedent of a conditional statement is a sufficient condition for the fact named in its consequent; and the fact named in the consequent of the conditional is asserted by the conditional to be a necessary condition for the fact named by its antecedent. If these conditions do not hold, the conditional is false. For example, the statement, "If you are dreaming you are asleep," is a true conditional statement. Being asleep is a necessary condition for having a dream and the fact that someone is dreaming is in and of itself evidence that he is asleep; that is, its being true that one is dreaming is a sufficient condition for its being true that one is asleep. On the other hand, "If you're asleep, you are dreaming" is not a true conditional, for one can be in a state of sleep without being in a dreaming state. Dreaming is not a necessary condition for being asleep, nor is being asleep a sufficient condition for dreaming.

A thing may be a *necessary* condition for something else without being a *sufficient* condition for it. For example, having gas in a car is a necessary condition for the car's running, but it is not a sufficient condition for the car's running. Although a car won't run without gas, it may have gas and still not run. Thus the conditional, "If a car is running, it has gas in its tank," is true: Having gas in its tank is a necessary condition of a car's running and the fact that a car is running is a sufficient condition of its being true that the car has gas. On the other hand, the conditional, "If a car has gas in its tank, it is running," is false: Having gas in its tank is a necessary condition for a car's running, but it is not a sufficient condition, as we all know.

Occasionally it is the case that the same thing is both a necessary and sufficient condition for some other thing. For example, being born is both a necessary and sufficient condition for dying: You can't die unless you were born, and if you were born, you will die. Thus, to say that a thing *P* is both a necessary and sufficient condition of another thing Q, we must assert two conditionals, "If P then Q" and its converse "If Q then P." The conditional "If P then Q" says that P is a sufficient condition for Q, and the conditional "If Q then P" says that P is a necessary condition for Q. The conjunction of two converse conditionals is called the *biconditional* and is expressed in words as "P if and only if Q." If one wishes to say that a thing P is both a necessary and sufficient condition for another thing Q, one needs to use a biconditional form of words, "P if and only if Q." To tell whether one thing is both a necessary and sufficient condition for some other thing, we must seek evidence that both the conditional, "If P then Q," and its converse, "If Q then P," are true.

Note that it is possible for a thing P to be a necessary condition for another thing Q without its being a sufficient condition for Q; and for a thing P to be a sufficient condition for Q without being a necessary condition for Q; and for one thing P to be both a necessary and a sufficient condition for Q. Logic does not usually tell us which is the case. We need evidence outside of logic to determine whether one thing is a necessary or sufficient condition of another thing, both things, or neither. What logic can do is tell us how to express the facts properly in a conditional statement of the correct form, and help us to understand sentences expressing such connections of fact.

Truth-Functional Equivalences

Another application of truth-functional logic in everyday reasoning is based on the equivalence relationships between various kinds of truth-functions. Many statements in legislation, regulations, warranties, instructions, and explanations contain truth-functional connectives such as *if, or, only if, unless*. Some familiarity with the relationships of equivalence and implication that hold between truth-functional statements of various kinds can illuminate the meaning of these statements. We have already considered a number of equivalence relationships in connection with the various forms of truth-functional argument. For example, in the case of disjunctions and conjunctions, statements containing the same components but in a different order are equivalent to each other. Any conditional statement is equivalent to its contrapositive, that is, a conditional in which the component statements are both negated and switched in position. We shall add to these two further principles of equivalence.

1. Any statement is equivalent to the negation of its own negation. It is obvious that "Not (Not-P)" is equivalent to P. But the rule also applies to disjunctions whose negations are conjunctions: Thus "P Or Q" is equivalent to "Not (Not-P And Not-Q)." Similarly, the negation of a conjunction, "P And Q," is a disjunction whose components are the negations of the conjunction's component statements: Thus "Not (Not-P Or Not-Q)" is equivalent to "P And Q." The negation of a conditional, "If P then Q," is a conjunction whose components are the antecedent of the conditional and the negation of the consequent of the conditional, that is, "P And Not-Q." Thus the negation of "If the sun shines, we go on a picnic" is "The sun is shining, but we are not going on a picnic." And then the negation of that conjunction is the equivalent of the conditional; that is, "If P then Q" is equivalent to "Not (P And Not-Q)." By applying this rule (that a statement is equivalent to the negation of its negation) to truth-functions whose negations are truth-functions of another type, we can generate a large number of equivalences whose variety makes explicit the truth claims of each truth-function.

2. Each type of truth-function has some equivalent in some other kind of truth-function. Every disjunction has two conditional equivalents. "Either P is true or Q is true" clearly says "If P is not true, then Q is true" and also "If Q is false, then P is true." In general, any disjunction is equivalent to a conditional whose antecedent is the negation of one component of the disjunction and whose consequent is the other component of the disjunction. Thus "P Or Q" is equivalent to "If Not-P then Q" and also to "If Not-Q then P." For example, "Either I go to the movies or read a book tonight" is equivalent to "If I don't go to the movies, then I will read a book tonight" and to "If I don't read a book tonight, then I'll go to the movies."

Every conditional statement has an equivalent disjunction. The conditional statement, "If P then Q," claims that either its consequent is true or its antecedent is false. Thus "If P then Q" is equivalent to "Either Q Or Not-P." For example, the conditional, "If the sun shines, we go on a picnic," is equivalent to "Either the sun is not shining or we are going on a picnic." A conditional statement is equivalent to a disjunction in which one component is the consequent of the conditional, and the other component is the negation of the antecedent of the conditional.

In obtaining equivalents for truth-functions, it is important to follow the rules exactly. In particular one must be consistent in handling negations of component statements and in not confusing the antecedent and consequent in conditional statements. According to the rule just mentioned, what is the disjunctive equivalent of "If Not-Q then R"? Is it "Q or R;" "Not-Q Or R;" "Q Or Not-R," or "Not-Q Or Not-R"? These are four different statements making four different truth claims. The rule states that the disjunction contains the negation of the antecedent. In this case the antecedent is already a negation, "Not-Q," so its negation will be Q; the other component of the disjunction is the consequent of the conditional, in this case, R. Putting the two components in a disjunction, we obtain "Q Or R" as the disjunctive equivalent of the conditional, "If Not-Q then R." Is "R Or Q" a correct answer? Yes, for the order of the components in a disjunction or a conjunction does not change its truth-values. In other words, "*R* Or *Q*" is equivalent to "*Q* Or *R*," just as "*Q* And *R*" is equivalent to "*R* And *Q*."

Some of the cumbersome statements which occur in contemporary legislation and in regulations relating to social policy and economic arrangements, can be disentangled by applying truth-functional principles. For example, suppose a regulation reads, "You are eligible for an additional $600 exemption on your income tax only if you are blind and are either over 65 or earn less than $20,000 a year." Applying truth-functional principles, we first translate the whole sentence into its basic conditional form, as indicated by *only if,* and work out the constituent statements of the consequent, separating various components by parentheses and brackets:

> If you are eligible for an additional $600 exemption on your income tax, then (you are blind And [either you are over 65 or earn less than $20,000 a year]).

A necessary condition for being eligible for an additional $600 exemption on income tax is stated by this complicated consequent. The consequent is a conjunction which has two components, one of them the simple statement, "you are blind." Thus to be eligible for this additional exemption, a person must be blind, for a conjunction is only true if both its components are true, and "you are blind" is one of them. The other component of the conjunction is a disjunction, "either you are over 65 or you earn less than $20,000 a year." Since a disjunction is true whenever any one of its components is true, in addition to being blind one must be over 65 or earn less than $20,000 a year. One does not need to be all three, but being blind alone is not enough; one must be blind and over 65 years of age or blind and earning less than $20,000 a year.

In working out the meaning of complicated sentences with truth-functional connectives, it is often useful to translate them into their equivalents: Put a disjunction into its equivalent conditionals, unpack the meaning of a conditional by reviewing its contrapositive or disjunctive equivalents, work out the exact truth claims of negations. The same rules are relevant whenever one needs to state one's views in a clear and unambiguous fashion to others.

EXERCISE 7I

1. Say whether each thing listed on the left is a necessary condition, sufficient condition, or neither of the thing listed on its right. Express each fact in a conditional.

    a. talking—breathing
    b. having an abortion—pregnancy
    c. being born in the United States—being a citizen of the United
        States
    d. being a teacher—having an advanced degree
    e. being married—being divorced

2. Which lettered statement is equivalent to or implied by the following:
    You may take Sociology 233 provided you have already taken and
    passed Statistics 100 or are taking Statistics 100 or have passed a
    qualifying examination in statistics.

    a. You may not take Sociology 233 if you have not passed a quali-
        fying exam in statistics.
    b. If you are taking Statistics 100 you may take Sociology 233.
    c. You may not take Sociology 233 unless you have already taken
        and passed Statistics 100.
    d. If you may not take Sociology 233 then you have neither passed a
        qualifying exam in statistics nor are you taking or have taken and
        passed Statistics 100.
    e. Only if you have taken Statistics 100 may you take Sociology 233.
    f. If you have taken and passed Statistics 100 you may take Soci-
        ology 233.

3. Express in truth-functions the New York Police Department policy on
    complaints of wife-beating:

        At least one officer must respond to every report of a wife-beating
    or threatened wife-beating, and a husband must be arrested for assault
    if there is reason to believe a crime has been committed, unless there is
    justification not to do so.

Review Exercise for Chapter 7

Which arguments are valid? Which are sound?

1. If the government does not institute comprehensive medical care, it
    will displease the unions. But the government can institute such care
    only if it raises taxes. If it does that, it may touch off a tax revolt. Thus
    the government must either forego comprehensive medical care or face
    a taxpayer revolt.
2. If the government takes measures to reduce unemployment, it will
    increase inflation. But if it does not take measures to reduce unem-
    ployment, it will lose the support of the black minority. Yet if inflation
    is not checked, the President will lose the confidence of the working

middle class. The President cannot be reelected without the support of the black minority and the working middle class. Therefore, the President will not be reelected.

3. Periodically suggestions are made to amend the rules for election to the presidency so as to make a majority of the total national popular vote a necessary and sufficient condition for election. If so, winning by a large plurality in the most populous states in the far east and far west will become a sufficient condition for election, and candidates will be tempted to appeal primarily to these voters. Consequently the President will not represent the interests of the whole country.

chapter 8

Inductive Reasoning

8A INDUCTIVE AND DEDUCTIVE REASONING COMPARED

Through deductive reasoning we are able to discover new truths implied by statements we already know to be true by applying rules of inference that are necessarily true. We can verify for ourselves that a statement is necessarily true by using our logical powers of reasoning. However, the greater part of the statements of concern to us in ordinary reasoning are neither necessary statements nor derivable from statements we have already found to be true by applying deductive rules of inference. For them we require evidence we can obtain only by observing the world, and by making use of the observations of others and of scientific instruments which expand human powers of perception.

The principles of inductive reasoning enable us to formulate arguments whose premises are such observations and whose conclusions are inferences about the existence or character of entities and events not included in the original observations. The conclusion of an inductive argument thus makes a claim that goes beyond the evidence provided by its premises; this very claim may often be confirmed or falsified by further observations other than those contained in its premises. This feature of inductive reasoning marks an important difference from deductive reasoning, one which makes its principles less foolproof, a matter of judgment as well as technical expertise. But inductive reasoning is indispensable and inescapable for many of life's purposes, and cannot be replaced by any form of valid deductive reasoning. It enables us to hypothesize about what may well happen before it does happen, permitting us to take steps to insure or avoid the occurrence of predictable events. Even when we lack the power to affect the course of events, our knowledge of its probable course enables us to adjust our plans and expectations accordingly. If our lives are not made better for such knowledge, at least our minds are more free than they were in a state of ignorance. It is extremely important to know how to draw conclusions by inductive reasoning and to assess those drawn by others.

Let us take a somewhat trivial example to illustrate the differences between inductive reasoning and the deductive reasoning we have been studying so far. Suppose a person wonders what his or her offspring may be like. There is a good deal of human experience drawn from past observation on this subject, as well as extensively developed theories that tell us how features of offspring correlate with those possessed by their parents, their parents' siblings, and their ancestors. There is considerable evidence, for example, that people who are brown-eyed have brown-eyed offspring, and there are theories of heredity to explain these observations. Putting this evidence together, we can make the generalization that in all probability all children of this brown-eyed person will be brown-eyed. We can easily put this argument in deductive form:

Brown-eyed people have brown-eyed children.
This person is brown-eyed.
_____

Therefore, all the children of this person will be brown-eyed.

However, any alert student will realize the premises of this argument will not produce a valid inference. The evidence drawn from observation does not justify our translating the first premise into "All brown-eyed people have brown-eyed children," for there do exist cases of brown-eyed parents having children whose eyes are blue or grey or black rather than brown. The premise must be rendered as "Most brown-eyed persons have brown-eyed children," and then the two premises will not guarantee the truth of the conclusion, since it does not follow necessarily from them.

The argument is, however, a sound *inductive* argument. For the conclusion makes a prediction about the characteristic of particular beings (the eye color of an individual's offspring) which can be confirmed or proved false by further observations (by what happens or fails to happen when the children are born). The conclusion relies on past observations of overwhelming correlations between brown-eyedness in parents and offspring. Genetic theory has also explained these empirical findings:

It has proven the existence of genes which control such physical characteristics as eye color and shown that brown eye color tends to be a dominant trait, whereas blue eye color is recessive. The conclusion that all the children born to this brown-eyed person will be brown-eyed is well supported by data from past observation and by theory relating to inheritable traits. Thus the argument is a sound inductive argument, although it does not qualify as a valid deductive argument.

Let us analyze the features of this argument that illustrate how inductive arguments differ from deductive arguments:

1. The conclusion of the argument goes beyond the evidence of the premises. It asserts something about things not mentioned in the premises, whereas the premises merely record the observation that many human generations of brown-eyed persons have regularly had brown-eyed offspring. But in a valid deductive argument, as we recall from diagramming, the content of the conclusion is already implicit in the premise or the combination of premises and never goes beyond them.

2. Since the conclusion goes beyond what is already asserted in the premises, the truth of the premises does not guarantee the truth of the conclusion (as in a valid deductive argument); rather it makes the conclusion *probable*. There is no *necessary* connection between the truth of the premises and the truth of the conclusion of a sound inductive argument. In any inductive argument, sound as well as unsound, it is possible for the premises to be true, whereas the conclusion may turn out to be false. For this reason, we speak of the conclusion as having some degree of *probability* relative to its premises rather than as following necessarily from them: The better the inductive argument, the higher the degree of probability (approaching virtual certainty). However, even in a sound argument such as our example, the conclusion is probable rather than necessary or certain: One of this brown-eyed person's children may turn out to have blue eyes rather than brown eyes, thus disproving the conclusion that all this person's offspring will be brown-eyed. Nevertheless the original argument is a sound inductive argument. Given the preponderance of evidence that brown-eyedness is generally inherited, we are justified in drawing the preceding conclusion.

Neither is it the case that the truth of the conclusion establishes the soundness of an inductive inference. Let us suppose it has been predicted that a particular person will take a long trip, on evidence based on this person's horoscope and the observation of astronomical events. The fact that the person subsequently does take a long trip, verifying the prediction, does not vindicate the reasoning process, which remains subject to many criticisms relating to the shakiness of correlations between events in individual lives and astronomical events.

3. In inductive reasoning, the degree of probability of a given conclusion is always relative to the evidence presented and may well change as new premises are added. Suppose we add to our evidence for brown-eyed offspring these additional observations: That this person has a number of blue-eyed and blond relatives and that this person's spouse also has a number of blue-eyed relatives. Now we know that the combined gene pools of the prospective parents contain blue-eyedness as a recessive character. These facts make it less likely that all the children of these two parents will be brown-eyed, and make it more probable that one or more might be blue-eyed. In the light of this evidence the conclusion that all the children of this pair will be brown-eyed is less probable. Theoretically speaking, we can keep adding indefinitely to the evidence that is relevant to the conclusion and thus materially change the degree of probability of the conclusion and the soundness of the argument. Practically, it is often possible to envisage available evidence that might significantly alter the soundness of the inference.

In deductive reasoning the situation is different. If the argument is a valid one and the premises true, no additional premises will affect the argument so as to make it invalid as it stands. On occasion we may be expected to supply unstated, obviously true premises which are required if the argument is to be valid, but we need go no further than this in assessing the validity of a piece of reasoning. However, in inductive reasoning it is seldom possible to assert that a given set of premises suffices to establish a conclusion beyond the shadow of reasonable doubt; part of assessing the argument itself is considering whether available evidence that would affect the soundness of the inference has been omitted from the stated premises. In examining an inductive argument our attention cannot be confined to the stated premises but must include all the knowledge available to us concerning the subject matter of the argument. To handle inductive arguments effectively one must have a broad fund of knowledge and, in many cases, detailed knowledge of the subject. The rules of inductive reasoning cannot provide this knowledge of the subject matter, but can make one aware of what kind of knowledge is relevant and point out how to utilize it effectively.

4. In inductive reasoning a subjective factor is sometimes present in the degree of probability assigned to a given conclusion by different reasoners examining the same evidence, as well as in the exact content of the conclusion drawn. One of two reasoners may think the evidence suffices to draw a conclusion, whereas another may think it deficient or likely to be reversed by additional evidence. In such cases, it is often the systems of belief, the interests, or the attitudes of the two reasoners which lead them to weigh the evidence differently or to find different considerations to be relevant to the issue. A government scientist, alert to public health dangers, might be ready to conclude that swine flu inoculations have not been factors in the subsequent deaths of aged persons receiving them, whereas a private physician or senior citizen might be more skeptical. Thus we need to recognize the possibility of subjective bias (perhaps quite unconscious) on the part of a reasoner when he or she is assessing the soundness of an inductive argument. This is especially important when the conclusion is about human affairs and is used to justify some policy or course of action. In deductive reasoning, the failure of two reasoners to agree on the validity of an argument usually involves a mistake on the part of one of the reasoners or some serious ambiguity in the statements of the argument. Whether the stated premises in deductive reasoning do or do not imply a specific conclusion is unequivocally settled by reference to rules of inference based wholly on the logical form of the statements independent of their subject matter, as we have seen in the last two chapters.

Let us briefly recapitulate the characteristics of inductive reasoning which distinguish it from deductive reasoning: The conclusion of an inductive argument follows from its premises with varying degrees of probability; the conclusion of a deductive argument either follows necessarily from the logical form of its premises, in which case the argument is valid, or it does not follow, and the argument is invalid. These are the only two possibilities in deductive reasoning: The argument works—the logical form of the premise statements implies the conclusion in accordance with some valid rule of inference—or the argument does not work at all and is invalid.

But in inductive reasoning we are always directly concerned with the subject matter of the statements, not just with their logical form. We project a factual claim that goes beyond the evidence provided by the given set of premises, and there is an unavoidable gap between what the premises assert and the claim of the conclusion. Some logicians speak of an inductive "leap" which occurs in going from premises to conclusion in inductive reasoning. In deductive reasoning, on the contrary, the steps are bridged by rules of inference which afford safe passage from premises to conclusion.

However, we do have principles of inductive reasoning which enable us to estimate successfully how big or how dangerous a leap will be from the premises to the conclusion of an inductive argument. We commonly use comparative terms such as *highly probable, unlikely,* and *somewhat improbable* to describe the soundness of an argument, not absolute terms such as *valid* and *invalid.* This difference does not reflect a superiority of deductive reasoning over inductive reasoning; the very premises of the former must often be established by the latter, and some things that can be proved by inductive reasoning cannot be proved by deductive reasoning alone.

EXERCISE 8A

Analyze the relation of the conclusion to the premises to determine whether each argument is deductive or inductive.

1. This man cannot be my first cousin: My mother is an only child and my father had just one brother, who died at six.
2. Most of the puppies in my dog's previous litters were pure white. So I expect to have all white puppies from this next litter.
3. All intentional killings of a human being are wrong. Since abortion involves the intentional killing of a human being, abortion is wrong.
4. All the children in the Jones family are blue-eyed and good-looking. Their parents must be blue-eyed and good-looking too.
5. According to my horoscope, persons born in Sagittarius are not good marriage partners for me. This blind date of mine says he was born in Sagittarius, so he is not a good marriage prospect.
6. All the times that I have won the lottery there has been a full moon. There is going to be a full moon next Saturday and so I shall not fail to buy a lottery ticket—my chances of winning are very good.

8B INDUCTIVE GENERALIZATION
AND INDUCTIVE FALLACIES

There are various types of inductive reasoning. The first two we will consider are distinguished by the logical character of their conclusions. In a previous chapter we distinguished *generalizations,* statements about a whole class of things, from *singular* statements, statements about identifiable individuals or sets of individuals. An important use of inductive reasoning is to help us arrive at generalizations about a class of things of a certain type, based on the observation of a limited number of things of that type. Usually we cannot observe every member of a class, but even when we can it is often too troublesome to be worth the effort.

The following generalization has fairly recently been formulated by biological investigations: "All female organisms have a matching set of two XX chromosomes." An older generalization is familiar to many generations of chemistry students: "All acids turn blue litmus paper red." The inductive reasoning which establishes such generalizations is called *universal generalization,* because its quantifier indicates a claim about every member of the group that is its subject term. This kind of reasoning may be schematized as follows:

UNIVERSAL GENERALIZATION

Instances *a, b, c . . . n* possessing property *S* are also observed to possess property *P.*

Nothing has been observed to possess property *S* which does not have property *P.*

Therefore, it is probable that all *S* are *P.*

The second type of premise, "Nothing has been observed to be *S* without also being *P,*" is important in a universal generalization. A universal generalization makes a very extensive claim, applying to all instances of the class, past, present, and future. It covers much more than the instances observed in the past—it also covers unobserved instances in the past as well as unobserved and perhaps unobservable instances in the present and future. Thus we must not only show that all the instances of *S* which have come to our notice have possessed the property *P,* but also include the evidence that no *counterinstances* of *S* which are *not-P* have been observed. The class which is the subject of the universal generalization, *S,* is called the *target population*—it is the class at which our reasoning aims in drawing some conclusion. Of the generalizations just mentioned, *female organisms* names one target population, and *acids* the other. The property *P* attributed to this target population in the conclusion is called the *projected property.* In our two examples, the projected property of the first is "possessing two matching sets of XX chromosomes," of the second, "turning blue litmus red."

Universal generalizations are extremely valuable in reasoning: They can be used as premises in syllogisms and other forms of deductive reasoning. Also, the projected property may be used as a criterion for the existence of a member of the target population and may even become its defining property, or part of it. However, good universal generalizations are hard to come by. We have already noted that even a well-supported generalization such as "Brown-eyed human parents tend to have brown-eyed offspring" does not qualify as a universal generalization because of the existence of counterinstances (children of brown-eyed parents who do not have brown eyes). Yet, even more limited generalizations are very useful. A generalization which asserts something about some proportion of the target population is often called a *statistical generalization.* Statistical generalizations may specify the proportion numerically (as 97 percent or 60 percent or 2 percent), but they may also include quantifiers such as *almost all, most, few,* and *an overwhelming number,* which are less definite.

Statistical generalizations must be schematized differently from universal generalizations. The second type of premise that is part of the evidence for a universal generalization need not occur, and the conclusion will not be universal in form.

STATISTICAL GENERALIZATION

A given proportion of instances of S are observed to be P.

Therefore, the same proportion of S are probably P.

We shall now list principles to apply to inductive generalizations of both kinds to determine how sound an argument is. However, these principles are *aids* to common sense, not *substitutes:* If they are applied mechanically they may override obvious facts about the target population or projected property, which affect the significance of the evidence. The principles tell us what kinds of things contribute to the soundness or weakness of inductive arguments *in general.* But knowledge of the subject matter is required in inductive arguments, and we must bring this knowledge to bear in applying inductive rules. It may happen that special facts about the subject matter of the argument indicate the need for a different assessment of the relevance of a bit of evidence. When such a situation arises, common sense takes precedence over a mechanical use of the rules that follow (the exercises will illustrate this fact).

We divide these principles into two groups: principles relating to the evidence presented and principles relating to the exact nature of the conclusion, in particular, to the target population and projected property designated.

The first set of considerations is designed to test the evidence, to see whether the observed instances mentioned in the premises represent a *fair sample* of the target population. We need to be sure that the properties possessed by the observed instances mirror those of the *whole* target population rather than those of some *subgroup.*

1. *The larger the number of observed instances of the target population, the more likely it is that their characteristics will mirror those of the entire target population.*

How large a number of observed instances is required for a sound inductive argument? A number of factors influence the size of the sample that is acceptable. The larger the size of the target population, the larger the sample that is desirable. A generalization concerning mammals needs to be based on a larger number of instances than one whose target population is white mice. The more variable the projected property is likely to be in the target population, the larger the size of the sample needed. Some physical properties and innate biological functions may reasonably be expected not to vary markedly in different members of a biological species, so fewer instances will do. However, the behavior of conscious beings and their mental attributes may vary considerably even among members of the same group. Reactions to drugs and responses to social factors also may differ widely.

A larger size sample is demanded in these cases because we have to be assured that the observed sample includes all the different factors that are at work in its target population. The group "American college students," for example, encompasses a large variety of subgroups: males; females; those who are wealthy, middle class, or poor; minorities; veterans; older women; recent high school graduates; and students at private, publicly supported, or church-related institutions. In cases where the target population is known not to include a large variety of subgroups, the size of the sample may decrease. Experiments on animals, for example, may produce reliable conclusions from a smaller sample. Sometimes a relatively small sample of a highly diversified target population may produce accurate results, provided the sample is carefully chosen to reflect the diversity of the target population. Predictions of the voting behavior of the American public based on responses of as few as 2,000 voters have been remarkably close.

2. The first rule relating to the *size* of the sample may be modified in view of the *character* of the sample. The more likely it is that the sample includes every kind of thing, or the major subgroups of the target population, the better chance it has of being a fair sample. Thus we must inspect the character of the observed instances as well as their number, to be sure that all the major relevant types in the target population are represented in the sample that is the evidence for the generalization. We approach the matter in two directions, observing both the extent to which the observed instances are *similar* to one another and the extent to which they *differ* from one another.

Of course all the observed instances are alike in that they all possess the property that defines the target population: If the target population is female humans then each of the observed instances is like every other in being a female human. But each female human will have many other additional characteristics: She will be white or black; married, divorced, or single; old, middle-aged, or young; and so on. It is essential to consider how much the observed instances resemble each other in these other characteristics. Suppose those in our sample of female humans also resemble each other in all being white and all being college graduates. Obviously they will not then be a fair sample of the whole variety of female humans, many of whom are not white or not college graduates. They might be a fair sample of only a subgroup of the target population, female white college graduates, but not of the whole class of female humans. The degree to which the observed instances of a target population are alike in additional characteristics is called the amount of *positive analogy among the observed instances*. The more the observed instances resemble each other in these additional characteristics, the less likely it is that they are a fair sample of the whole target population. Thus, our second rule: *The greater the positive analogy among the observed instances of a target population, the weaker is the argument.*

3. Correlatively, the less resemblance there is among the observed instances in their properties, other than that which defines them as members of the target population, the more likely it is that the observed instances do reflect all the different kinds included in the target population. The extent to which the observed members of the target population differ in these additional attributes is called the amount of *negative analogy among the observed instances*. For a target population of female humans, there would be a much higher degree of negative analogy if the observed set of instances included white women, black women, and oriental women; college graduates or high school graduates; single, married, and divorced women; women with children and women without; working women and housewives, than if it included only white women and college graduates of different ages. The set of observed instances with the higher degree of negative analogy is more likely to reflect the characteristics of the whole of the target population and thus be a fair sample of it. Our third rule: *The greater the degree of negative analogy among the observed instances, the sounder the inductive argument.*

The second type of consideration in assessing inductive arguments concerns the exact nature of the conclusion, which is inferred from the evidence about the observed instances.

4. The more vague and ill-defined the terms that describe the target population or the projected property attributed to the target population, the less reliable is the argument. In our two generalizations, "All female organisms possess a matching set of XX chromosomes" and "All acids turn blue litmus red," both the target populations and the projected properties are so well defined that we can readily decide which things are instances of them and which are not. But especially in generalizations concerning human traits and behavior, target population or projected property may be so loosely defined that it is not clear which things are true instances of them. The results of a poll of its readers by a popular woman's magazine were publicized as showing that a high proportion of "religious" women were "sexy." Yet one might well raise the question of what characteristics make a woman "religious," and thus a member of the target population, "religious women." Is it enough merely to indicate a definite religious affiliation? Attending church services with some degree of regularity? Affirming a belief in a divine being *without* any definite religious affiliation? Having a distinctive outlook on human life? Which women we would count as being "religious" might vary considerably depending on these various criteria, and this variation would bring the identity of the target population into question. As a consequence, any conclusion about what proportion of the target population does or does not possess some projected property will be in doubt.

A similar problem arises when the projected property is not defined well enough for us to be able to assert with confidence the presence of the property in a member of the target population. For example, what makes a woman "sexy"? Is it actually engaging in sex with a high degree of frequency with many different partners? Simply dressing and behaving in a sexually provocative fashion? Being thought by others to be physically attractive? Is the married woman who enjoys frequent intercourse with her husband but neither looks sexy nor behaves in a sexually provocative way an instance of a "sexy" woman? The principles of standard definition discussed in an earlier chapter may be applied in determining whether the target population and the projected property are sufficiently clear. Insofar as there may be reasonable doubt as to whether something is or is not an instance of a target population or whether an instance of the target population possesses the projected property, the significance of the findings themselves, as well as the very meaning of the conclusion drawn from them, are the subject of dispute. The fourth rule is: *The less well-defined the target population or projected property, the weaker the argument.*

5. The next rule is this: *The more sweeping the conclusion, the weaker is the argument relative to the evidence presented.* The more sweeping a conclusion, the greater the claim it makes about its subject matter, so that more of a leap is required to go from the premises to the conclusion. A universal generalization always makes a more sweeping claim than a statistical generalization about the same target population and projected property; a statistical generalization about a higher proportion of the target population is obviously more sweeping than one about a lower proportion. One can usually strengthen an argument by reducing one's claim about the proportion of things in the target population that are said to have the projected property or by naming a more restricted target population. The same evidence will support a weaker generalization more effectively than a more sweeping one.

In judging how extensive a claim is made by a conclusion, one must also take into account the nature of the property that defines the target population and the projected property attributed to the target population. Different properties may bring together a more or less extensive class of entities as the subject of the generalization, and, in consequence, widen or narrow the claim. The conclusion, "All female organisms have two matching XX chromosomes," is much more sweeping than one that says "All female humans have two matching XX chromosomes." The class of female organisms is much larger and contains many more types of things than that of female humans. Evidence that would support the former claim would need to be more extensive than for the latter; evidence that would suffice for a conclusion about female humans would be unconvincing for female organisms.

We must similarly analyze the nature of the projected property: The more precisely the projected property is specified, the more restricted is the evidence that can be found to support it. The property, "possessing a matching set of two XX chromosomes," is highly specific and only substantiated by a narrow range of phenomena. But the property, "having sex chromosomes," is much more generalized and thus capable of being substantiated by a much wider set of findings. Thus the more generalized the projected property, the weaker the claim made by the conclusion. Relative to the same evidence, the weaker the claim made by the conclusion—that is, the less sweeping the claim—the stronger the argument.

Students must take care not to confuse two very different things: the strength or weakness of the whole argument in the relationship between premises and conclusion, and the strength or weakness of the empirical claim made by the conclusion alone. The greater or more sweeping the claim made by the conclusion, the weaker will be the whole argument relative to the same premises. It is best not to use the term *strong inference* or *weak inference* at all: It is ambiguous, since the word *inference* may be used to mean the result of the inference, that is, the *conclusion*, as well as the *whole process* of going from premises to conclusion, which is the entire course of the argument. These two things vary inversely when we are comparing the extensiveness of the claim made by the conclusion alone and the riskiness of the leap from premises to conclusion. In other words, the "stronger" the claim made by the conclusion alone, the "weaker" the whole argument; and the "weaker" the claim made by the conclusion alone, the "stronger" the whole argument. We shall reserve the terms *more sweeping* and *less sweeping* for the strength of the conclusion, and use the terms more *sound* or less *reliable* for the strength of the whole argument. The student should always make clear whether he or she is referring to the strength or weakness of the claim made by the conclusion or by that of the whole argument.

In general, a conclusion that assigns a more generalized projected property to a more extensive target population is more easily confirmed by a greater range of evidence than a generalization that assigns a more specific projected property to a less extensive target population. The conclusion, "Americans are prone to violence," could be supported by data about television, sports, newspapers, and films as well as by crime statistics; whereas a statement such as "Many American white men killed their wives or girl friends in 1978" could appeal only to crime statistics of a limited kind. Relative to exactly the same evidence, changing a conclusion to make the target population less extensive or to make the projected property less specific will often generate an argument that is more sound. Although reducing the claim made by the conclusion will technically strengthen an inductive argument, it may also make it less significant. The conclusion that all females have matching XX chromosomes is an important, interesting one and leads to the further conclusion that the sex of offspring is effectively determined by the male parent. However, the more generalized conclusion, "All females have sex chromosomes," would not enable us to draw such an interesting conclusion. To reduce the claim made by the conclusion to the point where it no longer makes a claim worth considering may render the argument pointless.

6. Another thing to look for is the relationship of the projected property to the property defining the target population, given our present knowledge of the subject matter. The more likely it is that there is some causal relationship between the two properties, the more credible the conclusion. Since there is already evidence that women taking contraceptive pills have a greater susceptibility to strokes, an argument that claims that women taking contraceptive pills are susceptible to liver damage becomes more credible. In general, *the greater the probable relevance of the projected property to that defining the target population, given our present knowledge of the subject, the sounder is the argument.*

To assess the soundness of an inductive generalization (as well as other types of inductive argument), one should apply these principles, using common sense to decide on the applicability of each one to the particular subject matter. Then the student must exercise judgment in weighing and balancing the various considerations to reach an overall conclusion concerning the validity of the argument. It may well happen that the argument will show strength in one respect and weakness in others; simply adding up the factors is usually not possible. A monstrous failure to satisfy one principle (for example, the presence of a high degree of positive analogy among the observed instances) may be enough in and of itself to dismiss the argument as worthless. An unacceptable degree of vagueness in the target population or the projected property may justify skepticism from the outset. It is best to make a checklist of these factors and to judge each inductive argument according to each factor in regular sequence, as follows:

Rules For Inductive Generalization

Are the observed instances a fair sample of the target population?

1. The greater the number of observed instances, the stronger the argument.

2. The greater the degree of positive analogy among the observed instances, the weaker the argument. Are there too many of one kind of S in the observed instances?

3. The greater the degree of negative analogy among the observed instances, the stronger the argument. Are there enough different kinds of S in the observed instances?

What is the exact nature of the claim made in the conclusion?

4. The less well defined the target population and projected property, the weaker the argument.

5. The more extensive the target population and the more specific the projected property, the weaker the argument.

6. The greater the probable relevance of the projected property to the property defining the target population, the stronger the argument.

Finally, one should be alert for fallacies that undermine the reasoning. There are three different types of fallacies which commonly occur in inductive reasoning.

Fallacies of Inductive Reasoning

1. Hasty Induction   The most familiar inductive fallacy is that of leaping to a conclusion on the basis of insufficient evidence. It may be that the number of observed instances is far too few, the positive analogy among them too great, or the conclusion too sweeping.

2. Forgetful Induction   Another common fault is that of overlooking some obvious or well-known facts that cast doubt on or vitiate the reasoning. Government scientists reached the conclusion that swine flu inoculations would be safe for mass inoculations on the basis of tests made on a limited population, overlooking the fact that any serious side effects having a low incidence in the population would not be revealed by such tests.

3. Lazy Induction   It sometimes happens that a reasoner errs in failing to draw any conclusion at all from the evidence or in failing to draw a conclusion as strong as the evidence justifies. For example, the evidence linking cancer with heavy smoking was not recognized as warranting a conclusion about their causal connection for many years. This fallacy most frequently occurs when the conclusion warranted by the evidence is disagreeable to us. But a refusal to accept the burden of the evidence is just as much a fallacy as leaping to a conclusion that is agreeable to us.

EXERCISE 8B

Identify the target population and the projected property in the following inductive generalization. How do the lettered changes affect the soundness of the argument? Indicate any fallacy committed.

1. A national woman's magazine conducted a poll of its readers, receiving 1,210 responses. Of those answering, 475 of the 920 who considered themselves religious also described themselves as being sexy. The editors concluded that religious women are apt to be sexy, not prudish, as often thought. Let us suppose the following to be true:
   a. *Christian Century* conducted the poll.
   b. The readers had been asked to indicate the value of sex in comparison to money and social position, and placed sex first.
   c. *Playgirl* conducted the poll.
   d. The editors concluded that religious women are as interested in sex as nonreligious women.
   e. The editors concluded that a high proportion of their religious readers consider themselves sexy.
   f. The poll was conducted among 3,500 women of various income levels in 100 cities.

2. A starship orbits planet Eureka twice around its equator during its warm season. Noting green vegetation on most of the hillsides, the two scientists aboard conclude that all the vegetation of Eureka is green and grows on hillsides. Suppose the following:
   a. The starship orbits six times, taking a different course each time.
   b. They conclude that all the vegetation on Eureka is moss which grows on the hillsides.
   c. A woman pilots the starship during the second orbit.
   d. They conclude that most of the vegetation on Eureka grows on hillsides.
   e. The scientists are wearing blue-tinted glasses.
   f. The scientists observe brownish stubble on the plains.

8C INDUCTIVE GENERALIZATIONS ABOUT HUMAN AFFAIRS

In our own times, the search for knowledge has become one of the major human occupations. The conscious application of knowledge to all spheres of human life characterizes the social and political organizations of our own society and many others. In consequence the social sciences, in particular, have become a powerful social force. Their findings on subjects of human concern have been sought out and used to justify practices and policies affecting the lives of citizens to an extent inconceivable in earlier human times. Since the institutions of government themselves play a more pervasive role in everyday life than they did in previous times, it is particularly important for the citizen who wishes to exercise a responsible role in a democratic society to be able to make an informed and independent judgment of the generalizations of the social sciences. We shall note some additional factors to be considered in assessing such generalizations and offer some cautionary remarks about their application.

1. In assessing generalizations concerning human affairs, the attitudes, preconceptions, values, and political orientation of the investigators must be taken into account for their possible influence on the findings themselves, on the procedures by which they are obtained, and in the interpretation placed upon them. We have already noted the presence of a subjective factor in inductive reasonings; in generalizations concerning matters that touch human life, an awareness of this factor is essential. The situation of a social scientist in relation to the human phenomena he investigates is markedly different from that of a biologist or chemist in relation to his subject matter. The scientist's moral and intellectual beliefs, his personal history, and his professional situation may be expected to enter into his choice of a subject, his planning and execution of experiments and researches, what results he seeks, and his interpretation of those results. The way he himself behaves may influence the responses of his subjects, particularly when their background or outlook do not jibe with his own. The scientist is not immune from the influence of his client, whether that client is a public institution, a private industry, or political candidate. He is likely to be receptive to those studies whose results further his client's interests, interests which the investigator may share as a matter of personal, moral, or political conviction. Even the most competent social scientist cannot be thought of as a dispassionate observer of the results of his own professional work; an attitude of unconcerned objectivity toward the subjects he studies is not only unlikely but also perhaps even morally undesirable. As human beings social scientists cannot or ought not to be indifferent to the destiny of the

societies or groups they investigate and the role their own research may play in altering their members lives, for good or ill.

In reviewing the findings of the human sciences, one should not simply accept them at face value. Instead one should seek to become acquainted, as far as is possible, with the experimental situation, the conditions in which the findings were obtained, the procedures of the inquirers, and the exact responses of the subjects. Lack of such information is grounds for doubting the soundness of the reasoning. The results should be scrutinized for evidence of any skewing of the results, undue prominence given to some findings, or underestimation of others. Human responses are often many-sided and easily misinterpreted; the significance of unusual or unexpected responses may be lost on the interviewer or investigator.

A recent study suggested that government policy setters make only symbolic use of conclusions solicited from social scientists, that results were sought to support and rationalize a policy decision already made rather than to serve as a basis for decision making. Furthermore, the research actually used in decision making was often carried out by the government agency itself rather than by independent researchers.

2. The second rule relates to generalizations based on human behavior in so-called "controlled situations." For example, observations of the sexual responses of voluntary subjects or the effects of marijuana smoking are made in special places under so-called "laboratory" conditions set up by the investigators. First, one must raise the question of whether human behavior studied in such a "controlled" situation genuinely reflects the same type of behavior when it occurs in the natural human environment. The knowledge that he or she is being observed may affect the subject's performance and his or her interpretation of the "controlled" situation. Second, one may ask whether the subjects, simply by the fact of being volunteers, may not constitute a group whose responses are unrepresentative of a greater whole. Third, human behavior is affected by a number of factors and circumstances in the normal human situation; the isolation of a particular factor in an experiment may itself affect the kind of response elicited. Thus one needs to be circumspect in applying conclusions based on results obtained in specialized situations to behavior in the natural uncontrolled human environment. One must also query whether the kinds of people who voluntarily respond to surveys are likely to mirror the target population about which a conclusion is drawn. It is well known that some persons are reticent on certain subjects, and others may disguise their feelings or seek to impress the investigators.

Fourth, in generalizations about human attributes of mind (beliefs, emotions, attitudes, states of character), one must heed what particular behavior or verbal response or physiological symptoms are taken by the investigators to prove the presence of the mental attribute and to assess its validity. The way a question is phrased and the circumstances of the questioning may influence the answer given; one must take into account not only whether the quality is self-attributed or inferred from the responses of the subjects or others, but also the probable accuracy of this kind of attribution. The reasoner must judge whether what is taken as a sign (that a person is religious or sexy, for example) is a reliable indicator of the presence of the property, especially if that property is one that involves complex states of mind or behavior.

In the case of generalizations about future human conduct, it is appropriate to speculate whether any given class of human beings will continue to act in the future as they have in the past. Although there are many constants in human life, there are also processes of change which may alter human behavior (either imperceptibly or with drastic sudden-ness). One needs to consider whether the kind of behavior that defines a target population or projected property is apt to be stable or volatile and temper one's judgment accordingly. The birth rate has fluctuated mark-edly in the United States in past decades, as have buying and saving habits. Poll results may differ dramatically within a short space of time if sentiments concerning a subject are in flux. We must keep in mind the fact that inductive generalizations are based on past observations and ask ourselves how applicable they may be under future conditions.

Many generalizations about human affairs are couched in statistics. Although it is far from true that one can prove anything whatsoever with statistics (as is claimed), the pitfalls of statistical reasoning should not be ignored. It is most important to review the statistics themselves to test whether they bear out the conclusion they are said to support. Given the fact that a certain amount of statistical error must be allowed for, statistics indicating small percentage differences from one year to another or from one group to another do not provide sufficient evidence for significant comparisons. The greater the spread or change in the range of the statistics, the more confidence we may have that they signal something. In assessing the significance of the statistics presented, all the factors relating to a fair sample must be included. Furthermore, the possibility of hasty or forgetful induction is present; that is, there may exist some factor not taken into account in the argument that better explains the statistical facts than the conclusion drawn. Lazy induction may also occur. For instance, despite demographic projections of the decrease in numbers of the college-age population, administrators persisted in assuming that the college-going population would continue to increase.

Assess the following* by the rules for inductive generalization, including the considerations about human affairs.

1. Despite reports of declining church attendance in recent years, a recent study indicates that an overwhelming majority of American women describe themselves as religious, and a majority of them say they have become more religious in the past five years. Ninety-five percent of the American women surveyed by a national magazine described themselves as religious; three-quarters of the 65,000 women polled said they believe they have been in the presence of God, according to the survey by *Redbook* magazine. Thirty-three percent of the women identifying themselves as Protestants said they were "very religious" compared with 16 percent of Catholics and 4 percent of Jews. The magazine also said 86 percent of the women approved of the words "one nation under God" in the pledge of allegiance, and 75 percent wanted prayers restored in public schools.

2. New evidence that parents pass their marital tensions on to their children was reported by a team of two psychologists and a psychiatric social worker. They based their findings on a year's study of 33 Dutchess County families whose children had been treated for emotional disturbances at a clinic in Rhinebeck, N.Y. The Rhinebeck team asked the parents to fill out the questionnaire independently at home. Besides meeting the family together, they met separately with the children. Of the children, 24 were boys and 9 were girls. Their median age was 12 years, that of their fathers 40, and their mothers 37. They learned that 87 percent of the children mainfested problems in the same area as their parents. Matching the "severity" scores of the disturbed children with those of their parents, as determined through the questionnaire, they found that the scores in only one case—that of a 12-year-old boy—did not jibe.

Review Exercise For Chapter 8

Assess the following inductive generalizations.*

1. Two new studies suggest that certain abnormalities are seen in babies born of women who are chronic drinkers. A group of Boston researchers studied a total of 52 infants whose mothers fell into three groups: heavy

*Reprinted by permission of the *Baltimore Sunpapers.*

drinkers (women who had five or more drinks a day), moderate drinkers (those who had more than one a day), and abstainers. Only one of the nine babies born to the heavy drinkers was determined to be "normal" by the investigators. The infants were somewhat smaller in length and lower in weight, and they had head circumferences smaller than those babies whose mothers were abstainers or moderate drinkers. The smaller head circumference is particularly significant since it could mean the brain weights are less and the risks of problems in the central nervous system greater.

Another series of studies, carried out at the University of Washington Medical School and the University of California Medical School at San Diego, report similar findings. The West Coast researchers focused on infants whose mothers were severe and chronic alcoholics who continued to drink heavily throughout their pregnancies. Again, smallness, particularly in length and head circumference, was noted. Also, minor congenital abnormalities appeared more frequently among the children of alcoholic mothers.

2. Men, long believed to be nonchalant about their apparel, may be more fashion conscious than women, according to a Michigan State University study. The random sampling of families in Oakland County, in Michigan's populous southeastern corner, showed that clothing is closely tied to the way men feel about their lives. The three-month study, designed to find out what 482 men and women think about the quality of their lives, focused on middle-income families who live in rural, suburban, or urban areas. All of them have school-age children. The researchers said they believed Oakland County was representative of other highly populated areas near large cities.

The study also showed that men who saw clothes as a reflection of themselves had a higher level of self-esteem and were generally more satisfied with life. It also found large differences between what men and women value in life. Men valued highly their accomplishments, having fun, and being free from bother and annoyances. Lower on their scales were love and affection and financial security. Values at the top of the women's list were love and affection, freedom from bother, and beauty. Men said children brought them enjoyment, fun, and happiness, whereas women said children brought them self-fulfillment.

chapter 9

Further Kinds of Inductive Reasoning

9A   REASONING BY INDUCTIVE ANALOGY

In everyday reasoning we frequently use inductive reasoning to arrive at a conclusion about some one individual case; inductive generalizations are more commonly the fruits of systematic scientific research. An inductive argument whose conclusion is a singular statement rather than a generalization (whether universal or statistical) is called reasoning by *inductive analogy*. In inductive analogy a conclusion is inferred about the nature of a particular instance from its observed similarity to a number of previously observed instances. The general form of the reasoning may be schematized as follows:

INDUCTIVE ANALOGY

$a, b, c, d \ldots n$ have each been observed to be both S and P.
x is similar to $a, b, c, d \ldots n$ in being S.

Probably, x is similar to $a, b, c, d \ldots n$ in being P.

The similarity between inductive analogy and inductive generalization is apparent from a comparison of their general form. Both base their inferences on the observation of a regular correlation between two properties S and P in a number of previous cases. The essential difference between the two is in the logical character of their conclusions. In inductive generalization the conclusion relates to a *whole class*, the target population consisting of an indefinite number of instances of things which are S; in inductive analogy the conclusion usually applies to a definite individual case, which can be dated and placed, of something which is S.

Arguments of inductive analogy clearly must precede universal generalization on many occasions. When some researcher notes that a number of things which are S are also P, it is reasonable for him to expect on meeting another thing which is S that it will also turn out to be P. When such conjectures are borne out in a large number of cases, the next step is to broaden the inference to apply to the whole class of things which are S. Thus after noting that a number of female humans have XX chromosomes, whereas men have a set of XY chromosomes, it is reasonable to conjecture that this is a feature of the whole class of women, not just of the next woman.

It is sometimes said that an inference concerning an individual case should properly be understood as involving the application of a generalization to an individual instance which falls under the generalization—that a generalization always functions as a latent premise in such an argument. In our study of deductive reasoning we noted one type of syllogistic reasoning in which one applies a generalization to a particular instance. However, this strategy works reliably only with universal generalizations, in which case the reasoning is deductive. In many other cases, it is often a misrepresentation of the reasoning process to view it as the application of a generalization to an individual case. It often occurs that the reasoning process involves a direct comparison of an individual case with other cases either strongly or remotely analogous to it. It either makes no appeal to any generalization at all or is an additional step to the application of a generalization.

Sometimes there is simply no reliable generalization of the appropriate kind at all, or at least none known to the reasoner in question. He or she is left to ask whether this instance is sufficiently similar to other things of which he or she has acquaintance that a reasonable conjecture can be made about it. A hungry person lost in the woods coming upon a bush containing blue berries of an unfamiliar kind and needing to decide whether they are apt to be poisonous will proceed, quite naturally, to note the points of similarity and difference between these berries in front of him and other berries he knows to be poisonous or nonpoisonous. On other occasions, a reasoner may be interested in judging whether an individual case is likely to be an exception to a generalization rather than an instance of it. A doctor informed by phone of a sick infant with a high fever knows that infants with high fevers are very likely to have convulsions. In deciding whether to visit this infant at once or to attend to another child, he may well proceed by trying to estimate the probability that this particular sick infant with a high fever will soon fall into convulsions. Relying on his knowledge of the similarities in physiology, he will ask not only whether the child has previously had convulsions but also whether his parents or any of his siblings have ever had convulsions, or whether there is any family history of epilepsy.

Even in cases where there are appropriate generalizations, it is well known that the probability which can be assigned to a statistical generalization concerning a whole target population cannot simply be transferred to a conclusion about one definite instance of the target population. Let us suppose a statistical generalization states that six out of ten teenage boys from single-parent homes become involved in some kind of crime. A teacher cannot infer from this generalization that exactly six or even approximately six of ten such teenagers in his or her class have any kind of criminal record. And still less may the teacher reliably infer that any particular teenage student has been or will be involved in a crime. The generalization becomes more reliable as we apply it to larger and larger groups; in any individual case, we may have grounds for doubting its application altogether.

Even when there is a statistical generalization to which we can appeal, our reasoning proceeds in a different way in making a conclusion about an individual case: Usually we know more about the individual than merely that he or she belongs to a target population concerning which some relevant generalization has been made. This additional knowledge may make us either more or less confident about our ability to apply the generalization to the individual case. If we know that this teenager is not only from a single-parent family but has also recently taken to using drugs and staying out until late at night, we may well decide that the probability of his being caught in a crime is even higher than the statistics suggest.

In science some of the most fruitful theories have proceeded on the basis of an analogy between two very different phenomena. The biologist William Harvey's insight into the circulation of the blood arose from his perception of an analogy between the heart and the mechanical water pump; from this he hypothesized that the heart acted by pumping blood in and out of its various chambers and through the veins and arteries of the body. Analogy aids us in understanding the nature and predicting the actions of one phenomenon by drawing a parallel with some other phenomenon. Scientific reasoning that uses models (such as the familiar model of the chemical atom) is basically a form of reasoning by analogy.

The term *analogy* sometimes suggests a parallel or resemblance between two phenomena which are very different in kind—just as the heart, being a natural animal organ made of tissue, is quite different from a pump, a man-made mechanism made of metal. The point of resemblance or analogy between the two may sometimes be quite distant or abstract, and it is this which causes some logicians to distrust reasoning by analogy. Given the fact that reasoning by analogy often turns out to be fruitful, and that it is sometimes the only kind of reasoning open to us in a given situation, there is no need to reject it. Needless to say, however, we must be even more careful in applying the criteria for judging it to be sure that we are not misled. In formulating the rules for judging arguments of inductive analogy we will use the term *analogy* to mean a parallel or resemblance between two different sorts of things, in addition to the usual meaning we have already used in speaking of positive analogy and negative analogy in the criteria for inductive generalization.

Since both inductive generalization and inductive analogy are based on the empirical observation of a correlation between two properties in a number of instances in the past, the rules concerning the number and character of the observed instances that apply to inductive generalization also apply to the cases of inductive analogy. The greater the number of already observed instances used as the evidence for an inference in inductive analogy, the stronger the argument; the greater the positive analogy among the observed instances, the weaker the argument; and the greater the negative analogy among the previously observed instances, the stronger the argument.

However, arguments by inductive analogy involve an additional factor not found in inductive generalization: a comparison between the characteristics of the previously observed instances and those of that new instance which is to be the subject of the conclusion of the argument. In this comparison, the greater the resemblance between the new instance, about which we draw the inference, and the previously observed instances, which constitute the evidence for the argument, the stronger the argument will be. The closer the similarity between the new instance, whose character is in question, and the old instances, whose correlation of properties we know about, the more likely it becomes that the new instance will show the same kind of correlation of properties. On the other hand, the fewer points of resemblance there are between the new instance and the old ones—the more distant the analogy between the new thing and the other things with which it is compared—the less likely it is that the new thing will show the same correlation of properties as the already observed instances. For example, the more the blue berries on this bush are like previously observed blueberries that we know to be nonpoisonous—in color, texture, size, hardness, shape, and the size of their leaves—the more confident we may be that they will also be nonpoisonous. But the less like the previously observed nonpoisonous blueberries these new berries turn out to be, the more dubious we should be that they will share the property of being nonpoisonous.

One must be careful to distinguish this last factor, one of prime importance in arguments of inductive analogy alone, from a different one—the amount of resemblance and difference *among the previously observed* instances (that is, the degree of positive and negative analogy among them) which comes into play in both types of argument, inductive generalization and inductive analogy. In both types, the greater the amount of positive analogy among the previously observed instances, the weaker the argument; and the greater the degree of negative analogy among the previously observed instances, the sounder the argument.

In an argument of inductive analogy, we must undertake an additional comparison between the characteristics of the new instance, (the subject of the conclusion) and those of all the previously observed instances. Here the more likeness there is between the new instance and all the other previously observed instances, the more confident we may be that the new instance will be like them in some other respect; and the less like them, the less confident we may be that the new instance will possess the further property about which we are to draw an inference. Thus the rule of crucial importance in reasoning by inductive analogy concerns the degree of positive and negative analogy between the new instance, on the one hand, and all the previously observed instances, on the other hand. The greater the positive analogy between the new instance and all the previously observed instances, the sounder the argument; the greater the negative analogy between the new instance and the previously observed instances, the weaker is the inference.

The rules relating to the nature of the properties S and P also apply to reasoning by inductive analogy: The better defined these properties are, the sounder is the reasoning. When the analogy between the new instance and the old instances is remote or distant, this rule may provide a basis for dismissing the argument entirely. The rule relating to the extensiveness of the claim made by the conclusion must be modified when applied to reasoning by inductive analogy: Inductive analogy arguments make a claim about only a new specific instance, not a target population. However, the claim that a definite individual which has the property S will also have the property P is always a riskier one than the claim which says that a certain proportion of things that are S will also be P. However, the riskiness of the claim will also vary with the specificity of the property P (just as in inductive generalization). For example, the more specific conclusion that this infant will have *minor* convulsions is a riskier claim than the more generalized conclusion that this infant will have convulsions.

To summarize, the rules for inductive analogy are the same as the rules for inductive generalization, although suitably modified to take account of the fact that in one case the conclusion is a singular statement, in the other a generalization. Reasoning by inductive analogy requires us to consider in addition the degree of positive and negative analogy between the new instance and the previously observed instances. Just as in inductive generalization, one's application of the following rules needs to be tempered by common sense and by knowledge of the subject matter of the reasoning. They are not to be used mechanically, but with awareness of their relevance to the subject matter at hand.

Rules For Reasoning By Inductive Analogy

1. The larger the number of previously observed instances, the sounder the argument's inference as applied to the new instance.

2. The greater is the positive analogy among the previously observed instances, the less sound is the inference that the new analogous instance will possess the same combination of properties as the observed instances.

3. The greater is the negative analogy among the previously observed instances, the sounder is the inference that the new analogous instance will possess the same combination of properties as the previously observed instances.

4. The better defined the points of resemblance, properties S and P, the sounder the argument.

5. The more sweeping the conclusion relative to the evidence, the weaker the argument.

6. The more likely the relevant connection between the properties S and P, given our knowledge of the subject matter, the sounder the argument.

7. The greater the positive analogy between the new instance and the previously observed instances, the sounder the argument; the greater the negative analogy between them, the weaker the argument.

EXERCISE 9A

Identify the subject of the analogy and the projected property in the following arguments. Say how each of the lettered changes affects the soundness of the inference. Indicate any fallacy committed.

1. Mr. and Mrs. Green have just moved into Cosmopolis. One of Mr. Green's colleagues has recommended a real estate agent, a car repair shop, restaurants, and a shopping center, all of which turn out to be satisfactory. When Mr. Green has some disturbing physical symptoms, he decides that this same colleague probably knows a good doctor for him to consult.

   a. The colleague has recommended a pediatrician who turned out to be highly competent.

   b. Mr. Green seeks advice on a furniture repair shop.
   c. Mr. Green concludes his colleague will know of some doctors for
      him to consult.
   d. Mr. Green decides his colleague's advice may not be desirable,
      his colleague being a Christian Scientist.
   e. Mr. Green concludes his colleague will not know of any good
      doctors.
   f. His colleague has a brother who is a doctor.

2. When Mrs. Brown takes a whole chicken, bought the day before from
   her local grocery, out of its plastic bag, she finds it covered with a
   jellylike film. Noting that it smells and looks fresh, she recalls that on
   several occasions previously ham and frankfurters had been covered by
   a sticky film but proved safe to eat. She infers this chicken is safe to eat
   too.

   a. The chicken was greenish and smelled odd.
   b. On previous occasions other chickens have been covered with
      film.
   c. The other meats had been smoked, whereas this chicken is
      supposed to be fresh.
   d. She decides the chicken is not safe to eat.
   e. On the last occasion, the cooked meat tasted a little odd and
      several members of the family suffered from cramps and diarrhea.
   f. She bought the chicken at a discount store at a very cheap price.

9B   CAUSAL REASONING

A most important type of inductive reasoning is the discovery of *causes*.
The conclusion of a causal argument may be either a generalization, such
as "Smokers often die of lung cancer," or a singular statement, such as
"Jones' death was caused by a drug overdose." Thus a causal argument
will fall under the category of inductive generalization or inductive
analogy, and the rules for inductive generalization and inductive analogy
respectively are applicable to arguments of causal reasoning. Since causal
generalizations often figure as premises in causal reasoning leading to
singular conclusions, we shall first examine inferences to causal generalizations.

A causal generalization is often expressed in locutions such as the
following:

> X brings about Y; X's produce Y; X tends to make Y happen;
> Whenever X occurs, Y will follow; Y is the effect of X;
> Y results from X.

The following are familiar instances of causal generalization:

> Smoking produces lung cancer.
> Maternal alcoholism increases the incidence of birth defects.
> A high cancer rate is the effect of industrial pollution in a neighborhood.

In order to apply the rules for inductive generalization, it is sometimes desirable to restate the generalization so as to specify the target population and the projected property. For example, in the causal generalization, "Smoking produces lung cancer," *smoking* is the *cause*, or *causal factor* and *lung cancer* is the *effect. Smokers*, or cases of people smoking, are the target population; and the projected property needs to be expressed in terms that are apprpriate to the target population, as in a phrase such as "persons susceptible to lung cancer." The sentence, "Maternal alcoholism results in birth defects," might be rephrased as "Women who are heavy drinkers are likely to have children with birth defects"; "heavy-drinking women" then defines the target population, and the projected property becomes "likely to have children with birth defects."

The first step in assessing a causal generalization is the same as that for any inductive generalization. We must determine whether the cases being observed are a fair sample of the target population. Our second step is to analyze the nature of the causal conclusion to determine whether the causal factor and its effect are sufficiently well-defined. The extent and specificity of the causal claim in relation to the evidence presented must then be examined. Finally it is extremely important, in the case of causal generalizations, to take note of our knowledge of the subject matter as it exists independent of the argument in question, to determine whether it tends to support or discredit the causal claim made in the generalization.

In judging the reliability of a causal generalization certain special considerations enter in, making it useful to analyze the notion of causation. *Causation* has been the subject of much philosophical theorizing, the details of which need not be repeated here. But in order to judge correctly whether one thing is a cause of some other thing, it helps to be clear about what is meant by a *cause*. To begin with, a *cause* is generally in existence for some period of time before its effect. No one would attribute lung cancer to smoking if it existed in patients prior to their taking up smoking. Thus "X causes Y" implies that "X comes before Y."

However, we are all aware of the fact that if one thing comes before another it is not always a cause of the later thing. A common form of fallacious reasoning occurs when one draws the inference that X is the cause of Y on the basis of the fact that X took place before Y. This fallacy goes by the compact Latin phrase, *post hoc, ergo propter hoc*: "After this, therefore because of this." In many cases it is easy to spot: No one would think that the migration of birds causes the change of seasons, even though it precedes the change. But in other circumstances the existence of a fallacy in this pattern of thinking may be widely disputed.

In general when a distinctive unexpected change occurs immediately following some out-of-the-ordinary happening, we suspect a causal connection between the two because we think (correctly) of an effect as that which follows its cause.

For example, when the roof of a large stadium under construction near O'Hare International Airport collapsed moments after a jetliner had passed unusually low overhead, witnesses immediately linked the collapse with the aircraft's passage. In order to reach a sound conclusion about a cause, however, we need to know more than simply the fact that one thing took place before another. We need grounds for supposing that something is capable of bringing about the given effect. In the case of the collapse of the roof, we know that sudden intense local vibrations do cause spans such as bridges and roofs to cave in, so it is not unreasonable to conjecture that the low passage of the jetliner set off the vibrations which immediately preceded the crumbling of the structure. In judging a causal conclusion we must look for evidence that will show that the factor hypothesized to be the cause is not just accidentally associated with the effect, but that its occurrence is what produces the effect.

Modern science has been remarkably successful in identifying causal factors. This success is due in part to the ingenuity of investigators who have devised ways to isolate factors so that genuinely causal ones can be separated from others that are linked with instances of an effect only by accident or by regular association. One such device is a *control group*. Let us suppose that investigators wish to determine the effect of a given drug upon a particular disease. A number of individuals with the disease are separated into two groups: one group is given the drug, the other—called the *control group*—is given a pill containing nothing but sugar, or some other form of treatment. The results obtained in this group are examined for differences with the results obtained in the group given the drug being tested. Any significant difference in the results in these two groups can then be inferred to have been caused by the administration of the drug.

Procedures with control groups are often quite sophisticated. When feasible, the individuals in the groups are matched in relevant features— age, sex, length or seriousness of disease, previous kinds of treatment, occupation, and so forth—so that the composite nature of both groups is quite similar. When matching is not possible, individuals are randomly assigned to one or another of the groups, on the assumption that random selection will eliminate special factors that would affect the comparative results in the two groups.

A set of principles formulated by the British philosopher J. S. Mill is useful in analyzing the results of causal investigations. He called them *the method of agreement, the method of difference, and the method of concomitant variations.*

The method of agreement states that *a factor which is present whenever the effect is present, and absent whenever the effect is absent, may be a causal factor.*

This commonsensical principle is widely used, and expresses the notion that the cause of a given type of event is regularly correlated with the existence of the effect. Many causal hypotheses originate with the observation that one type of event has been followed by another type of event. The many cases in which persons exposed to a chill have come down with colds has given rise to the popular belief that it is the chill that causes the cold. This principle is very much subject to the fallacy of hasty generalization, especially when based on a small number of instances. Nevertheless, observation of a regular correlation between two events is surely grounds for positing a causal connection between them. However, the method of agreement must usually be supported by the method of difference if the fallacy of hasty generalization is to be avoided.

The method of difference states that *a factor present in cases in which the particular effect is absent is unlikely to be a causal factor.*

This principle enables us to reject a factor as a cause by explicitly checking for counterinstances—cases in which the factor is present but the effect does not occur. The causal generalization that exposure to chill causes colds has been brought into question by the results of studies by a British group; it found that the number of people who caught colds immediately following prolonged exposure to chill was not significantly different from the number of people who did not catch cold. Here the factor present in all cases is prolonged exposure to chill; the fact that a substantial number of persons did not experience the effect of catching cold even though this chill factor was present argues against the chill as a causal factor in colds.

By using the method of difference in conjunction with the method of agreement, we can test whether the common factor found by the latter is indeed the causal factor. If the common factor does not pass the test of the method of difference, its status as a cause of the phenomenon being studied is undercut. If it does pass, its claim as a causal factor is supported. It is desirable to use the method of agreement and difference together in establishing a causal generalization; and the use of control groups is an effective method for the joint application of the two. In and of itself, however, the method of difference very often enables one to reject a factor as a cause.

The method of concomitant variations states that *a factor present whenever the effect is present, whose variations in degree are closely correlated with variations in degree of the effect, is likely to be a causal factor.*

In some cases it is impossible to use the methods of agreement and difference because the candidate factor cannot be easily isolated or removed from other factors. Thus we look not for the absence or presence of the factor or the supposed effect, but for some kind of regular variation of the effect with a variation in the candidate factor. The existence of such regular variation confirms the possibility that the factor is a cause; nonexistent or irregular variation discredits it. For example, the causal generalization that food additives cause an increase in hyperactive behavior has been argued on the following evidence. Among several groups of hyperactive children, some were given a diet eliminating food additives as much as possible, and others were given diets with varying amounts of food additives ranging from high to low. A comparison of the behavior of children in the various groups showed that hyperactive children whose diets contained a minimal or lower amount of food additives were said by parents and teachers to show markedly less hyperactive behavior than those with diets containing the higher amounts of food additives.

In analyzing the evidence for a causal generalization, one should look for the use of techniques such as those just discussed (the existence of control groups, the application of one or more of Mill's methods), whose results support the generalization.

We can summarize the principles for testing a causal generalization as follows:

Rules for Assessing a Causal Generalization

1. Apply the principles of inductive generalization to determine whether the evidence for the causal generalization is a fair sample of the instances of the causal factor or target population.

2. Apply the rules of inductive generalization in analyzing the extensiveness and specificity of the causal claim made by the conclusion in relation to the evidence, and in determining whether the causal factor and the effect are sufficiently well-defined.

3. Note whether the causal claim is supported by methods (control groups and the methods of agreement, difference, and concomitant variations) which reliably establish causal factors.

4. Note whether independent findings relating to the subject matter support the causal claim.

1. Say how the soundness of the following causal argument is affected by each of the lettered changes.

Professor Brown has been teaching logic courses over twenty years to students in various kinds of undergraduate programs: a private eastern women's college, a large private coeducational university in the Midwest, a coeducational public university, a local college giving evening courses to part-time students. He has noted in recent years that students have difficulty with deductive reasoning, which requires concentration on the exact meaning of statements. One night he reads a newspaper article reporting the results of a Gallup poll as follows:

> Drug use continues to be a serious problem on the college campuses of America, with marijuana use at a high point. Since the late 1960s the percentage of students saying they have tried marijuana has grown from 5 percent in 1967 to 55 percent in 1974 to 66 percent in a survey conducted during the present college year.
>
> In a 1970 survey, 16 percent of a nationwide sample of college students said they had tried amphetamines such as "speed." Just one year later the comparable figure was 22 percent. In the current survey, 21 percent say they have tried these drugs. In 1969, one-tenth of the college population said they had tried barbiturates such as Quaaludes. In the current survey, the proportion is 14 percent. In terms of hallucinogens like LSD and mescaline, 1 percent of the student population said they tried these drugs in 1967. Today's figure is 14 percent.*

Putting these results together with his own observations, Professor Brown hypothesizes that marijuana use by college age students may be decreasing their capacity for deductive reasoning.

a. At a conference of logic teachers, members report that college students' performance in logic has been declining steadily in the past decade, and a resolution to study this problem is passed unanimously.

b. Brown's logic courses during the last ten years have included both inductive and deductive reasoning, whereas previously the courses only covered deductive reasoning.

c. Brown concludes that drug use may contribute to students' difficulty with deductive logic.

d. Brown infers that there is no connection between drug use and students' performance in logic courses.

*Reprinted by permission of the *Baltimore Sunpapers.*

e. Another report concludes that marijuana smoking does not affect reasoning, based on these findings: 25 students were given 10 arithmetic problems to solve before smoking marijuana, and then tested again after smoking, and there was no significant difference in scores.

f. Brown has been polling his students on marijuana use for the last five years: These results show that 85 percent of the students who receive failing grades or drop the course reported regular marijuana use for two years or more.

g. Another newspaper article quotes elementary school and high school teachers' remarks that students using marijuana found it difficult to concentrate in reading.

2. Identify the causal factor and the effect in the following.* Assess the causal argument.

a. Most fatal or potentially fatal auto accidents are caused not by drunk drivers but by drivers with particular personality traits, according to a recently completed study. "It's the personality traits that result in a person who has many problems in living, including use and abuse of alcohol in conjunction with driving," said Dr. C. W. Schmidt, chief of psychiatry at Baltimore City Hospitals. Dr. Schmidt and Dr. J. Schaffer, assistant professor of medical psychology at the Johns Hopkins Medical School, studied the personalities of men and women who survived or were killed in 310 car crashes in the Baltimore area during a 7-year study.

Relatives and friends were asked to complete written tests to rate the dead drivers' personality traits. Those drivers then were compared by age and sex with drivers in a pool of data drawn primarily from random population samples in Carroll County. The study said that male drivers involved in the accidents had personality traits generally defined as more bizarre, anxious, belligerent, hyperactive, verbally expansive, and psychopathic than the general male population. Women drivers studied, however, were actually more stable than the general female population. Most of the male victims in the study were from low socioeconomic backgrounds, whereas most of the women were from middle-class families.

b. The tendency toward sudden-infant-death syndrome (SIDS), also known as crib death, apparently isn't inherited, Dr. D. R. Peterson, University of Washington professor of epidemiology told a research group. He said the condition occurred only at a

*Reprinted by permission of the *Baltimore Sunpapers.*

very slightly higher rate than average among parents who had multiple births and occurred at an average rate among cousins of the victims in the study.

Peterson said the odds are about 500 to 1 that any couple will encounter SIDS, 60 to 1 that it will occur in the next child born to an SIDS couple, and 40 to 1 that it will happen to any of the couple's subsequent children. After an SIDS incident, the relative risk of an SIDS incident increased 11 times of what might be expected in the community. In a companion report, Dr. John Emery, of the University of Sheffield, England, said his studies suggest that the greatest risk factor is socioeconomic. He said SIDS occurs more often in lower-income and minority families.

9C   SINGULAR CAUSAL INFERENCES

Like most inductive generalizations, causal generalizations are commonly the results of scientific research. In everyday reasoning, we often engage in reasoning whose conclusion is a singular causal statement, to the effect that some particular thing or action is the cause of some other particular event. What is the cause of yesterday's airplane crash in Colorado? Why am I having trouble starting my car this morning? Why has the neighbor's teenage boy started taking drugs?

Sometimes reasoning concerning the cause of a specific event falls under one or the other types of argument already considered. It may be a straightforward application of a causal generalization to a particular instance, as in this case:

Cars have difficulty starting when their batteries are old and weak. My car battery is five years old and weak. Therefore, my car is difficult to start because its battery is old and weak.

On other occasions, it may not be so evident what causal generalization a case falls under, so that reasoning by inductive analogy may be called for. Suppose a particular car has failed to start one day when it is raining steadily, and a mechanic tells us that the ignition system is wet and is preventing power from flowing from the battery. On a subsequent rainy day when a neighbor's car will not start, it is reasonable to make an analogy between the performances of the two cars and draw the conclusion that the neighbor's car has a wet ignition. In this way arguments by inductive analogy can lead to singular causal conclusions from observations of correlations of events in one's own past. Indeed, using the rules of inductive analogy and Mill's methods, an individual may be able to hit on the causes of particular events with an accuracy rivaling that of an expert. In the case of medical problems, for instance, the causes of allergies and indispositions may be numerous, and the individual's self-observation may be a valuable source of evidence.

In the foregoing cases the operative sense of *cause* is not different from that in cases of inductive generalization. However, in some kinds of everyday reasoning we use the term *cause* in a related but somewhat different way. When we inquire as to the causes of human actions, or of events that take place in a human context, it is often not possible to isolate one factor as the cause in the strong sense that term bears in inductive generalization and inductive analogy. We recognize that there is a whole chain of events and circumstances, a whole causal network, which leads to a particular outcome. In these cases when we ask about *the* cause, we are looking for some especially significant factor, often one within human control, while we are also acknowledging the presence of other factors as necessary or contributing in a substantial way to the outcome. Here the notion of the cause is weaker: The cause is the factor (often related to human action or inaction) in the absence of which the particular event would not have occurred.

Very often we need to ascertain in particular whether some human action or negligence was a causal factor in this weaker sense. Was the airplane crash caused by bad weather, the inattentiveness of the pilot to a warning signal, or the failure of the control tower personnel to give timely warning? In such a case, there are sometimes a number of contributing causal factors in the weaker sense, some human and some nonhuman— poor visibility, unfamiliar terrain, icing on the wings, malfunctioning of an engine. What we need to know is the precise relevance of the human factors in order to decide whether an individual should be held responsible for the event, either legally or morally.

Drawing conclusions about the cause of a specific human action is another important task of everyday reasoning. Once again, it is often found to be essential in assigning moral and legal responsibility, guilt or innocence, praise or blame. It is worthwhile to take note of how much weight to give to empirical generalizations in such reasoning. Causal generalizations of a psychological or sociological kind are surely relevant to such reasoning, but we must be aware of limitations in their use. Empirical generalizations are seldom universal, but statistical, holding only for a certain proportion of the target population named. Even the most firmly grounded generalization about the cause of a type of human action asserts only that there is a fairly high degree of probability that a factor is causally related to the behavior of a certain proportion of individuals who fall in a certain class. Thus we cannot simply go from the generalization that poverty is a causal factor in stealing by some members of minority groups, to the conclusion that a particular person belonging to a minority group stole a television set because he was poor. It is dubious whether an individual's behavior can be adequately explained by his or her being a member of a class for whom a causal generalization is well established. A statistical generalization licenses a conclusion only about groups of individuals—it does not justify our picking out any individual and pinpointing his behavior as the effect of membership in a group. Generalizations select certain features commonly found in many individuals and report broad correlations among generalized patterns of behavior and situation. Yet the action of an individual is the specific action of an actual person with unique traits, operating under concrete circumstances. Any adequate explanation of an individual's action must be based on these specific facts, especially if we are making judgments of legal or moral responsibility.

Our knowledge of an individual can always be much fuller than mere generalizations based on class characteristics, and this detailed knowledge can be even more relevant as evidence in explaining his or her behavior. Together with our knowledge of human nature, based on long human experience, this evidence often will enable us to reach sounder conclusions about the causes of individual human actions than statistical generalizations will. The "blanket" nature of the generalization is sometimes of little use, either in understanding the behavior or attributing any moral quality to it. A psychologist may explain to a mother that sibling rivalry causes her son to strike his younger brother. But sibling rivalry will generate a variety of types of behavior in different situations, to which various moral attributes apply. In order to determine whether in a particular instance it is sibling rivalry of a blameworthy kind, the parent must inquire into the particular circumstances. In deciding whether to assign moral or legal responsibility to a person for an action he has performed, empirical generalizations alone do not suffice either to inculpate or exonerate: Not only is their validity as applied to the individual case questionable, but also their blanket character usually does not enable us to draw the specific kind of conclusion required.

It is sometimes said that the existence of causal laws governing human behavior makes it inappropriate to hold an individual morally responsible for an action, since it must be viewed as an effect following from the operation of causal factors in his or her past. Given these past causal factors, it is argued, the individual could not have acted other than in fact he or she did. Thus, he or she lacks moral freedom, the concept of which justifies holding an individual morally responsible for what he or she does or fails to do. However, as we have noted, empirical laws governing human behavior are framed in abstract and generalized terms, such as *sibling rivalry*. The actions that fall under a law are of many kinds, and of significantly different moral character: Sibling rivalry could lead a boy to work hard to achieve higher grades than his brother or to clobber him on the head. That for which one holds a person morally responsible is a specific action in specific circumstances. It is the specific moral quality of the act that is relevant, not the fact that it falls under some causal generalization about human behavior. Let us postulate the existence of even a quite detailed psychological law to the effect that a jealous person like Shakespeare's Othello in circumstances like those of Shakespeare's play would, on the stimulus of what he believes to be proof of his wife's infidelity, commit an act of violence. Any one of the following actions would be in conformity with this law: Othello kills Desdemona; Othello kills his wife's alleged lover; Othello kills himself; Othello kills Turks in battle. Although all of these instances equally satisfy our psychological law as the predictable effects of the causal factors operating on the individual, they are all acts on which we would pass different moral judgments, ranging from praise to blame.

In concluding this discussion, we should observe that a person's knowledge of the probable results of his or her actions or the probable consequences of his or her behavior is itself one factor to be considered in determining whether he or she should be held morally or legally responsible. Both in law and morality people are held accountable for results they may not have intended or wished to bring about but which they could foresee to be the probable consequence of their action. Thus, inferring the probable effects of one's own actions is a kind of reasoning which every morally responsible person is required to undertake, for his or her own good and for that of others.

Principles for Determining the Cause of a Specific Happening

1. Note whether the happening is explained by the application of a reliable inductive generalization or analogy.
2. Note whether there is some factor in whose absence the particular happening probably would not have occurred.
3. Could the doer be expected to know the probable consequences of an action causally connected with the happening?

EXERCISE 9C

1. In which of the following cases is it reasonable to say that the causal relationship of an action to an event is such that the doer may be held morally responsible for it?

   a. A retarded fourteen-year-old girl who puts her newborn child into a trash can on her mother's instructions.

    b. The fourteen-year-old girl's mother, who is of normal intelligence and gave the instructions above.

    c. King Henry IV of England, whose remark, "Have I no friend will rid me of this living fear?" prompted one of his followers to kill the deposed King Richard II.

2. Is it reasonable to hold Mr. F. responsible for Mr. D's death or mental deterioration?

    Mr. F. contacted Mr. D. on December 1, 1976, and offered to help treat his father, who then was in a coma. Mr. F. told the younger Mr. D. that he was an expert in hypnosis, psychology, and conditioned reflex therapy. However, before treatment could be arranged, the senior Mr. D. died. Because of his father's death, Mr. D., who held a degree in music from Bucknell University, and who had been working as a pianist, organist, and arranger, took over the running of his father's business.

    Mr. F. contacted Mr. D. some weeks after his father's death and asked about his state of mind. When Mr. D. replied that he was depressed over his father's death and the fact that he had to abandon his music career, Mr. F. advised him to undergo therapy sessions with him. Throughout the first half of the year, Mr. F. had treated Mr. D., using hypnosis, psychoanalysis, and tape recordings at night. In a chart supposedly given to Mr. D. by Mr. F., the young man was characterized as having a high neurotic tendency, as being introverted, living within himself, submissive, and self-conscious with feelings of inferiority. Another exhibit, the typewritten card, "Feeling Talk," urged Mr. D. to "deliberately force his true feelings out," to act spontaneously. "Do not plan your response," the card said; "At the split second that the emotion is felt, give it oral expression." An additional card to him stated, "MAKE ALL PERSONAL DECISIONS ON YOUR OWN EVEN IF IT KILLS YOU."

    On June 1, 1976, Mr. D. drove his van to an isolated road, hooked up a hose to the exhaust pipe, and pumped exhaust fumes into his van. As the fumes entered the van, he wrote down his feelings in his diary up until the moment he lost consciousness. The diary was found next to him in the van. One notation read: "My lungs burn, the windows are steamy. Numb extremities, like a high actually. . . . Carbon, play on."*

9D   EXPLANATORY HYPOTHESES

We often engage in reasoning to provide an explanation for an occurrence which is puzzling, unexpected, or an apparent exception to what is usually

*Reprinted by permission of the *Baltimore Sunpapers.*

the case. For example, the mass suicide of over nine hundred members of the Jonestown cult community of Guyana in November 1978 is the type of event that seems so contrary to normal human behavior that it needs explanation. Much serious scientific work consists in the development of elaborate theories to account for the specific character and workings of common natural phenomena. The atomic theory of matter, relativity theory, and the "big-bang" cosmology are examples of scientific explanatory hypotheses familiar, at least by name, to many laymen. Such theories systematically relate complex notions, detailed observations, and experimental results within a whole framework of statements designed to make the subject matter intelligible. If we are to assess these explanatory hypotheses, knowledge of the subject matter is indispensable. Still, there are some general principles for assessing explanatory hypotheses which are applicable both to them and to the kinds of reasoning we ordinarily carry on.

Many of the forms of inductive reasoning that we have already discussed could be interpreted as providing simple explanatory hypotheses. For instance, the conclusion of an inductive generalization or inductive analogy argument could be viewed as an hypothesis proposed to explain the facts asserted in the premises. This alternative way of looking at these types of argument will also provide some new principles (in addition to the usual rules) for judging their soundness.

Let us take the following as a sample of reasoning which seeks to provide an explanatory hypothesis. On December 2, 1977, there were two high-altitude explosions observed about 5 to 10 miles offshore from Connecticut to South Carolina. These were followed by five more explosions on December 8. Some of these blasts were equal in force to 100-ton dynamite blasts and shattered some windows. They were felt mostly along the shore, but residents from areas as far as twenty-five miles inland felt vibrations from them. Here we have a whole series of unusual occurrences for which an explanation is sought. These occurrences are the data, or evidence, for which we seek some explanatory hypothesis. We can immediately see that a number of possibilities suggest themselves: Earthquakes, supersonic aircraft, missile explosions, or even the passing nearby of extraterrestrial spaceships. In the kind of reasoning we are considering, we do not proceed by examining just one hypothesis; we need to look at the various possible explanations and rank them in relation to one another. What we are seeking is *the most probable* of the various hypotheses, the one that provides the best explanation of the occurrence. Thus we need to consider the merit of each hypothesis not just singly, but in competition with other rival hypotheses. Our principles are designed to enable us to select that one out of a number of hypotheses which is the most likely explanation of the occurrence in question.

One obvious rule is that the hypothesis that explains all or more of the data is the preferred hypothesis. An hypothesis that will not fit a substantial part of the data is unsatisfactory. In this case the explosions were said to be too violent to be caused by any one supersonic aircraft, which was one hypothesis immediately offered.

A second rule is to delineate the different consequences of each of the rival hypotheses. Then we must either engage in further observation or check the existing evidence for the presence or absence of these consequences. For example, earthquakes are regularly monitored by seismic equipment: If the hypothesis that earthquakes triggered these blasts were correct, then the occurrence of earthquakes in the area would be registered on the readouts from seismic equipment for those dates. However, a check of those readouts showed no earth movements at the time of the booms. Since a clear consequence of the idea that the booms are earthquake-related has been proved to be false, we must eliminate the hypothesis of earthquakes. Should a particular consequence be verified, of course, the hypothesis is supported against the claims of its rivals.

To test the hypothesis of missile explosions at sea, we have to begin with the logical conclusion that they were set off either by our own country or by some foreign power. Missile explosions set off by a foreign power so close to our shores might be expected to bring out our own defenses in force. Since no such dramatic and clearly perceptible confrontation happened, we may reject this possibility. If, on the other hand, the missile explosions were our own, then the Pentagon, or some defense office, should be able to confirm military testing in the area. However, a Pentagon spokesman said defense officials knew nothing about the booms or any testing in the area. Do we now need to eliminate this hypothesis? Not if we are willing to defend it by proposing an *auxiliary hypothesis*, an additional hypothesis serving to explain an apparent failure of the original hypothesis. We might maintain the hypothesis of U.S. missile testing and explain the Pentagon denial by the auxiliary hypothesis that the Pentagon is putting out a "cover story" for security reasons. Similarly, the hypothesis of supersonic aircraft need not have been eliminated quite so early; it might have been supported by the auxiliary hypothesis that a number of supesonic aircraft were either flying in formation or were at least aloft in the same area. Of course, we then need to test the auxiliary hypothesis as well as the original one. In general, the more auxiliary hypotheses one needs to square the original hypothesis with the evidence available, the weaker is the original hypothesis.

When an hypothesis is of a kind for which no testable consequences at all are conceivable, it is unsatisfactory from a logical point of view because we have no way of verifying or falsifying it. An example of an unverifiable hypothesis of this kind is that of alien extraterrestrial vehicles which are invisible and undetectable by radar. Although there might be an abstract possibility that this hypothesis could be true, from the practical viewpoint it is better to seek out some testable hypothesis, one which we could know to be true or false on the basis of appropriate evidence.

One scientist suggested the hypothesis that methane gas, produced in the decomposition of organic wastes dumped offshore by the states of New York and New Jersey, might be the cause of the explosions. He pointed out that there would have to be a buildup of gases over some period for this to be so. This hypothesis is testable: One could study the area's wind currents and general weather conditions in the period preceding the blasts to see whether they are consistent with the hypothesis.

A third principle for judging the relative worth of any hypothesis is that of *simplicity*. In general, an hypothesis is preferable to others if it is *simple*. By *simple*, we do not mean easier to understand or uncomplicated in its terms. An hypothesis is simple when it refers to kinds of entities and ways of behaving that are not unusual, that function as principles of explanation in well-grounded or widely accepted scientific theories or commonsense knowledge. The hypothesis that aliens from some other part of the universe are operating extraterrestrial vehicles near the East Coast is not simple, in the sense of this rule. The hypothesis is easy to understand—extraterrestrials are common in science fiction—but not *simple* in the logical sense we are giving the term. Rather it is a farfetched hypothesis, and not just in a punning sense. The more farfetched an hypothesis, the less confidence we can place in it—if it goes beyond reasonable bounds, we may even speak of the *fallacy of a farfetched hypothesis.*

We can apply these rules to arguments of inductive analogy and inductive generalization in the following manner. Consider the conclusion of the argument to be an hypothesis proposed to cover the observations contained in the premises. Devise one or more alternative hypotheses which will also account for the data of the premises. Compare the original hypothesis with the alternative hypotheses, applying the rules we have just outlined. We can summarize the principles for judging a set of hypotheses offered as the explanation for an event as follows:

Rules for Judging
an Explanatory Hypothesis

1. Does any of the hypotheses account for more of the data than the others, or account for it more successfully? The hypothesis that accounts for all the data or more data than the others is preferable.
2. What different consequences are implied by each hypothesis? The hypothesis whose consequences are confirmed by additional available evidence is preferable. An hypothesis with no testable consequences is unsatisfactory.
3. Do any of the hypotheses require a greater number of auxiliary

hypotheses than the others? The more auxiliary hypotheses that are needed, the weaker is the hypothesis.

4. Does any of the hypotheses commit the fallacy of farfetched hypothesis? A *simple* hypothesis, one that makes use of well-known entities and usual modes of operating, is preferable.

EXERCISE 9D

1. Another hypothesis for the blasts of December 2 and 8: Intense cold made vibrations from supersonic aircraft operating out of New York and New Jersey perceptible a greater distance. Compare this hypothesis with that of U.S. missile explosions or methane gas in accordance with the rules listed in the text.

2. Which hypothesis offers the best explanation of the data in the following? How could each hypothesis be tested?

   a. On going downstairs one summer morning, Mrs. White is surprised to see that the screen on the open casement window is up. The front door is standing open, and the portable television is not in its place on the sunroom table.

      (1) Mrs. White's husband neglected to lock up the house properly on going to bed the night before.
      (2) A burglar had entered the house and stolen the television.
      (3) Some family member was sleepwalking during the night.

   b. On returning home after a holiday, Mrs. Black's son tells her of a "little problem" with her car. His friend Keith had stopped by the previous weekend to see whether the family had returned. In the alley near their garage he found a key which he tried in the lock of Mrs. Black's car, where it broke off. Keith explains that he thought it was dangerous to leave the key in the alley since it might belong to her car. The extra key kept in the container in the bumper of Mrs. Black's car is gone.

      (1) Keith intended to take the car for a joyride, knowing the family was away, but was foiled when the key broke in the lock.
      (2) Neighborhood boys fooling around in the alley discovered the key in the bumper and threw it away as a prank.
      (3) Keith is telling the truth.
      (4) An intruder, seeking to steal the car from the garage during the family's absence, opened the car door with the extra key but was unable to start it without the ignition key.

c. A Vela nuclear-detection satellite, lofted into orbit in 1970, registered a brilliant flash in the general vicinity of South Africa on September 22, 1979—a curve of light was bright, brighter, then less bright, like a large explosion. Satellite data indicate the power of the possible atomic explosion was equal to about 2,000 tons of TNT, a small nuclear blast. There was no corroborating evidence from acoustic devices or radioactivity-measuring devices. South Africa denied any knowledge of the explosion and has promised not to develop nuclear devices or perform nuclear tests in its territory. It has a pilot uranium enrichment plant that could produce weapons-grade material, but it is not known whether they have accumulated enough nuclear material to produce a nuclear bomb.

(1) South Africa exploded a nuclear device, which did not completely burn its fissionable material.
(2) The burst of light was caused by a combination of natural events, such as lightning flashes, meteors, or sun glint.
(3) There was a malfunction in the satellite.
(4) Russia exploded a nuclear device from a submarine in the Indian ocean.

Review Exercise for Chapter 9

1. Assess the inductive reasoning in the following arguments.* What alternative hypotheses could account for the data?

a. People who suffer from "math anxiety"—including many women and minorities—are blocked from advancing in two-thirds of the country's professions, says T.S., head of a consulting firm that treats fear of mathematics through seminars and counseling. "Math anxiety is panic, muddled thinking, and an inability to concentrate," T.S. said. Fear and hatred of mathematics, which keeps most women and many men from studying advanced algebra and calculus, forces many people into dead-end jobs, T.S. said in an interview. Any job that entails planning, drawing up an annual budget, using computers, or analyzing finances requires the ability to think mathematically, said T.S., who studied a federal dictionary of occupational skills to make the estimate that two-thirds of the professions in the country use these skills.
b. Robert Jastrow, one of the world's best-known scientists, believes that science has found the God of Genesis in space. What

*Reprinted by permission of the *Baltimore Sunpapers*.

the scientists are confronted with is a theory of the creation of the universe which is best explained by a single act of creation by a force of unimaginable power. The theory was first proposed when scientists discovered that all galaxies were rushing away from us in space. The farther out they were, the faster they were moving, with some of those on the edge of the observable universe pushing the speed of light, Einstein's cosmic speed limit. The only logical explanation for this phenomenon was a gigantic explosion that blasted these clouds of stars hurling outward. That explosion was Creation. "I find it salutary ... in this funny creation theory that astronomy has developed, there is implication of some forces or circumstances that are not within the boundaries of science at this time," says Jastrow. "This is a convergence of science and religious thought ... because there is an effect without a cause, which is another name for God."

c. "Dear Dr. Steincrohn: I'm 42 and getting closer to the 'heart attack' age. I'll confess I smoke too much and work too hard. But I go right on doing what I shouldn't because of poor heredity. It seems every other male in our immediate family has had a heart attack. My father died of one at the age of 46. So did an uncle at the age of 49. It's evident that I have poor heredity. Therefore, there's no sense in taking care. I've become a fatalist. Whatever I do, chances are I'll have a coronary attack. In view of my poor heredity, I think you will agree that it's silly for me to be careful."

d. Women who smoke cigarettes during pregnancy are nearly twice as liable as nonsmokers to lose their babies through spontaneous abortion, a study says. A spontaneous abortion—as opposed to one that is induced artificially—is defined as one in which a woman naturally loses a fetus less than about 20 weeks old. The researchers did not distinguish between a spontaneous abortion and a miscarriage, which is generally defined as loss of the embryo or fetus during the first three months. Earlier studies have shown that babies of women who smoke are smaller than normal and are likely to die at birth. The researchers were not sure why women who smoke have more spontaneous abortions, but they said that there are two main theories. One is that smoking women eat less than nonsmokers. The other is that fetuses of smoking women do not get enough oxygen. Researchers compared the smoking habits of 574 women who aborted spontaneously to those of 320 who delivered after full pregnancies. They found that 41 percent of the women who aborted were smokers, compared to 28 percent of the women who had normal pregnancies.

2. Is it reasonable to hold some person responsible in the following incidents?*

    a. Three horrified schoolmates watched helplessly as Jimmy X., a seventh-grader, toppled to the floor after fatally wounding himself with a bullet in the head during a game of Russian roulette. The children told police the gun misfired the first time the boy pulled the trigger. When the gun simply clicked and failed to fire, the youth said, "Aw, shucks," the children told officers. Jimmy had "a surprised look" on his face as he fell to the floor, the children said. "They were dumbstruck," said the principal of the school. "It was just such a shock." Jimmy is the youngest of four children. The rest of the seventh-grade class was outside the room during the lunch break yesterday when the shooting occurred, said D. P., Jimmy's teacher. Jimmy and three other children had brought their lunches and were to eat in the classroom, she said.

        The three children told police Jimmy showed them his father's revolver, which he had brought to school. His father is a meter reader. There was no explanation of how or why Jimmy brought the pistol to school. "I'm sure it was an accident," said Ms. P. "There's not a single kid in my classroom who would even contemplate suicide. Jimmy's a happy-go-lucky kid. He gets along well with other kids and with his family; he wouldn't do something like this on purpose."

    b. Robert F., Sr., 52, could tolerate the fighting with his crazed and drunken son, but when the son threatened to demolish the family car with a 15-pound maul his father shot and killed him. The father gave a statement saying his 18-year-old daughter summoned him from the neighborhood tavern to deal with the son, who was behaving wildly. F. told police he tried to put his son out of the house but he resisted and began cursing, evidence showed. The father went upstairs and got his .22 caliber revolver, which he held behind him as he returned to the first floor, according to the statement. The younger F. attacked his father and the two rolled and struggled on the floor until the defendant whacked his son across an eyebrow with the pistol and drew blood . . . The victim became enraged, grabbed the maul from under the kitchen sink and strode from the house, threatening to batter the car, the elder F. told police.

        The victim stood by the car and lifted the maul and his father shot him . . . Another son of the defendant was prepared

---

*Reprinted by permission of the *Baltimore Sunpapers*.

to testify that the victim's swing seemed to indicate that young F. was attempting to heave the maul at his father . . . When police arrived, the defendant confessed to the killing and told them the gun was in his pocket. He had never been arrested before he shot his son. The younger F. had been committed to a veterans' hospital nine times in the past six years and had been released about eight months before the killing . . . The victim had been refusing to take his medicine and disobeying doctors' orders against drinking.

chapter 10

Other Kinds
of Everyday Reasoning

10A REASONING BY ANALOGY

In the previous chapters we have put forward principles for assessing various kinds of deductive and inductive arguments, the two major forms of reasoning extensively studied by logicians. We shall now examine some familiar kinds of everyday reasoning which do not readily fall into either category. One common type is reasoning that uses analogies.

In an analogy a comparison is usually made between two very different types of things, which are called the *terms* of the analogy. The philosopher Montaigne once drew an analogy between marriage and a birdcage, with the birds outside wanting to get in and the birds inside wanting to get out. In this analogy, one of the terms—a birdcage—is something concrete and perceptible, and the other term—the institution of marriage—is something invisible and abstract. By correlating an abstract and intangible thing with something whose character and workings are obvious and well-known, we often gain a better "handle" on it: We are then able to integrate our knowledge of it with our understanding of other sorts of things more successfully. Complex scientific theories involving intricate notions often make use of so-called "models," which relate data about things not observable by the senses to things of our common sense experience. Occasionally, as was the case in Harvey's analogy of the action of the heart to the workings of a water pump, an analogy will even suggest testable consequences and function somewhat as an explanatory hypothesis, enabling us to understand the nature of a thing and even to predict or speculate about its further properties.

In following an analogy, as well as in developing one, reasoning is involved. It may be intuition that makes us see an analogy between two sorts of things, but it is reasoning of a logical kind that carries it through to any significant conclusion. The first step in following an analogy is to precisely identify its terms: the two different kinds of things which are compared. It is important to focus the "unseen," or less familiar term—for example, "marriage" in Montaigne's birdcage analogy—as sharply as possible. Failure to identify the two terms accurately will lead one to misinterpret the analogy, just as failure to specify the exact conclusion may mislead one in following an argument.

Second, one must make a careful correlation between the features of the two terms of the analogy, making appropriate allowance for the different forms these features will take, given that they belong to two different sorts of things. In the analogy of marriage to a birdcage, the physical enclosure provided by the birdcage corresponds to the social, psychological, and legal bonds of marriage: Just as marriage both brings partners together and also separates them from the outside world, so the birdcage encompasses its occupants. To the unmarried—the birds outside the cage who want to get in—marriage appears an attractive haven or love nest; but to marriage partners—the birds in the cage who want to get out—marriage is like a prison they seek to escape.

The value of an analogy does not lie simply in the number of like features but in the significance of the features it singles out. Montaigne's analogy is not only amusing but apt because it exposes the very features of marriage that produce ambivalent attitudes toward it. A successful analogy—as in the case of the heart and the water pump—sometimes works by indicating that although two things may be of very different kinds, the interrelationship between their parts and their overall structure is comparable. Or, as in the birdcage-marriage analogy, there may be a correlation between the ways two different things function in relation to other entities and to their environment.

Analogies are often used in literature to describe or explain the nature of a thing. In poems, the quality or content of a human experience, which may be very difficult to articulate, is set before us by means of analogies to incidents of everyday life or to concrete objects. Much of the New Testament consists of parables—stories which use complex and extended analogies to illustrate religious conceptions, such as the nature of the Deity or the character of divine justice. The story of the Prodigal Son, for example, outlines a novel view of the attitude of God toward sinners, one that stresses reform and repentance rather than retribution. Just as in the analogies used in empirical science, it is essential to trace the lines of an analogy with care in order to comprehend the notions of the writer.

Another important use of analogy is to make or buttress a point in an argument: By means of an analogy, it can be claimed that the subject of discussion has some particular character which supports the conclusion drawn by the reasoner. In such cases, the analogy functions as a kind of premise supporting the conclusion. Here is an argument by a doctor in which an analogy of the human embryo to the foundation of a building supports the conclusion that abortion is not murder:

> Abortion is not killing a child. No one would accept a house from a contractor-builder with only the foundation finished. The embryo is the foundation of a prospective human being. When we stop the building in the early stages it is not killing a human being—it is stopping the progress of a potential human being. It is for this reason that the Supreme Court, as well as the Church of England, agreed that abortion in the first sixteen weeks of pregnancy is permissible and is not considered killing or murder.*

Here the terms of the analogy are the human embryo and the foundation of the building. The point of the analogy is that the embryo should not be identified with a human being, just as we do not identify the foundation of a building with the whole house. Thus, a doctor's termination of the development of the embryo is comparable to a contractor's termination of construction of a building after laying the foundation: These are not acts of destruction, but simply failures to continue construction. Thus, with the support of the analogy, the likeness of abortion to the killing of a human being is denied.

When an analogy is used to support a definite conclusion, we must consider not only how to understand the analogy but also how to assess it for its strength as a premise of the argument. As usual, we must reflect on the *aptness* of the analogy: Does it enable us to understand the significant features of the less understood or controversial term of the analogy by reference to the correlated features of the better understood term? An analogy is *strained* when it compares two things whose features cannot be put into significant correlation. Such an analogy may serve not to illuminate the nature of the less understood term, but to mislead us or even cover up the term's essential features. When an analogy functions as a premise of an argument it should expose some feature of the subject that is highly relevant to the conclusion drawn by the argument.

Let us examine the foregoing argument of the embryo and the foundation to determine whether the analogy is an apt one and supports the conclusion drawn from it. We begin by looking for significant correlations between the mature human and its embryonic state, on the one

*Reprinted by permission of the *Baltimore Sunpapers.*

hand, and between a completed building and its foundation, on the other. The final building and the mature human develop from foundation and embryo, respectively, and both do so by gradual steps over a considerable number of months. In each case the finished product is larger and has more working parts than the formative one, and each entity undergoes a radical change in appearance. The characteristic functions and powers of the finished product, whether house or human, are not to be found, in the main, in either the foundation or the embryo. These facts do suggest that we should have different practical attitudes, and perhaps also different feelings, toward the early and final stages of both house and human. Thus, an attitude toward the embryo may also have a different moral character from a similar attitude toward a fully developed human being.

But in testing an analogy, we must go beyond finding similarities and look for *disanalogies* between the two terms as well. We must consider whether one term has crucial features which have no correlate in the other term, and whether these differences significantly affect the conclusion based on the analogy. The analogy of the embryo to the foundation of a building turns out to be a weak one, despite similarities we have mentioned, because there exist more striking disanalogies between the two which undermine the conclusion the analogy is used to prove. For example, the sense in which the embryo is the foundation of a "prospective human being" is a very different one from that in which the foundation is that of a prospective building. The whole embryo becomes the human being; unlike the foundation of a building, which can and often does survive the superstructure placed upon it, it is not a distinct, relatively unchanged part of the final product. It is possible to resume construction of the building's foundation at a later time if the contractor stops work on the building; it is even possible to raise a number of different structures on the very same foundation; but stopping the growth of the embryo in abortion is an irrevocable act. The human relationships between the embryo, the future father and mother, and even the doctor in the case, have a strong emotional significance. Hence these relationships have a profoundly different moral quality from those between the contractor or the prospective owners and the foundation of a building. Thus, when we consider the full human meaning of the two actions, destroying the embryo is *not* very much like leaving off construction once its foundation is laid. Since these disanalogies undermine the conclusion drawn about the moral acceptability of abortion, the analogy can be seen to be a strained one which does not offer strong support for the conclusion.

Another technique in testing an analogy is to see whether the analogy can be turned against itself and used to support a conclusion opposite to that originally drawn. In this case, one might argue that the same analogy justifies infanticide, since the infant is in the same sense the "foundation of a prospective human being." Another strategy is to look for *counter-*

analogies, new analogies which contradict the conclusion originally drawn. For example, one might argue that abortion is comparable to bombing the foundation of the building, rather than merely stopping work on it, and that it is thus an impermissible destructive act. Or one might offer an entirely new analogy, such as that between the embryo and a rare plant that has just started to take root, in which abortion is likened to the willful, violent uprooting of a unique being before it has had a chance to bloom. In these ways we may discover the strength or weakness of an analogy and thus contribute to our understanding of the subject of the argument.

The use of analogies is pervasive and popular in everyday reasoning, and should not be dismissed as an inherently inferior technique. It is a technique capable of both criticism and justification, although admittedly the rules for judging an analogy are somewhat looser than those for other types of reasoning. Especially when an analogy is made to support some substantive conclusion, we can apply the following rules in order to estimate the validity of the analogy or the soundness of the argument:

Rules for Judging an Analogy

1. Identify the two terms of the analogy and examine in detail their corresponding features. The *apter* the analogy, that is, the more significant or illuminating the features of the unfamiliar or controversial term brought out by the comparison with the other term, the better the analogy.

2. Look for disanalogies or differences in the corresponding features of the terms of the analogy. The more *strained* the analogy, the weaker is the argument based on it. A fallacy of *strained analogy* occurs whenever the differences or disanalogies are so striking that they undermine the conclusion rather than support it.

3. Attempt to construct a *counteranalogy*; that is, try to suggest a more or at least equally plausible analogy which contradicts the conclusion of the argument offered.

EXERCISE 10A

Identify the terms of each analogy in the following. Assess the aptness of the analogy and its support of the conclusion.

1. The Soviets feel no need to disguise the contempt they feel for the United States. The sentencing of Mr. Orlov expresses contempt for "human rights" rhetoric and is an analogue of Mr. Brezhnev's contemptuous "response" to Mr. Carter's decision against producing the

neutron weapons needed to counter the Soviet advantage in conventional forces in Europe. Mr. Brezhnev's declaration that the Soviet Union, too, will forego such weapons has prompted this comparison: A man plagued by rats considers purchasing a cat. The rats respond that if he will not purchase a cat, they will not purchase a cat.*

2. A very bad doctrine is being invoked in the selection of Mrs. M. to replace her late husband as a member of the House of Delegates. This is not to say, or even suggest, that she is not qualified for the job. It is a comment on the way she is being chosen by the district's Democratic Committee. The chairman is quoted as saying, "Since Art won the seat, and since his widow has professed interest in finishing out his term, the only moral thing is to let her do it. She is the heir apparent and I think it's only fair that she have it for this interim period." Heirs are persons who inherit decedents' property. To say that Mrs. M. is "the heir apparent" connotes that public office is a piece of property owned—at least for a term—by the person who was elected. It is, of course, no such thing. Voters chose the official, and nobody else, to represent them.*

3. If the fetus is going to die anyway without even possessing self-awareness or the capacities to make decisions of any kind, the only thing that we can do for it is to ensure that it does not suffer in the time that it remains alive. If there is any possibility that the fetus is suffering, then suffering should be ended by total anesthesia for the remainder of the life of the fetus. So long as this provision is scrupulously observed, I cannot see that the commission's prohibition on shortening or lengthening the life of the fetus can make any difference to the fetus at all.

   For those inclined to reject this solution, I suggest the following thought experiment: Suppose that for some reason we can do nothing to save a dog which is dying. There is an experiment we can perform on it before it dies which has reasonable prospects of leading to a significant medical advance. The experiment can be performed under total anesthesia and the dog will die before recovering from the anesthetic. Is there any rational basis for objecting to such an experiment? So long as we are sure the dog will feel nothing, I cannot see any. Nor do I think it makes any difference whether the experiment shortens or prolongs the unconscious animal's life. †

4. In a crackdown on prostitution, the mayor of New York City initiated a policy of reading the names of male clients of prostitutes on daily radio

---

*Reprinted by permission of the *Baltimore Sunpapers.*

†P. Singer, "Bioethics," *New York Review of Books,* August 5, 1976. Copyright © 1976 Nyrev, Inc. Reprinted with permission.

broadcasts. He said this is the modern equivalent of the colonial punishment of putting a minor offender into the stocks for a day as a deterrent to crime.

10B   REASONING ABOUT PROPER CATEGORIES

Another type of argument involving analogy uses a form of reasoning concerned with the proper way to categorize a particular instance or whole class of things. Is it an act of suicide if a man who is about to be executed will not permit further legal appeals? Is abortion a kind of murder? Is alcoholism a disease? Such questions, common in everyday reasoning, are not merely semantic. As we noted earlier, a dispute is verbal only when people choose to use words differently; no difference in their beliefs is at issue. However, such questions as whether obtaining or performing an abortion is murder are serious moral issues. They cannot be settled by making arbitrary decisions about how to use a word, for such decisions have implications in morality and social policy. As in the case of arguments by analogy, there are still definite principles to help us assess such arguments even though there are no formal rules to apply to such reasoning.

Our first step is to marshal whatever evidence is available concerning the thing to be classified and the projected classification. If it is an individual case, particular facts about the persons involved, the actual circumstances, and the events and consequences related to the matter at issue are relevant. When we are categorizing something such as alcoholism, all the information we have about its causes, effects, symptoms, and characteristic features should be brought into view, along with the typical range of cases that come under that heading. If we are considering whether alcoholism is a disease, we must in the same way review those things that are classified as diseases and note their features. In particular we should distinguish the typical features of clear-cut instances of the projected classification (so-called "paradigm" cases) and see how they differ from controversial or borderline cases of the projected classification. Cancer and tuberculosis, for example, are "paradigm cases" of the disease classification.

In reviewing the information about the thing to be categorized and the projected classification, it is important to note whether further facts are obtainable that would help to settle the issue. For example, if it were discovered that people with abnormal genetic makeup or irregular neurochemical functioning (not an effect of alcoholism itself, of course) were peculiarly subject to alcoholism, such evidence would support the classification of alcoholism as a disease. In such cases the question of classification may be partly empirical, and the techniques of inductive reasoning can help in deciding the issue.

The second step is to make a detailed comparison of points of likeness and difference (positive and negative analogy) between the thing in question and clear-cut cases of the projected classification. For example, one would compare alcholism to various sorts of diseases with respect to causes, effects, symptoms, prognosis, treatments, clinical course, onset, and the typical kind of victim. In general, the more similar to clear-cut cases of the projected classification the thing in question is, the better the argument for the projected classification. The greater the negative analogy between the thing in question and clear-cut cases of the projected classification, the weaker the argument for the classification. However, as in other arguments by analogy, merely counting up the number of likenesses and differences is not a reliable way to determine the strength of the analogy; it is the significance of the features elicited in the comparison that determines the appropriateness of the projected classification.

Also as in other arguments by analogy, one can attempt to devise counteranalogies by reviewing features of the thing which suggest alternative classifications that may be equally or even more plausible. Is alcoholism in its main features more like obesity, drug addiction, or psychosis than it is like cancer or pneumonia? Here again, one should note positive and negative analogies between the thing in question and the alternative classifications. Evidence about borderline cases is relevant here, in that such evidence may bring to light features that are the grounds for preferring one classification to another. If the psychological and behavioral characteristics of alcoholism are more comparable with those of obesity or drug addiction than with those of disease, it might be preferable to classify alcoholism with them as a behavioral disorder.

The last principle is extremely important in deciding issues of classification: We must examine the implications of the projected classification and perhaps compare them with the implications of other projected classifications. Exactly which implications are relevant will, of course, depend on the subject matter in each case. However, among the implications to consider are the following:

1. *Is the classification consistent with the rest of our knowledge of the subject matter?* For example, would classifying alcoholism as a disease be consistent with theories of disease and harmonious with medical knowledge? The greater the consistency of a given classification with this knowledge, the stronger the argument for it; a classification which conflicts with basic knowledge of the subject matter is defective and requires additional argument. To prove that a given classification is desirable or superior to others, one must often disarm the competing classifications, or counter-classifications. In doing this, one may consider the alternative classifications as rival hypotheses and apply the principles of explanatory hypothesis in comparing their relative strengths and weaknesses.

2. *Is the classification consistent with well-grounded or widely accepted beliefs of a moral, social, religious, or aesthetic kind?* For example, the legal implications of considering alcoholism as a disease should be explored, since there are special laws regarding alcohol. It sometimes happens that the purpose of an argument in favor of a given classification is to alter beliefs, or actions or policy based on beliefs. Some prefer to regard alcoholism as a disease rather than a moral weakness, for example, in order to encourage a more sympathetic approach to the problems of alcoholics or to stimulate social action in their behalf. When such an approach to classification is used, we need to balance its desirability against its negative effects on the coherence of our other beliefs and on our organization of the subject matter. In particular, it should be questioned whether reclassifying something is the most suitable way of bringing about a changed attitude toward it.

3. *Does the classification represent a useful or desirable extension of our concepts? Does it raise problems, confuse our thinking, or reflect some partisan bias?* For example, does putting alcoholism in the category of diseases because it commonly produces serious physical malfunctioning represent a justifiable extension of our notion of disease? Smoking heavily also has serious physical effects—should we then call smoking a disease? The view that alcoholism is a disease is associated with the proponents of a particular form of treatment for alcoholism; it has been suggested that thinking of alcoholism as a disease stands in the way of other approaches to the problem which are worthwhile alternatives.

Questions concerning the proper classification of a thing are often difficult to resolve, especially when moral issues are involved. Thoughtful and persistent application of the preceding principles helps in many cases to reveal the salient facts and also the advantages and disadvantages of a suggested classification, permitting the justness of a given classification to come into view. In any event, the crucial features of the things to be classified, those that must be reflected upon, usually come to light in the course of the deliberation.

Principles to Assess Reasoning about Proper Classification

1. Review the information available concerning the thing to be classified and the projected classification.

2. Note significant points of similarity and difference between the thing to be classified and clear cases of the projected classification. The greater the positive analogy, the stronger the argument.

3. Devise counterclassifications, that is, alternative plausible classifications. Compare the strengths and weaknesses of the various classifications by testing the degrees of positive and negative analogy, consistency with the data, and simplicity.

4. Test the implications of the proposed and alternative classifications for (a) consistency with knowledge of the subject matter; (b) consistency with moral, legal, political, religious, or aesthetic beliefs relevant to the subject matter; (c) the desirability or undesirability of any changes in our notions that would result from the proposed classification.

EXERCISE 10B

Discuss the appropriateness of the following classifications, applying the principles listed in the text.*

1. Is the "Stone Field Sculpture" a piece of sculpture?

   Artist C. A.'s arrangement of thirty glacial boulders on a grassy area in downtown Hartford has drawn criticism from Mayor G. A. and others, who question whether it is art. The mayor puts it this way: "Webster defines sculpture in terms of shaping, carving, forming. This guy did nothing. He took a pile of rocks and shifted them to another rockpile in downtown Hartford. And he got $87,000." Dean B. H. of the Hartford Art Center says the dictionary definition has become meaningless in the second half of the twentieth century. "The individual should be able to relate to a work of art, and the work should relate to the outside world," he said. "You can get into this work and lose yourself in it."

2. Should the kinds of behavior described be classified as "time theft"?

   "Theft of time," which will cost the American economy as much as $70 billion in 1977, is the biggest crime of them all, according to a leading employment authority. R. Half, president of Robert Half Personnel Agencies, the world's largest financial executive and data processing employment specialists, defines *time theft* as those deliberate employee actions which result in the "massive, growing misuse and waste of our most precious and irreplaceable commodity—time." Included among Half's examples of time theft are arriving at work late,

*All are reprinted by permission of the *Baltimore Sunpapers.*

leaving early, taking unjustified "sick" days, extensive socializing with co-workers, turning the water cooler into a conversation area, inattention to the job at hand, and reading novels and magazines.

3. Should the Nazi Party's march through Skokie be banned as a public nuisance?

The relevant body of law in this case is not the First Amendment but nuisance statutes. People are not allowed to wander nude on downtown streets, or to defecate there. Public nuisance statutes can be abused, but normally they are not. The law is not invoked often against uncurbed dogs, unmufflered cars, spitting on sidewalks, or noisy parties. But after warning and repeated offense, the law can (and should) be invoked. I know that all my parallels will be thrown aside as irrelevant because the Nazis scream their insults in words, and the First Amendment protects speech. Well, the woman tortured by repeated obscene phone calls is afflicted by another person's speech. Is that speech protected by the Constitution?

The Nazis who want to parade in Skokie are not engaged in the rational airing of views but in the provoking of irrational (but predictable) responses. They are, in effect, broadcasting an obscene phone call to a whole neighborhood instead of a single house.

10C   MORAL REASONING

Moral reasoning takes many forms. As the two previous sections illustrate, moral issues are often at stake in the various forms of reasoning by analogy. An analogy sometimes figures in the premises which lead to a moral conclusion, as the analogy of the fetus to the foundation of a building was accepted to support the conclusion that abortion in the early stages of pregnancy is morally acceptable. Sometimes the subject of the analogical reasoning is itself a moral question, as when we argue about whether homosexuality is a vice or an alternative life style, or whether capital punishment is cruel and unusual punishment.

Not uncommonly, moral reasoning takes deductive form, as when we derive a moral principle from other principles or pursue the implications of moral concepts (the application of a moral principle to a particular case is often expressible in a syllogism). However, the principles of deductive inference seldom suffice to judge the soundness of a piece of moral reasoning put in deductive form. In such reasoning, the soundness of the argument frequently depends on the truth of some moral premise. Thus we need to be able to pronounce on the truth of the moral premises if we are to establish the soundness or weakness of the argument. For example, the following bit of reasoning could readily be put into valid syllogistic form:

> Any action which fulfills the desire of the person doing it is right. Since Alice would very much like to have a cocktail, it is right for her to do so.

But the fact that the argument is of valid syllogistic form does not certify the soundness of the reasoning. We also need to know whether the premise, "Any action which fulfills the desire of the doer is right," is a true one, a morally acceptable premise. Philosophers call this premise the *egoistic principle*. Although defended by some as an ultimate moral principle, it is usually not accepted as a general rule either by philosophers or laymen. In general, only principles and values which are widely respected and approved are persuasive in everyday reasoning. When one asserts a controversial principle such as the egoistic principle, the argument only becomes plausible if one has demonstrated that the principle is acceptable, at least in the particular ethical situation to which it is being applied.

Stating, testing, and refining the principles, values, and concepts of morality is the purpose of ethics and social philosophy and of much religious thinking. In such discussions we seek to arrive at conclusions about the goods and evils of human life and how they are to be attained or avoided. In such inquiries we put together ideas from many sources. These are not just derived from our own desires and disappointments, our conscience and remorse, and the norms embodied in our own social forms, but are also communicated to us by the ethical writings of the past and present, implied by advances in the natural and social sciences, or made feasible by technological developments. Ethics is a persistent, continuing form of inquiry which structures human striving for goals beyond mere survival. We must constantly rehearse and learn our moral lessons within the context of the present human scene in the light of the specific limitations and opportunities that the world provides for our thoughts and actions.

In this text we have neither leisure nor liberty to engage in ethical thinking except insofar as it touches logic, but fortunately we can make a start at judging moral reasoning without a formal investigation of the subject. Common sense includes many moral maxims in its store; history, religion, literature, and art all express many of the goods and evils that define our lives as beings who act, think, and perceive in a moral world. There are a large number of moral principles whose truth is widely acknowledged. For instance, The Ten Commandments and The Golden Rule are principles first propounded by prophets but adopted by both religious and nonreligious thinkers. Tenets formulated by philosophers have become deeply entrenched in our common moral thinking: Kant's thesis that each human being should always be treated as an end, not as a means; Aristotle's conception of happiness as virtuous activity fulfilling the highest human capacities; the Epicurean values of friendship and peace of mind; the Stoic ideal of self-mastery; the utilitarian social ideal of the greatest good for the greatest number; Locke's conception of basic human rights; the democratic notion of justice as equality before the law. In the moral issues which come up in everyday reasoning, we appeal to such shared standards and values, invoking them as premises for our moral deliberations.

Moral reasoning often occurs in conjunction with other forms of reasoning we have already considered; when it does, part of the task of moral evaluation is to test this auxiliary reasoning in the usual ways. Inductive generalizations frequently function as premises for further conclusions of a moral kind, as when the generalization that alcoholic mothers tend to have babies with birth defects is used to support the moral injunction that expectant mothers ought not to drink. When the inductive reasoning is undertaken because of some moral concern over the subject matter, that concern may affect not only the weight we give to the available evidence but the amount of evidence we demand as well. When drawing one conclusion instead of another will seriously affect the welfare of a person or group, we have to be more circumspect. Sometimes skepticism is desirable—as when drawing a particular conclusion that may convict a person of a serious crime—but at other times it is proper to draw a conclusion from lesser evidence to be on the safe side—as in predicting the probable effects of a drug on its users. We also need to be aware that the moral position of the reasoner may even affect his or her interpretation of the results of his or her investigations, and we must be ready to discount the reasoning because of its subjective bias. In cases of this kind we should be guided by the thought that irremediable harm may be done to actual individuals or to the permanent vital interests of a particular group as a result of our believing or disbelieving the conclusion offered.

In many cases, moral reasoning is a matter of deciding which principle or value has priority, or whether the principle or value cited is the appropriate one to apply in the given situation. Few moral principles apply universally without any qualification whatsoever; moral insight involves recognizing legitimate exceptions. The injunction against killing, for example, is set aside in cases of legitimate self-defense. Some principles are acknowledged to have only limited validity: The egoistic principle is generally acceptable only when no harm is done to others or when any evil or risk is suffered only by the adult individual himself. Debates about whether motorcyclists ought to be required to wear helmets have involved the question of the egoistic principle and its limitations. In other cases, the reasoning may be called on to resolve a conflict between two moral principles that justify opposite conclusions when applied to a situation.

For example, the conclusion of the argument that expectant mothers ought not to drink contains the implied moral premise, "Expectant mothers ought not to do things that jeopardize the child's proper development." But suppose the expectant mother wants a drink very much and does not want the child much at all? According to the egoistic principle, we may then infer it is quite right for her to drink. These are the sorts of cases that call for moral judgment in everyday reasoning. We shall now formulate some principles to be considered in reaching a moral conclusion.

A common form of moral reasoning attempts to reach a conclusion as to whether a general type of action or some particular course of action is right or wrong. Often it is not possible to separate these two questions, since whether a particular action is right or wrong may depend primarily on whether it is an instance of a *type* of action that is right or wrong. For example, the question of whether it is wrong for a particular person to engage in extramarital sex with another particular person may hang on whether extramarital sex in general is right or wrong. However, it often happens that certain facts about an individual or his or her circumstances have significant weight and affect the conclusion. In analyzing moral reasoning, it is important to keep in mind whether the subject of the moral conclusion is a particular action or a general type of action. In general, all of the following principles can be applied to this kind of moral reasoning, although one or another may have more weight, depending on whether the moral judgment is a singular one or a generalization.

First, one must ask, what are the motives or psychological causal factors of the action? By a motive or psychological causal factor we mean those mental factors, conscious and unconscious, which lead a person to act in a certain way. Often the person is aware of them and will offer his or her conscious motives as the explanation of the act. Sometimes we may reasonably attribute a motive to a person, regardless of whether he or she admits to it, on the basis of such evidence as the individual's appearance, statements, manner of acting, and past history, and the circumstances of the action, or of subsequent actions. Motives such as anger, jealousy, hatred, greed, resentment, revenge, envy, or vanity are usually blameworthy and are harmful either to the doer or to others. Motives such as love, compassion, kindness, generosity, courage, consideration, loyalty, or friendship render an action praiseworthy and morally good. Other motives, such as fear or prudence, may be neutral, good, or bad, depending on the circumstances and on the nature of the action performed. It is seldom hard to determine to which category a given motive or complex of motives belongs: Common sense, long human experience, and philosophical and religious beliefs usually converge. In general, an individual's proceeding from a praiseworthy motive tends to make an action right, or helps to excuse it at least in part; proceeding from a blameworthy motive tends to confirm the wrongness of an action.

Very seldom, however, does knowledge of the motive of the action alone enable us to conclude that an action is right or wrong. We need to consider also the individual's intention, the end which the doer seeks to bring about through the action. There is usually an intimate connection between motive and intention: If a person's motive is anger, his intention usually is to perform an action that will do harm to someone or something. A goal that is recognized to be of value—promoting someone else's good, for example—is an end that tends to make the action morally right, just as goals or purposes that are bad or questionable make the action morally wrong. Such unacceptable goals often involve promoting the agent's own interest at the expense of that of others, or jeopardizing something of value for an immediate pleasure or for something of lesser or insignificant value. As with motives, there is a broad fund of human experience and knowledge concerning the goals and purposes that are morally acceptable and those that are morally unacceptable. As in the case of motives, there is sometimes a complex of goals, not all of which carry the same moral weight. We may need to decide which one of these goals is paramount or whether, on balance, the purposes of the action "pass muster." One of the tragic features of human life is that the intended goal and the actual effects of an action may not coincide: The purpose of the action may be laudable but it may not turn out as expected or intended. Thus we must also consider another set of facts, the consequences of the action.

By the consequences of an action we mean its results, whether foreseen or unexpected. We have already noted that in general we hold a person morally responsible for the consequences of an action that could reasonably be expected to follow from it, whether he or she took them into consideration or not. In general, an action is wrong if its consequences injure someone's well-being, result in the destruction of something of value or interfere with some good; an action is right if it promotes someone's well-being, averts an evil, or produces something good. It may happen that an action has both desirable and undesirable consequences, in which case we must consider whether the good outweighs the evil. To evaluate such an action we must take account of not only its motive and purpose but also of one final important matter, the nature of the action itself.

We need to look at the character of the action: Is it the kind of action that is recognized to be morally acceptable even independently of its consequences? Lying and breaking promises, cheating, disloyalty, stealing, selfishness, cruelty, inconsiderateness, and ingratitude are some of the qualities thought to have an intrinsically bad character. Truthfulness, honesty, fairness, and respect for others are among those actions that are good in themselves. In general, the actions that exhibit good character— that is, virtues such as courage, benevolence, self-control, wisdom, moderation, love, or friendship—are morally good whereas those of weak or bad character—acts revealing cowardice, insolence, self-indulgence, pride, egotism, or cruelty, even indifference to those one should care for or respect—are evil. It is essential to consider whether an action is in accord with morality and law. An action that violates a fundamental principle of morality and justice is usually wrong for that reason, regardless of motive, intention, or consequences. An action that is in accord with a generally accepted moral principle or rule of justice is right—or at least not clearly wrong. Actions that are offensive, embarrassing, or considered contrary to decency and good taste—for example, many involving the body—are subject to moral criticism in some circumstances, especially if performed in public. Actions that are widely practiced or in accordance with social convention are generally viewed as morally unobjectionable.

In applying these principles to determine the rightness or wrongness of a course of action, we cannot mechanically punch them in and add them up to arrive at an answer. As in the case of inductive reasoning and arguments using analogy, we must treat them as independent factors and reach an overall conclusion only after weighing each one. If the reasoning we are assessing does not make reference to any of the four factors (motive, goal, consequences, intrinsic moral character), one must attempt to supply them using the facts provided together with one's understanding of the morally relevant features of the subject at issue. Lack of reference to one or another of these factors does not mean that the reasoning is at fault, for these premises are often so much a part of common knowledge or such obvious facts that they need not be mentioned.

In determining the soundness of a piece of moral reasoning about the rightness of an action or the desirability of some course of action or social policy, it is important to be aware of the relevance of all four factors, for disputes often arise when one of them is valued differently or overlooked in favor of another. It may be, as in inductive reasoning, that an action proving morally acceptable in relation to a majority of the factors may so grossly violate one of them (a moral rule deeply entrenched in daily life, for example) that the moral estimate of the action is determined by that principle alone. More often, however, the principles relating to the four factors will converge to support a conclusion. It sometimes happens that a conclusion based on one factor will be in conflict with a conclusion based on another. In public discussion of university affirmative action programs, for example, supporters defend them because they believe the goal to be laudable, whereas critics perceive in them the violation of a fundamental democratic principle. Cases such as these are the most troublesome ones, and they demand true wisdom and moral imagination for their resolution. The great majority of cases of moral reasoning yield a fairly straightforward answer; the difficulty lies less in reaching a conclusion based on sound reasoning than in reconciling the interests of those adversely affected by the conclusion.

In general, the two factors of motives and intentions are more important in decisions about a particular action of an individual person. In discussing the rightness of a *type* of action, priority is commonly given to the other two factors, that is, the consequences of the action and its conformity with accepted or enlightened moral practice (intrinsic moral character). But in both cases, we need to give attention to all four factors, both in presenting arguments and in evaluating the reasoning of others. To summarize, we ask these four questions:

1. Are the motives of the action praiseworthy or blameable?
2. Is the intention or purpose of the action good or bad?
3. What are the actual or potential consequences of the action on human well-being?
4. Is the character of the action in conformity with moral principles and law?

As in inductive reasoning, the soundness we attribute to the reasoning depends on the extensiveness or sweep of the conclusion in relation to the evidence: An argument which concludes, "Expectant mothers ought not to drink at all," requires stronger evidence than one which concludes, "Expectant mothers ought to limit their drinking."

We will show how principles relating to the four factors work by examining two cases, one concerning the action of an individual person, the second concerning a general type of action.

Suppose our neighbor Mrs. Green is thinking of leaving her husband, and asks whether it is the right thing to do. We know that he is frequently drunk; she confides that he often beats her on these occasions and even abuses their children. She says that she fears for her own safety and for that of her children; she believes that the only way to convince her husband of the brutality of his behavior is to leave him.

Here, the motives of fear and desire for security are ones of which reason and morality approve. But we must also look for other motives that Mrs. Green does not mention, or perhaps does not even recognize. It is not uncommon for people to disguise their motives, or even to hide them from themselves. To verify Mrs. Green's motives, we have to inquire into Mrs. Green's character and circumstances, paying particular attention to her relationship with her husband and family. Is the motive she offers consistent with her past behavior? If she has often been visited by an admirer when her husband has been absent, we might suspect that she wants to be free to carry on an affair—not a motive that meets with moral approval. In attributing motives we need to employ all of our knowledge of human psychology, for motives may be not only hidden and disguised but also mixed and conflicting—reflecting emotions, beliefs, and attitudes with differing moral qualities. In assigning a moral character to a person's motives, we attempt to determine which motive is paramount and possesses the greatest moral significance. In figuring this out, it is helpful to analyze the motives in relation to the second moral factor, closely linked with them—the intention, purpose, or goal of the action.

As in the case of motives, we must consider not merely the avowed intention but also those purposes we may reasonably attribute to the agent. To do this we must call on both our detailed knowledge of the person's character and situation and our common-sense knowledge of human affairs. We do not stop with Mrs. Green's acknowledged intention, we probe for others that might also be operating. Is Mrs. Green's goal limited to inducing her husband to change his ways? or does she propose to start a new life apart from him? These are two quite different intentions which we may judge differently as we learn more details. One thing we need to discover is whether the probable consequences of the action will accomplish a morally good intention, for sometimes the actual predictable consequences of an action are not even consistent with the agent's intention. Is leaving her husband the way to get him to stop drinking, if that is her aim? If her intention is to separate from him permanently, we might ask whether such a drastic step is demanded by the circumstances and whether she can manage successfully on her own.

In estimating the third factor, the probable consequences of the action, we engage in inductive reasoning concerning probable effects of the action, unintended as well as intended ones. Then we weigh the favorable and unfavorable consequences, not just for Mrs. Green but also for the others—her husband and children—whose lives are vitally affected by her course of action. If the probability is high that Mrs. Green and her children will lead distinctly better lives apart from her husband, or that he will be shocked into more reasonable conduct by her leaving, the desirability of her proposed action is confirmed. But if her leaving is likely to bring hardship on herself and her family without any beneficial effect on her husband, its moral quality is questionable.

Finally, we must take account of the fourth factor, the intrinsic moral quality of the action. Ordinarily, abandoning one's husband is not a morally acceptable action, for it is a rejection of one's duty to one's spouse and may indicate lack of loyalty or some weakness of character. Nevertheless, there are circumstances in which a husband forfeits the claim he has upon his wife, and constant physical abuse is generally accepted to be one of them. To decide whether Mrs. Green's action falls under this category, we would have to be confident of the correctness of her charge. To do this we would use the techniques described in the previous section.

In arriving at a final judgment about Mrs. Green's intended action, we must take account of all four factors (motive, intention, consequences, intrinsic moral character) in their interrelationship with and impact upon one another, not just one by one. Usually the results will converge to produce a firm moral assessment of whether the action is the right thing to do under the given circumstances. When judging the moral quality of one's own actions, performed or intended, the doer and the judge are one. Often one has to engage in a process of self-examination if one is to counter self-deception about one's own motives and intentions. In this task a candid consideration of the two other factors—the consequences and the intrinsic moral character of the action—may be revealing. Usually one needs to entertain alternative courses of action (like rival hypotheses in inductive reasoning) in order to discover a course of action whose consequences may be more assured, more in keeping with moral perceptions and the intentions, feelings, character, and circumstances of persons involved, than the action in question. Perhaps Mrs. Green might do better to encourage her husband to join Alcoholics Anonymous, or seek out an advisor for a discussion of family problems.

The two factors of consequences and conformity with moral principles are prominent when the issue is the rightness of a type of action or the desirability of a social policy. Also in cases such as this, one must compare the relative advantages of alternative courses of action to see, in particular, whether extreme or lesser measures will be effective or desirable. Since one of the exercises in this chapter argues for decriminalization of marijuana smoking, let us see how the four factors enter in when the opposing view—that marijuana usage should not be decriminalized—is presented.

A study of the motives of those opposing decriminalization does not yield any morally decisive results, since those motives tend to be varied and of mixed moral character. Some people are suspicious of a new and unfamiliar practice, others fearful of its potentially harmful effects, and others may have religious scruples. The stated intentions of the two opposing parties will usually be different, and thus should be compared for their relative moral or social priority under the actual circumstances, yet each side is likely to present an objective that is morally acceptable and socially approved. Clearly many who favor decriminalization are marijuana smokers claiming to promote legitimate interests in the name of freedom and the egoistic principle, just as those against it are primarily non-smokers claiming to safeguard the interests of society or of particular groups they believe to be threatened. The debate tends to become a standoff, incapable of resolution simply through a consideration of the motives and intentions of the opposing camps.

As is true in many issues of social policy, it is primarily the consequences of decriminalizing marijuana that are critical. Those in favor maintain it will free police to investigate more serious crimes. Yet there is little evidence that police spend so much time pursuing offenders of marijuana laws that decriminalization would enable us to decrease the size of a police force or promote more effective enforcement of other criminal laws.

In any case, such an effect would be only a side effect, a consequence not capable of tipping the moral balance on the issue. The serious issue is whether marijuana smoking is a sufficiently serious threat to the welfare of those engaging in it to warrant its legal ban, as a necessary measure to discourage its use. To decide this issue, inductive reasoning about the harmful effects of marijuana smoking is germane.

Proponents of decriminalization say there is no firm evidence that marijuana smoking is addictive or otherwise harmful to the body; at any rate, they often assert, it is less harmful in its physical and behavioral effects than drinking alcohol, which is legal. But this claim overlooks the fact that marijuana smoking has not been prevalent long enough for us to have reliable knowledge about its effects, whereas the effects of alcohol are well known because it has been used regularly by large numbers of people over a long period of time. Furthermore, the fact that smoking nicotine cigarettes has been proved harmful is grounds for suspecting that smoking marijuana is not risk-free; the fact that a lesser number of cigarettes are consumed in smoking marijuana is offset by the fact that marijuana has a hotter burn. Recent studies indicate that the effects of heavy smoking of marijuana parallel the effects of heavy tobacco smoking: irritation of the airways, chronic bronchitis, and potential cancer. Its adverse physical effects may not come to light or be substantiated scientifically for several decades, as was the case with ordinary cigarettes. Furthermore the increasing youthfulness of current marijuana users, the greater frequency of use, and the greater potency of smoked material all increase the risk and justify caution about its safety for these users.

It is therefore rash to hold that marijuana smoking has no long-term injurious effects or even that it is less harmful than alcohol, which, taken in moderation (even on a regular basis), is known not to be harmful, and indeed even beneficial. As added evidence, marijuana is known to have negative psychological and behavioral effects on regular users. These effects are not as obvious or offensive to others as those arising from alcohol abuse, but just for that reason they are more insidious, as they escape the attention of both the user and the observer. The passivity induced by marijuana that prevents the user from behaving violently also prevents him or her from engaging in desirable activities, ones important for his or her future. Teachers report that regular use of marijuana decreases the student's academic achievement and even the capacity to cope successfully with the ordinary problems of life. Since there is a considerable backlog of human experience to suggest that reliance on drugs in general weakens character and impedes a person's ability to function effectively in everyday life, these observations cannot be discounted. Declining scores on academic achievement tests correlate with the increase of marijuana use among school-age children, so that some kind of causal connection is not implausible. Here again, there is a parallel with cigarette smoking—common sense and nonscientific observation point to a connection long before scientific research compiles statistics to verify it.

We are thus led to the fourth factor, whether decriminalizing of marijuana is in accord with moral principles and social norms. The notion that a democratic society should not restrict the freedom of its citizens has important qualifications with respect to children and to substances harmful to their users. In the case of children, we think it mandatory to protect them from things prejudicial to their own future well-being. Marijuana serves no essential human need; the need it does serve is one that can readily be fulfilled in safer and better ways. It is consistent for society to take legal steps to eliminate or discourage use of a substance which leads children into patterns of behavior detrimental to their own future prospects. The precedent of the legal status of alcohol argues against rather than for decriminalization, since the use of alcohol is legally restricted in order to keep it from children. Since the decriminalization of marijuana would serve to make it more accessible to children and less easy to discourage its use, it is most consistent with our social norms to prohibit a practice that threatens the well-being of the young, and, through them, the future well-being of society itself.

Principles for Determining the Rightness of an Action

1. Are the motives of the action praiseworthy or blamable?
2. Is the intention or purpose of the action good or bad?
3. What are the actual or probable consequences of the action on the well-being of persons?
4. Is the character of the action in conformity with moral principles and law?

EXERCISE 10C

Apply the principles relating to the four factors of motive, intention, consequences, and intrinsic moral character to determine the rightness of the action or social policy discussed in the following.

1   George Black is a law-school student with a part-time job doing clerical work for one of his law professors. At income tax time, he learns he is required to pay income tax on these earnings. He believes this is unfair, since he is a student with no other source of income who only just manages to meet expenses. He reflects that he is unlikely to be caught by the government and decides not to report his earnings.

2. In an article, "External Human Fertilization," Clifford Grobstein discusses various social and scientific issues relating to research on the subject, one of them being ectogenesis, the continuing development in the laboratory of human embryos fertilized in the laboratory. He remarks:

> Such true "test-tube babies" and the human hatcheries envisioned in Aldous Huxley's *Brave New World* are not feasible in the current state of knowledge, nor are they known scientific objectives. Whether they will ever become human objectives is for the future to decide.
>
> The fifth question emphasizes the importance of the careful consideration of the fourth [ectogenesis]. The value of organ and tissue transplantation in the therapy of degenerative and traumatic disease has been demonstrated by the spectacular (if not fully successful) surgical efforts involving skin, kidneys, and the heart. Transplantation from cooperative donors and from victims of accidental or other premature death is limited by the availability of sources and by the recipient's immunological rejection of foreign tissue. Human embryonic tissue and organs could constitute an additional resource, with the potential for greater abundance and conceivably less vigorous immunological resistance. The culturing of preimplantation human embryos to the stage of early organ formation might provide a practical therapeutic source, since many early organs of other mammalian embryos have been shown to continue to develop externally in isolation from the rest of the embryo.*

Should research and experimentation in the development of human embryos in the laboratory as a source of replacement for human organs be promoted?

3. John Grey has gone to a store having a sale on calculators of a model he wants. He is about to buy the last one, when he realizes he has left his credit cards in his car. On the way to the parking lot a friend asks directions to the store "with the sale on calculators." Fearing that his friend will buy the last calculator, he gives him wrong directions.

4. Decriminalization of marijuana can no longer be considered a radical idea. Eight states have already taken such a step. National organizations, including the American Bar Association, the Consumers Union, the American Public Health Association, the Governing Board of the American Medical Association, the National Education Association, and the American Academy of Pediatrics, have called for it. President Carter has endorsed it, and legislation is now before Congress to make it federal law.

There are many reasons for decriminalization. Most convincing among these is that criminalizing marijuana use has simply proven to be totally ineffective in reducing its use. A 1975 study by the Maryland Drug Abuse administration has shown that both in Baltimore city and

---

*Reprinted with permission from the *Scientific American,* June 1979.

Baltimore county over 60 percent of high school seniors have used it, over a third are currently using it, and about 20 percent use it daily or several times a week. And the cost of enforcement is very high. It has been estimated that a single marijuana arrest costs the state between $1,000 and $1,500.

Marijuana may be dangerous, although this has not been proven conclusively. In any event, it is not consistent with American beliefs for the state to dictate what an individual citizen does so long as that act does not injure anyone else. In this case, criminalizing the use of marijuana is doubly indefensible, as being not only inconsistent with our beliefs but also ineffective. When the effect of such law enforcement distracts our police from the prevention of serious crime and alienates thousands of otherwise non-criminal citizens, it is time to change our policy.*

Review Exercise for Chapter 10

What kind of reasoning occurs in the following?* Assess the soundness of each argument by applying whatever rules are appropriate.

1. "I wish to correct several false impressions in the article, 'A Prescription for Destroying Public Schools.' It quotes from the *Washington Post*, 'If you don't like swimming in the neighborhood pool, that's up to you.' In this case, where education is concerned, "swimming" is required BY LAW, so it is NOT 'up to you' as stated, but a required action. To carry the analogy further, if the neighborhood pool has snakes in it or is not kept at a comfortable temperature, then I may choose to build a pool in my own backyard. This choice is made so that I am able to obey the LAW that requires my children to swim. In the event of a tax credit (HR 3946) parents would not have to pay that amount in taxes that it costs these conscientious parents to obey the LAW in a manner that is acceptable to them. They are not asking 'the federal government to help pay for the private pool in the backyard.'"

2. Christian Barnard, the man who made medical history with the renewed life he brought through transplants, is engaged in a quiet personal campaign to legalize euthanasia—mercy killing. "The primary goal of medicine is to improve the quality of life," says Barnard, "to alleviate suffering." This, he notes, was the purpose of heart transplants. "These operations I do are never intended just to prolong life— but to improve the quality of life for the patients." Even those who died after a few months or years had renewed vigor in the time they survived,

*All are reprinted by permission of the *Baltimore Sunpapers.*

he says. Barnard stresses he has never practiced mercy killing, because it is illegal. He believes the law will someday change and doctors will be permitted to stop treatment "when the treatment serves only one purpose—and that is to prolong the suffering of the patient." "It's important to realize," says Barnard, "that death is sometimes good medical treatment. Sometimes it achieves what medicine cannot achieve—it stops suffering." Barnard made headlines in his native South Africa when it was learned that he and his brother have a death pact. If one brother should be incapacitated—a vegetable kept alive by machines—the other brother would kill him.

3. "It's that time of the year for spring concerts in the schools. Then the curtain opens. The instrumental music teacher gives the signal with baton, and the concert begins. But all is not as it should be. For while the student orchestra is playing and the student chorus is singing, the conversational buzz of the audience resumes. These talkative parents are setting a terrible example of audience behavior for their children. What is worse, by their inattentiveness they are communicating to their children the message that they feel the children's efforts are not important enough or of a quality good enough for their listening pleasure. Does such a message inspire the children? Does it teach the children how to behave at public gatherings? Do those rude parents ever stop to consider that there might be some people in the audience who would like to hear the concert?"

4. "There are several bills currently before Congress, and others in the making, which would require the registration of American youth. Such bills all represent preparation for war. Training of our nation's youth in military philosophy and spirit, and in the use of arms, would have several detrimental effects. First, such training would encourage our young to support U.S. intervention by force and by the threat of force in the internal affairs of other nations. Second, training of our young in the use of arms and the dependence upon violence undermines the principles upon which our country is founded. Further, it teaches the use of violence as a solution to personal and social problems. Such training would also encourage the population to become comfortable and accepting of the unthinkable destruction, and indeed suicide, that must accompany modern war with nuclear weapons."

5. There is no doubt where Golden Ring Junior High School students stand on the issue of television monitors in the classroom—they are against it. A letter to *The Evening Sun* urged installation of TV cameras for central monitoring "100 percent for any class in session. This will disclose the troublemakers without placing an instructor or student informer in jeopardy."

   At Golden Ring, two English classes decided to let *The Evening*

Sun know how they felt about the issue. Some 49 of them wrote letters. The score on TV monitoring; against—44; for—3; maybe—2; The most-often voiced concern of the students was the probability that television cameras in a classroom would be distracting both to teachers and pupils. The second most frequent complaint was the cost. The Golden Ring students seem acutely aware of the burden of a school system on the taxpayers and they questioned whether an expensive TV monitoring system was affordable, even if worthwhile. The students are also prone to be aware of the dangers of vandalism. A large number were aware of the energy requirements of the monitoring system and questioned whether its installation would be wise in an era of diminishing energy resources. Many of them resented the implication that they could not be trusted and therefore should be under camera surveillance. Several said the eye of the camera would make the students "paranoid." And a few suggested that if there were discipline problems, coping with them was the teacher's burden, not the job of someone watching television screens in some distant monitoring room.

chapter 11

Further Principles
for Everyday Reasoning

11A OFTEN FALLACIOUS WAYS
OF REASONING

In this section we will look at some common forms of reasoning which are
sometimes *fallacious*: The reasoning looks valid and so may be persuasive,
yet careful attention to how the premises lead to the conclusion exposes a
serious flaw. Sometimes a fallacious principle of reasoning resembles a
valid one, and so may easily be confused with it. We have already discussed some of these fallacies: the fallacies of affirming the consequent,
denying the antecedent, hasty induction, and strained analogy. What we
now consider are not distinct types of argument but commonplace ways of
thinking. These are quite legitimate in some cases but they contain loopholes; logicians have baptized some of them with distinctive names, sug-
gestive of the type of thinking involved.

The first of these is often called *black-and-white thinking*. An ancient
way of thinking is to make distinctions in terms of opposites. The first
scientific thinkers, the natural philosophers of ancient Greece, even
posited the fundamental principles of the natural world to be those of hot
and cold, wet and dry, male and female, odd and even. In human affairs,
we readily classify people as heroes or cowards, friends or enemies,
professionals or lay people. Yet this way of thinking can lead us to confuse
contrary terms with *contradictory terms* and then to draw conclusions that

are correct for the latter but not for the former: We cannot properly infer from the fact that Jones is not generous that he is stingy, or that a person who is unwilling to help us intends to harm us. Very often it is the case that there is a middle ground between the two opposites, as there is here between being generous and being stingy. Or there may be a neutral ground or indifferent point, as here between helping and harming, that is the state of doing neither. Sometimes it happens that a thing can be partly in one category and partly in an opposite one, as in the case of many political designations: The terms *conservative* and *liberal* are taken to be opposites, but it may be that the same person has a conservative position on one social issue and a liberal position on another. Therefore, we must be cautious in operating from the premise that a thing must fall either into one category or its opposite; or in supposing that the falsity of a statement implies the truth of its contrary or of a statement implied by its contrary. Thus the falsity of the statement, "All vegetarians eat eggs," does not enable us to conclude that its contrary, "No vegetarians eat eggs," is true. It only enables us to assert its true contradictory, "*Some* vegetarians *do not* eat eggs." Black-and-white thinking occurs when we leap from the truth or falsity of a belief to the truth or falsity of another statement which appears to be its opposite. This leap is made safely when the situation admits of only *two* possibilities, like an electric switch that has only two positions, *on* and *off*. We need to analyze the subject matter to know whether this situation exists or whether there are other possibilities that jeopardize the leap from one opposite to the other.

A strategy useful in detecting fallacious instances of black-and-white thinking is the technique of *reductio ad absurdum* (reducing the argument to absurdity): See if another conclusion, one that is clearly false, may be drawn from the statements supposed true in the argument. If so, the original argument is discredited, since the statements assumed or inferred to be true (premises or conclusion) lead to a nonsensical conclusion. When this happens we must suspect that something is wrong either in the statements assumed to be true or in the principle of the argument.

For example, in a logic exercise a number of students assumed it to be true that "No human beings are perfect." They drew from this quite plausible assumption the implication that "All human beings have bad habits" is true. This inference, at first blush, seems plausible too. But this move supposes that "being perfect" is the logical opposite of "having bad habits," and thus that because no one is perfect therefore everyone must have some bad habit or other. If this were so, it would also follow that "not having bad habits" implies "being perfect." But we know that that is not so at all; being perfect implies much more than merely not having any bad habits—it implies having *all and only good* habits. Indeed, a little reflection will show that there are many people who really do not have bad habits but who are by no means perfect. Thus going from "No human beings are perfect" to "All human beings have bad habits" is an example of black-and-white thinking that is clearly fallacious.

However, there are cases when going from one opposite to the other is not fallacious—when only two actual possibilities exist. One large class of such cases is that of universal necessary statements and their contraries. For example, we can infer from the fact that "All mothers are female" that "No mothers are male," there being only two sexes. Statements which reflect how we classify things also fall into this category: It is reasonable to say that it is either true that "All fetuses have human rights" or that "No fetuses have human rights," even though the two statements are logical contraries, not contradictories. It would appear that *as a class* fetuses either have human rights or do not, so that it does not seem reasonable to assert that some fetuses have human rights and others do not. But some people actually do take a position that implies this belief, in saying that unwanted fetuses do not have human rights whereas wanted fetuses do, or that fetuses of a certain age have human rights but younger ones do not. In a case such as this, whether a black-and-white fallacy is being committed will itself be a subject of controversy.

In testing black-and-white thinking for the existence of a fallacy,

1. analyze the subject to determine whether another alternative or a middle ground between the extremes posed in the reasoning exists. If so, a fallacy has been committed.
2. Use *reductio ad absurdum* to determine whether the statements taken to be true lead to another conclusion which is false or highly dubious. If so, the reasoning is discredited.

A second popular way of thinking is called *"bald-man" reasoning.* Some of the distinctions we make are not based on the presence or absence of some property, but on the *degree* to which some kind of thing is present or absent. Whether a man is to be called bald, depends not just on his having hair or not having hair but also on whether the perceptible amount of hair he has qualifies him as being bald. Since we cannot draw any precise line concerning how much hair a person must have or lack to be called bald (because its distribution over the head matters), we speak of being bald or not being bald as a *difference of degree* (how much or how little hair) rather than one of *kind* (such as being male or female). Questions often arise about whether or at what point a given degree of a thing needs to be recognized as making a difference in kind. Suppose a person argues that being an alcoholic or not being an alcoholic is a difference in degree of drinking and not a difference in kind, for it depends not only on how much one drinks but also on how often and for how long a time. Thus, one can't really draw a distinction between a user of alcohol and an abuser of alcohol. In the case of alcoholism, it is obvious that differences in degrees of drinking do add up to a difference in kind: The difference between a user and an abuser of alcohol is revealed not just in how much alcohol is consumed but in the perceptibly different behavior, appearance, and speech of the alcoholic, and the role and effect of drinking in his life, all of which put him into a different category from the user of alcohol. The "bald-man" fallacy occurs most frequently in cases such as this, when someone argues that a difference in degree does not make a difference in kind, when in fact it does.

As in detecting black-and-white fallacies, we need to analyze the subject matter of a "bald-man" form of reasoning to see whether the difference in degree is such as to make a difference in kind. The following are guidelines for deciding when a "bald-man" fallacy has been committed:

1. There is a *perceptible* difference of a major kind between one state and another. For example, the difference between day and night is not just that of more or less light—a bright moonlit night is perceptibly different from a cloudy day.
2. The *cause* or *effect* of one degree of a thing is very different from the cause or effect of another degree of it. The difference between *necking* and *going all the way* is not a matter of degree, because of the possible effect of pregnancy in the latter case.
3. The difference in degree gives a thing a totally different moral significance from others in the same range. For example, the parent who spanks a child in disciplining him is in a different moral category from one who beats him so severely as to break an arm.

"Slippery-slope" reasoning is very like "bald-man" reasoning. Typically, a speaker presents evidence that leads one to grant part of what is said, or grant its plausibility in some instances at least; he or she then argues that no significant difference exists between the cases on which you agree and the remaining cases, and that therefore you ought to grant his or her whole argument. The image of a slippery slope is very graphic in illustrating the trend of such reasoning: Once you grant one or more of the proponent's points there is no definite stopping point, and you are pushed into going the whole way and accepting his or her conclusion. For example, pro-abortion arguments often begin with cases in which abortions are clearly acceptable (as when the mother's life is jeopardized by pregnancy, or the fetus is seriously defective) and proceed to cases involving victims of rape or incest on to cases of economic hardship or unwed teenagers, or threat to the psychological well-being of the mother, until the conclusion demanded of one is that it is not possible to separate acceptable from unacceptable abortion, so that abortion is permissible in all cases. As the foregoing example shows, whether a fallacy is committed in

"slippery-slope" reasoning is itself frequently a point of controversy, for reasons similar to these we noted in connection with black-and-white and "bald-man" reasoning.

The guidelines for determining whether a fallacy is being committed in a piece of "slippery-slope" reasoning may be adapted from those in "bald-man" reasoning. A fallacy is likely when

1. there is a perceptible difference between the features of the cases accepted and those in dispute;
2. the cause or effect in the accepted cases is quite different from that in the disputed cases;
3. some feature of the accepted cases has a different moral significance from the features of the disputed cases.

Another form of "slippery-slope" reasoning consists in arguing that one thing leads to another in a chain of consequences that cannot be broken at any one point. Thus, it is often argued that teenagers should not experiment with marijuana because it leads to experimentation with other more serious drugs, resulting in serious psychological dependency and ending in drug addiction. In assessing this type of "slippery-slope" argument, one needs to estimate the likelihood of the chain of effects and their seriousness, utilizing our long-term experience with the subject matter, our commonsense understanding of human nature, and the results of scientific knowledge when available. A fourth guideline in such cases is

4. apply common sense and the principles of causal reasoning to determine the likelihood of the chain of effects, events, or conditions described in the reasoning.

The *reductio ad absurdum* technique is often effective in exposing fallacies in "bald-man" and "slippery-slope" reasoning as well. The strategy in these cases is to find a parallel series of cases, but one in which the parallel conclusion would clearly not be drawn. For example, one could make a parallel between the pro-abortion argument previously outlined and homicide: One might then argue that even though there are many cases in which killing another person is excused, such as in self-defense, protection of others, legal executions, wartime, unavoidable accidents, and so on, no one would conclude that killing another human being is generally justified.

EXERCISE 11A

Point out any black-and-white, "bald man," or "slippery-slope" reasoning. Indicate any fallacies.

1. In a ruling, the Supreme Court majority held that a law saying that affirmative action was "not required" implied that such action was *permitted.* The minority in its dissent maintained that the intent of the legislators, shown by their speeches in support of the bill, was rather to deny that any form of discrimination was sanctioned by the law.

2. Was it determined by a deliberate conspiracy back in covered-wagon days or is it just happenstance that buying clothes is made so much simpler for men than for women? Women, it is generally agreed, do come in assorted sizes and shapes. Why, then, is it assumed by the clothing manufacturers that all women have uni-sized arms? Men's shirts are available in a wide range of inseam sizes. Slacks made for women may infrequently be found in three lengths, but the vast majority of them are available in only one length. There certainly can be little logical reason for these inconsistencies. Isn't it time that store owners and clothing manufacturers worked toward ending them?*

3. During a recent trip to Vermont I was impressed with that state's law which places a five-cent deposit on all beverage bottles. I do not know what the economic implications of such a law would be, but the aesthetic value is obvious. No state from here to Vermont was as free of litter. The economic impetus to not throw away bottles rubbed off on other throwaway items, and Vermonters seemed to be less inclined to discard cans, cigarette butts, and so forth on public land.*

4. Doctors should freely provide prenatal tests to women who want to determine the sex of their unborn child, even though they might have an abortion if they are unhappy with what they learn, a federal researcher says. Doctors who agree that women have a right to control their reproduction cannot logically withhold this information, says John C. Fletcher of the National Institutes of Health. "One must be willing to accept the fact that some abortions will be performed for trivial reasons," he wrote in today's *New England Journal of Medicine.*

   The test, called amniocentesis, is intended primarily to find out if a fetus will be born with a genetic defect, such as Down's syndrome. However, it will also reveal the sex of the child, and sometimes a woman will have an abortion if she learns that she is carrying a boy when she wants a girl, or vice versa. "I personally believe that sex choice is not a compelling reason for an abortion," Fletcher wrote. "The first moral response of most who think about the issue is close to queasiness." But Fletcher noted that the Supreme Court ruled that the mother-to-be has the sole right to decide whether she wants an abortion, and she does not have to tell anyone her rationale.

   "It is inconsistent to support an abortion law that protects the

---

*Numbers 2, 3, and 4 reprinted by permission of the *Baltimore Sunpapers.*

absolute right of women to decide and, at the same time, to block access to information about the fetus because one thinks that an abortion may be foolishly sought on the basis of the information," he maintained.*

5. A medical researcher describes his research: "I noted that a mild electric charge of negative ions stimulated the growth of bone tissue, so I reasoned that an electric charge of positive ions might destroy bone tissue and could be the basis of a treatment of bone disease."

11B SOMETIMES FALLACIOUS APPEALS IN REASONING

Another set of fallacies commonly recognized involves appeals that are introduced to persuade an individual to accept a premise or conclusion of an argument. Often an argument will cite the belief of an acknowledged authority which concurs with a statement of the argument. In the abortion argument discussed in Chapter 10, appeal is made to the view of an ecclesiastical authority, the Church of England. The fact that an ecclesiastical body—one concerned with moral matters, in particular one emphasizing the sacredness of life—does not condemn abortion in the earliest stages of pregnancy lends weight to the argument. In general, an appeal to authority is not fallacious when the authority has a special competence in the subject which makes his or her views relevant to the issue. A second consideration in an appeal to authority rests on whether the view of the authority correctly applies to the case being discussed. Especially when an authority from the past is cited, one must reflect on whether changes in the course of time have made his or her views questionable. Advocates of isolationism frequently cite Washington's Farewell Address because of its warnings against foreign entanglements, but the great changes in the condition of the nation since that time must make us skeptical of its relevance. Even when the authority is contemporary, one should note whether the case in question is comparable to those on which the authority has pronounced.

In general an appeal to authority should be an auxiliary point in an argument, not the main point. But in matters of specialized knowledge or where lay knowledge is inadequate, the views of authorities may rightly play the prominent role.

In assessing an appeal to authority, one needs to take account of these two factors:

1. whether the person cited as an authority is unusually competent in the subject under consideration, so that his or her opinion has weight;

2. whether the opinion cited applies correctly to the case being considered or the subject under discussion.

A so-called *ad hominem* argument (a Latin term for an argument directed "toward the man" rather than his statements) is the contrary of the appeal to authority: It points out some facts about the advancer of an argument or opinion as grounds for *disbelieving* what he or she says; something about the person—his or her position, character, action, circumstances—is cited to discredit his or her statements on the subject. Often it is improper to do this, since criticism should be directed to the argument itself, to the truth or falsity of the premises and their power to support the conclusion. But whenever the facts about the speaker are such as to lead us to doubt his or her honesty or the soundness of his or her views on the subject being considered, *ad hominem* arguments have their place; indeed the proceeding is institutionalized in our law courts as arguments designed to discredit the testimony of a witness by proving that he or she is unreliable.

It would not be unreasonable, for instance, to be skeptical about the views of a man who claims to be an expert in marriage counseling but who, it turns out, is constantly embroiled in marital difficulties himself. We also have a right to expect consistency between a person's actions and his or her beliefs, so that actions which appear to conflict with a person's stated views require explanation. Similarly, inconsistency between present statements and previous ones on the same subject may justifiably arouse suspicion and demand explanation. Even if legitimate, an *ad hominem* argument by itself is seldom conclusive; it needs the support of more usual forms of criticism of the premises and the mode of inference used in the speaker's actual argument.

An *ad hominem* appeal is fallacious whenever

1. the facts presented about the arguer have no bearing on the views expressed in the premises or conclusion of the argument he or she is making;
2. the facts do not discredit his or her truthfulness in general.

The last type of appeal (and often, a last resort itself) is the appeal to force. (The Latin term *ad baculum,* meaning "to the stick," indicates the threat of punishment.) Strictly speaking, appeals to force often contain no reasoning, in the usual sense; on occasion there may not even be language, as when a robber motions with a gun, and says "Give me your wallet!" In such an "argument" there may be no attempt at all to persuade a person of the rightness of what he or she is asked to do, say, or believe, so that one might object that there *is* no argument in a logical sense. Without the presence of reasoning of any kind, one cannot speaking meaningfully of anything even being a "fallacy" in the ordinary sense. However, often the appeal to force is made in conjunction with reasoning, language is usually the medium of its appeal, and rational considerations do enter into the response. We can usually convert an appeal to force into an argument by formulating a premise that asserts the prospect of inevitable painful consequences as a reason for accepting some conclusion.

The strength (it would be odd to say *legitimacy*) of an appeal to force thus depends on two factors:

1. the seriousness and certainty of the threatened consequences (causal reasoning and moral reasoning both enter into judgment of this factor);
2. the threatened consequences being worse than any other alternative (here moral reasoning primarily decides the issue, but an estimate of probabilities is also relevant).

This resort to the threat of punishment frequently occurs when there are no justifiable grounds for a conventional argument, and therefore many condemn this appeal as always improper. Nevertheless, there are situations in which acceptable premises do exist, but they may prove ineffective, or the need for immediate action may dictate an appeal to force, such as the following:

1. The mental state or particular circumstances of the person may be such as to make a rational appeal ineffective, or an appeal to the fear of negative consequences more effective. For example, with young persons, people in hysteria or confusion, or hardened criminals, the appeal to force may be advisable.
2. The seriousness of the situation, considerations of the person's own good, or the possibility of harm coming to others make an appeal to force legitimate.

In all the modes of argument discussed in this chapter one cannot infer, simply from the fact that a particular instance appears to fall under one or another of these headings, that the argument contains a fallacy. The guidelines listed under each type of reasoning are designed to indicate what to look for in testing soundness or unsoundness in each case. It is not unusual for a piece of reasoning to fall under more than one type; in such cases, the guidelines for *each* type should be applied, to obtain a thorough and fair judgment. It sometimes happens that the decision about whether or not a fallacy is being committed depends on moral or factual beliefs about the subject matter which figure as key premises; in these cases the question cannot be resolved without discussion of the plausibility or implausibility of these beliefs. This matter, in turn, we can settle in most cases by applying the principles of inductive and moral reasoning formulated in our previous chapters. Identifying a piece of reasoning as one of the kinds we have taken up in this chapter is not by itself proof of a fallacy in reasoning, it is only grounds for suspicion and caution. Nor is the presence of such kinds of reasoning in a larger argument grounds for condemning that argument through guilt by association.

EXERCISE 11B

What kind of appeal is made in each of the following? Is it legitimate or illegitimate?

1. The great physicist, Albert Einstein, believed that the existence of God is demonstrated by the marvelous complexity of the natural laws operating in the universe. Thus, the existence of God, far from being disproved by science, is proved by it.

2. Buy the *National Inquirer* at your local newsstand—the weekly whose reporting of Earl Butz's racist comments forced him to resign as Secretary of Agriculture. If your news dealer doesn't carry the *Inquirer,* remind him what happened to Earl Butz.

3. Joe DiMaggio, former star of the New York Yankees, has been making a series of commercials for a New York bank which advises viewers to steer clear of the stock market and sock it away in his bank instead. It's certainly true that the market has not been performing well recently, so it would be wise to take his advice.

4. The Nobel prize winner in chemistry, Linus Pauling, insists that massive doses of Vitamin C are effective in preventing and curing colds. But we should not be influenced by his prestige into going along with this quackish notion. After all, he's not a medical doctor.

5. Albert Einstein rejected the indeterminacy thesis, which states that certain basic processes of nature are random events which cannot be predicted. "God," Einstein said, "does not throw dice." However, we should not pay any attention to his view, since it is well known that he was a religious man.

11C   ETHICAL STANDARDS AND EMOTIONS IN REASONING

A common misconception about what constitutes sound reasoning is that it should be *dispassionate:* that a reasoner should neither express emotions nor attempt to influence the emotions of his hearers; discourse that does so is sometimes stigmatized as *rhetoric*. But rhetoric, in its original sense, is simply reasoning which aims to *persuade*. Surely the best kind of reasoning is that which not only sets forth the truth about its subject matter but does so in a way that will lead others to see that truth. In many of the subjects about which we reason in everyday life it is impossible, unnecessary, and even undesirable to keep our emotions out of play. What we need to do instead is to locate the proper role of the emotions in argument.

Clearly we ought to suppress those emotions that get in the way of reason itself: emotions like anger, hatred, and fear. A speaker undergoing such emotions should recognize that they can distort and paralyze thinking, and that getting them under control is the first order of business. If his or her hearers are in the grip of these emotions, the first step is to calm or neutralize those emotions, so that they will be in the proper state of mind to follow his thinking. The way to do both is the same: Enlist the aid of *other* emotions, such as sympathy, a sense of fair play, or even the fear of the serious consequences of rashness. Pointing out the gravity of a situation or its triviality—putting the matter in a larger perspective or appealing to a sense of humor—are often effective. (Benjamin Franklin once brought an explosive meeting during the American Revolution to reason with the pun, "Let us all hang together or we shall all hang separately!")

There are some feelings that have no place in a good argument, and a judicious thinker will neither express them nor seek to arouse them. These are emotions that both interfere with our reasoning and incite us to actions unjust or damaging to our own well-being or that of others. In addition to anger and hatred, which we have already mentioned, these feelings include prejudice, vengeance, resentment, jealousy, and those of a perverted, sadistic, or masochistic kind. An argument that appeals to such emotions may be faulted for doing so. It is unlikely to present the facts fairly or in such a way as to remedy a difficult situation, but will more probably encourage ways of thinking and feeling damaging to the mental and moral development of both the arguer and those he addresses.

Instead, a reasoner should evoke sentiments that promote sound habits of mind—ones that enable a matter to be seen in proper perspective, with all sides fairly represented; that promote the making of needed intellectual and moral distincitons; that encourage a balanced skepticism or enhance conviction, as the argument itself warrants. Such sentiments include the desire for knowledge, a respect for truth, sympathy, good will and generosity toward others, and trust, hope, or fear, as the circumstances justify.

In addition to these generalities we need to consider whether the particular emotions expressed or appealed to in a piece of reasoning are *well placed,* that is, whether the emotions are appropriate to the subject of the reasoning or whether they are out of place. In matters relating to public affairs, there is a place for appeals to patriotism, fraternal feelings, indignation, desires for progress and justice, and to the concepts of civic duty, honor, and loyalty; in matters concerning personal relationships, appeals to love, considerateness, compassion, forgiveness, pity, respect, shame, and pride, are all acceptable as well. As a rule, one must have evidence that the emotions are rationally grounded in the situation under consideration—that the situation has moral features that warrant exactly those emotions. Whether pity or righteous indignation is appropriate in regard to the actions of a political figure, for example, should be demonstrated in the reasoning itself and not merely assumed beforehand.

A good argument not only instructs its hearers, but also, through its method of reasoning, encourages the development of the better emotions while weakening the hold of inferior or morally bad types of feeling. The emotions reason ought to generate are those which promote or preserve rather than jeopardize human good. Emotions that are either indexes of morally good human dispositions—such as justice, courage, prudence, and benevolence—or that lead to them fall into this category; emotions that are evidence of faulty character or lead to bad habits are ones that reasoning should counteract.

In general, an argument is not sound or unsound merely on the grounds that it appeals to or expresses emotions. We must consider

1. whether the emotion is of the kind that is appropriate to reasoning;
2. whether the particular emotion is well-placed or misplaced in the particular subject matter of the argument;
3. whether that emotion is justified by the argument.

One so-called "fallacy" mentioned by logicians is the appeal to *pity.* But whether the appeal to pity is legitimate or illegitimate depends on the subject of the reasoning, and sometimes on the circumstances of the reasoning. In determining the moral quality of an action or a person's moral responsibility for it, pity for that person or for those affected by his or her fate is usually an irrelevant, often distracting consideration. Yet in making a decision on the possible existence of extenuating circumstances or extraordinary considerations which might influence what the punishment for an action should be, an appeal to pity is not out of place.

In this discussion we have been applying ethical standards to judge whether reasoning that involves the emotions is sound or unsound. Before we take up other ethical constraints that affect our assessment of an argument, let us reflect on why we ought to apply ethical standards to reasoning, using some of the principles of moral reasoning set forth in Chapter 10.

In general, reasoning has two goals: (1) to discover the truth about a given subject matter, and (2) to convince others of the truth of some particular belief. Truth is a human goal whose value has been attested to by many generations of mankind. It is prized for itself as an achievement involving the fulfillment of the highest human faculties. Also undeniable are the power and usefulness of knowledge in improving the material conditions of human life and in advancing the moral well-being of the species and of individual societies. It is thus of the highest importance that reasoning be carried on with utmost diligence. Reasoning's second goal, that of convincing others by argument, cannot be separated from its first goal, the discovery of the truth about the subject matter. The aim in reasoning should be to convince one's hearers by instructing them, leading them to see the truth about the matters under discussion.

To accomplish this task, the reasoner must first be committed to finding out what the truth is, and then to presenting the facts in a way that is not misleading but engenders insight as well as conviction. Only in this way does the reasoner respect the human capacities of those whom he or she engages in argument. One should avoid temptations to use short cuts in one's thinking processes, especially when the matter is a vital one. It is a duty to seek out and inspect the available relevant facts rather than simply to rely on those facts which are at hand, are obvious, or generally agreed upon. The reasoner who deliberates attempts to put the facts together as they fit: One should neither ignore them, nor play them down, nor overemphasize them under the influence of one's own preconceptions or desire for a particular outcome. The effective reasoner does not slant his or her discussion by choosing only those facts which point to the desired conclusion and by suppressing counterconsiderations.

The language used in describing the facts should present them in the proper moral perspective, so as not to misrepresent them. This does not mean that the arguer avoids language with moral or emotional connotations or refrains from arranging the premises so that they converge toward the desired conclusion. Such practices are often essential if there is to be a readily intelligible argument that does justice to all the dimensions of the subject matter. But the argument should provide its audience with enough of the relevant evidence, including counterconsiderations, to enable them to join the reasoner in the process of testing whether or not the evidence supports the conclusion.

Finally, let us review the motives and consequences of that kind of reasoning that aims merely to persuade, and does so by consciously or unconsciously ignoring, overlooking, or misleadingly slanting the facts in order to make them fit some predetermined conclusion. The most common motives leading to such ways of reasoning are laziness, the desire to gain some advantage for oneself or others, and disrespect for the truth. None of these are motives or dispositions of which one can approve. Although seeking advantage for self or others is not in itself a disreputable motive, seeking advantage unfairly or discreditably is.

Furthermore, the consequences of arguing poorly or dishonestly must be reckoned with: An argument that overlooks relevant facts is apt to be unconvincing and will be overturned, if not immediately, then in the course of time. Such an argument reflects negatively upon the intellectual powers of whoever advances it. A temporary advantage may indeed be gained, but a person who habitually tampers with the facts is likely to be found out; one who deceives others, for whatever reason, will discover that his or her credibility as a reasoner has been damaged. One should also mark the effect of such practices upon one's own reasoning powers: Sloppy, careless, and prejudiced reasoning does not develop the mind, but weakens and degrades it.

A genuine moral issue arises when the conclusions of sound reasoning appear to conflict with the moral goals of an individual or society. As reasoning beings, it is not open to us to manipulate the facts or bend our principles, even if it is to make an argument conform to long-range, generally approved social goals. Rather, we should engage in a more searching review of our conceptions, including those that relate to the conditions of human well-being, in order to reconcile them with the truth. Finally, we should learn to reconcile ourselves to the truth.

These ethical questions are to be applied to all kinds of reasoning:

1. Does the reasoning neglect, misrepresent, or manipulate the facts in order to reach a preferred conclusion not supported by the evidence?
2. Is any conflict between the conclusions of sound reasoning and the interests of the individual or a social group recognized and properly confronted?

The possession of reason has long been recognized as the power which both distinguishes and ennobles the human species. It is a duty to self and to one's fellow human beings to safeguard the integrity of reasoning, so far as one is able, and to enhance its creative exercise in oneself and others.

EXERCISE 11C

Assess the emotional appeal made in the following.*

1. "I love music. I love people. I cannot tolerate music and/or people who degrade human beings. The record that is being played over the radio

*Reprinted by permission of the *Baltimore Sunpapers*.

every day, called 'Short People,' is completely abhorrent to me. Merely listening to the words should prompt the listeners to switch the dial.

I know that hit songs make the cash registers ring. I also know there is such a term as *conscience,* which would dictate that any gains made by degrading people would be tainted. The mere fact that someone categorized short people as 'got no reason to live, they got little hands, little eyes, and they go around telling big fat lies' indicates that the singer is the type of person who is prejudiced, ignorant, and not worthy of even having his or her words repeated, much less publicized.

I feel the radio stations should be severely criticized for allowing this record to be played. Banning such a record is not violating freedom of speech; it is protecting a human being's dignity."

2. "Why is a mother who breast-feeds her child not permitted to nurse in the open? Why must she be ashamed of her preference in infant feeding methods? Unfortunately, our society is obsessed with sexuality and therefore with the female breasts. Our consciousness is saturated with advertisements that accentuate the sex appeal of the woman's bosom. But let a woman modestly nurse her child and the word 'disgusting' comes to the lips of some. It just doesn't seem fair that mothers deny themselves and their babies the warm and intimate relationship implicit in being a 'nursing couple' simply because society doesn't want to see it. For childbearing women have to accept breast-feeding as natural; they have to be able to see others doing it comfortably. If it's all right for women to walk about in the advanced stages of pregnancy, then they should also be able to nurse without harassment. Let babies have the opportunity to enjoy the most precious gift of love a mother can offer— herself, through the act of breast-feeding."

Review Exercise for Chapter 11

What modes of reasoning or kinds of appeal are contained in the following arguments?* Assess the soundness of each argument.

1. "You have printed many letters concerning abortion, and there is one point of view which occurs over and over in many of these letters. If an unborn child is unwanted then it is acceptable to dispose of this unborn child ... As the policy of unwantedness is now socially acceptable it should be expanded to include the wrecks and remnants of persons ... persons who are senile. To bring the policy of unwantedness to its maximum benefit we should also include those people who may be

*Reprinted by permission of the *Baltimore Sunpapers.*

physically intact, but who are born troublemakers. A well-known example of this type of person was Jesus Christ . . . His preaching deeply disturbed a lot of very important people and he had to go . . . The policy of unwantedness permits us to slice off all our social warts; when properly executed this policy will bring forth an ideal society where everyone is neat and nice and comfortable—like me."

2. "One of your correspondents, bleeding profusely, insists that the state itself commits murder when it executes a convicted murderer and thus piles murder upon murder.

This simplistic argument ignores the distinction between murders and other homicides. While all murders are homicides, all homicides are not murders. When a vehicle driver strikes and kills a pedestrian crossing the street in a crosswalk, this is a homicide. The pedestrian is just as dead as if the driver, with malice aforethought and premeditation, had killed him with a bullet; he is just as dead as an executed murderer. Yet the driver is not guilty of murder any more than the state is when it executes a murderer, although the driver may be guilty of manslaughter. If a pedestrian, carelessly crossing a street between intersections, is struck and killed by a lawfully operated car, its driver is not guilty of any criminal act.

The state, in taking the life of a convicted murderer, is not only complying with the dictates of our laws but is really carrying out the imperative commands of the first and highest of the natural laws: the rule and right of self-preservation and the protection of the innocent. From the dawn of the human race this rule and this right have been recognized and enforced, not as a matter of vengeance but of absolute necessity, as *homicidium ex necessitate*. Without it we would have anarchy, the law of the jungle . . . The right to kill murderous predators, whether animal or human, must be observed and enforced if civilization is to survive."

3. The trend in higher education is to prepare students for a job, but not every educator approves of that trend. The Rev. C. Stephen Mann believes people should pursue liberal education for its own sake. Education, he said in an interview, should be for creating human beings, not merely doctors, lawyers, business administrators, or social workers. To become a human being, he said, is enormously complicated, and the seminal college years are vital to that process. "The job is, I concede, a serious issue. But it is certainly not the only one. I might go so far as to say that education should be the very antithesis of profession. It should be for all those hours of one's life outside of how he earns his bread and butter."

Overemphasis on training for a job, he said, leads to an oversimplified view of the world, of human life, and of the individual's responsibility—both to society and to himself—as a human being. "It shrinks the universe. It diminishes the magnitude and the glory of the human enterprise. It makes a human being a mere technician. In that respect it is like education in the Soviet Union. Their education, too, turns human beings into mere technicians. But in Western civilization, man has always been regarded as greater than merely a cog in a vast machine. Yet in our institutions of higher learning we ignore the responsibility of asking our students to . . . discover and express their own place in it all . . . Instead, during the most thoughtful, probing period of their lives, they are permitted to view their role in that enterprise as merely finding and holding a job. . . ."

He criticized psychiatry and psychology, which have been providing the world view implicit in most education today. That view, he said, is that the individual's primary responsibility is to make himself and his family as comfortable, as safe, as he can. "If the psychiatrists' answer to the discomforts bothering man is so suitable and true, then I'd like to know why their profession has one of the highest suicide rates in the world?"

Index